PEOPLE VS. DONALD TRUMP

An Inside Account

MARK POMERANTZ

Simon & Schuster
NEW YORK   LONDON   TORONTO
SYDNEY   NEW DELHI

Simon & Schuster
1230 Avenue of the Americas
New York, NY 10020

Copyright © 2023 by Mark Pomerantz

First Simon & Schuster hardcover edition February 2023

SIMON & SCHUSTER and colophon are registered trademarks
of Simon & Schuster, Inc.

For information about special discounts for bulk purchases,
please contact Simon & Schuster Special Sales at 1-866-506-1949
or business@simonandschuster.com.

The Simon & Schuster Speakers Bureau can bring authors to your
live event. For more information, or to book an event, contact
the Simon & Schuster Speakers Bureau at 1-866-248-3049
or visit our website at www.simonspeakers.com.

Interior design by Paul Dippolito

Manufactured in the United States of America

1   3   5   7   9   10   8   6   4   2

Library of Congress Cataloging-in-Publication Data has been applied for.

ISBN 978-1-6680-2244-3
ISBN 978-1-6680-2246-7 (ebook)

To Judy

*Thank you for fifty-four years of love,
devotion, and patience*

CONTENTS

INTRODUCTION

In February 2021, the media ran stories about a new lawyer who had joined the staff of the Manhattan district attorney to work on the investigation of Donald Trump. The press described the lawyer in favorable, almost breathless terms. He was new to the investigation but no fresh-faced rookie. The media labeled him a seasoned prosecutor and a veteran defense attorney. He had handled cases involving organized crime and complicated financial scandals. He knew the white-collar world. He was said to be "the real deal," and a "heavy hitter." The reporters and pundits predicted that "he would get the job done."

That new lawyer was me. When I joined the Trump investigation, I got countless emails and telephone calls from friends and colleagues, urging me to "go get him" and wishing me luck. A year later I resigned from the district attorney's office and told the DA that he was responsible for a "grave failure of justice" because he would not authorize Trump's indictment. There was another media wave, and again I got emails and telephone calls from friends, and many from strangers, thanking me for my service but expressing sadness and disappointment that I had resigned. Some of the messages were not so friendly. One postcard informed me that I was "the scum of the earth" and said, "no one gives a flying fuck" about what I think.

Mostly, though, people who contacted me wanted to know one thing: "What happened?" Why had the investigation, which by all accounts had been gaining steam and seemed likely to lead to criminal charges against the former president, come to a sudden stop?

This book explains what happened, at least as I saw it. Over the months that I and others worked on the case, we developed evidence convincing us that Donald Trump had committed serious crimes. As we put the facts together, many of us came to believe that we had enough evidence to convict him, and we could present a solid case in court that would lead to a guilty verdict. The district attorney agreed and authorized the prosecution. But then the district attorney's office went through one of its very infrequent regime changes. The new regime decided that Donald Trump should not be prosecuted, and the investigation faltered. What happened? Grab something to drink and find a comfortable chair. I will tell you all about it.

CHAPTER ONE

OUTSIDE COUNSEL

In December 2020 I was a quietly content older lawyer, living a retired life in a suburb of New York City. The coronavirus pandemic was raging. When people asked me what I was doing to fill my days, my standard answer was, "I'm doing nothing, and I don't start that until noon." I was planning how to celebrate my wife's seventieth birthday and pondering the looming New York winter, with its short days and somber skies. My calendar had few entries, and I was hunkered down in the split-level ranch house where we had lived for the last thirty-five years.

Some months earlier, I had come through two surgeries for an aggressive and life-threatening form of cancer. The surgeries were successful, but the diagnosis prompted me to have an intimate conversation with myself about life and death. I decided to appreciate more fully the rich and bountiful life I had lived. That life had included a large and close family—my wife and I had raised twin daughters and twin sons, and the four children had blessed us with four spouses and seven (now eight) grandchildren. I had had a long and successful legal career. After graduating from the University of Michigan Law School in 1975, I had been a law clerk for a distinguished federal judge, a law clerk at the Supreme Court of the United States, a law professor, a federal prosecutor, and a criminal defense attorney for many years. I had prosecuted and defended cases involving murder, drug trafficking, political corruption, tax evasion, and financial fraud in many of its infinite variations.

Before I retired, I was a senior partner at a prominent New York City law firm. There I spent many years juggling cases and clients. My work life had been frenetic, filled with phone calls, meetings, travel, court appearances, and big black document binders that I had to study for whatever case I was preparing. By December 2020, that frantic activity had long faded from my life's rearview mirror. I missed the excitement and joy of working on significant cases with engaging colleagues, but I had no desire to head back into the maelstrom of practicing law.

Then the telephone rang. It was Carey Dunne, counsel to the office of Manhattan district attorney Cyrus ("Cy") Vance, asking if I would consider joining a group of outside lawyers who would advise Cy Vance in connection with his pending investigation of Donald Trump.

Cy Vance had become Manhattan's district attorney in 2010. As the district attorney for New York County (the formal name for Manhattan), he had the authority to bring criminal charges based on violations of New York State law that took place in Manhattan. He could not bring federal criminal charges—that was the job of the United States attorney. However, since Donald Trump ran his business operations from headquarters in Manhattan, Cy Vance had jurisdiction to investigate Trump and the Trump Organization for all sorts of criminal conduct, including fraud, issuing false financial statements, falsifying business records, and any other behavior that was illegal under New York's Penal Law.

I did not know Cy well; I was already beginning to wind

down my career as a criminal defense attorney when he became district attorney. But after I joined the investigation team, I got to know both Cy and Carey Dunne very well. Physically, they are cut from the same bolt of cloth. They are both lean and handsome men, of a similar age (midsixties), with distinguished shocks of gray hair. They had served together as assistant district attorneys in Manhattan during the 1980s. Both are unfailingly polite and well-spoken. They both have country homes in Connecticut, consistent with what I thought of (perhaps wrongly) as their "patrician" lifestyles. Cy was the son of Cyrus Vance Sr., a prominent lawyer who had served as secretary of state under President Jimmy Carter. He reminded me of my old boss, Potter Stewart, a justice of the United States Supreme Court for whom I had served as a law clerk in 1976–77. Cy, like Justice Stewart, was mild-mannered, almost deferential in his speech. Stewart had been a Yale law student along with Cy's father. Cy seemed to have inherited the persona of a thoughtful and considerate gentleman who believed in public service and who exuded a certain noblesse oblige. There is another, less visible aspect to Cy's personality: his weekend hobby is riding his motorcycle on Connecticut's back roads.

Carey, like Cy, is whip-smart, but more intense. He is always poised and in control of himself, not shy but never overbearing. He is smooth; some might even describe him as "debonaire," though for years he has played the drums in an all-lawyer rock band. Consistent with his former position as general counsel in the district attorney's office, he is a lawyer's lawyer. We were not friends in December 2020, but our paths had crossed several times over the years. We had represented different parties in several high-profile criminal cases. Carey represented Im-Clone Systems in a widely publicized insider trading case that led to prison terms for my client, ImClone CEO Sam Waksal, and television personality Martha Stewart. Carey also represented Credit Suisse in an investigation in which I represented investment banker Frank Quattrone. Quattrone, after being charged with obstruction of justice, ultimately was exonerated and the criminal and regulatory charges against him were all dismissed. Our clients in those cases had different interests, and we were not close, but I knew Carey from those and other matters. I also knew that Carey had a formidable record of accomplishment as a past president of the New York City Bar Association and a longtime partner at Davis Polk & Wardwell, one of the country's leading law firms. Carey had retired from Davis Polk in 2017 to rejoin the district attorney's office as its general counsel.

When I got Carey's call at the end of 2020, asking me to join a group of lawyers to advise on the Trump investigation, I was delighted. There was no talk of specific responsibilities or assignments. It seemed like the group would just consult from time to time as thorny issues might arise. Participating in the group would not take a lot of time and would allow me to peek through the window at whatever the district attorney was doing in his investigation of Donald Trump. I had not followed the investigation closely, but I knew it was active.

The invitation was flattering. I did not know why I had been asked to be part of the group, but I assumed that my professional background had something to do with it. Before I retired I had handled many high-profile cases, including some with political figures. My clients had included governors and senators, business leaders, financial institutions, and also gangsters and murderers. I had represented Steve Jobs in a federal investigation, and Matthew "Matty the Horse" Ianniello (said to have been the acting boss of the Genovese crime family) as well as Anthony "Bruno" Indelicato, who had been charged as a Mafia hit man. My roster of clients also had included companies like Citigroup, Lehman Brothers, and Deutsche Bank, along with their seniormost executives. And I had been a federal prosecutor for a number of years. I don't know which of these experiences prompted Cy Vance and Carey Dunne to ask me to join the group of lawyers consulting on the Trump investigation, but I immediately accepted.

Although I was pleased, the concept of a public prosecutor's office convening an advisory group of private lawyers to help with a pending investigation seemed a bit odd. During the two stints I had worked as a federal prosecutor, it would have been unthinkable to involve outside lawyers in our decision making. The United States Attorney's Office for the Southern District of New York, where I had worked, was famously independent. We had barely tolerated the participation of the lawyers from the main Department of Justice in Washington, D.C., let alone sought case advice from outsiders.

I later learned that the district attorney's office (widely known as "DANY," an acronym for District Attorney for New York County) had convened a group of "legal eagles" to help plan strategy for its litigation in the Supreme Court of the United States involving a subpoena it had issued for Donald Trump's tax returns and financial records. Trump, who was the sitting president when the subpoena was served, had claimed that no local prosecutor should have the power to investigate the president. When the case reached the Supreme Court, DANY recruited a group of experts to help refine its legal position, advise on the nuances of Supreme Court practice, and coach Carey Dunne as he got ready for his oral argument before the justices. Having gotten good help from outside lawyers for the Supreme Court battle, Carey and Cy had decided to convene a similar panel of private lawyers as they moved forward with their investigation of Donald Trump, and they obtained a judge's approval to allow them to do so.

We had our first detailed telephone conversation during the second week of December 2020. Carey gave us some background on the pending investigation. He explained why Trump's tax returns and accounting records had not yet been produced: while the Supreme Court had decided that Trump could not defeat the district attorney's subpoena just because he was president, it had not ruled on any other, garden-variety objections that Trump could raise. Following the Supreme Court's decision, Trump had brought a new proceeding attacking the subpoena and claiming that the investigation of him was very narrow and related only to his payment of "hush money" to adult film star Stephanie Clifford. That payment had been orchestrated by Trump's personal lawyer and self-described "fixer," Michael Cohen. Trump argued that the district attorney did not need his tax returns and accounting information to pursue that narrow investigation.

In fact, the district attorney's investigation of him was much broader, and would grow to cover many aspects of his business operations. The lower courts, recognizing that the district attorney had the right to probe the operation of Trump's multifaceted business, had rejected his argument. However, Trump had the right to ask the Supreme Court to reconsider his case, and the Supreme Court had not yet issued an order requiring the tax returns and other documents to be produced. So, even though Trump's objections had failed to persuade any court that had heard them, the district attorney had yet to get his hands on the records. Trump's lawyers had perfected the art of delay through litigation, as we would see time and again in the coming months.

The main topic of the conversation, and the issue that

seemed to have prompted the formation of the "outside advisors" group, dealt with a building in Manhattan's downtown financial district. That building, located at 40 Wall Street, was a residential and office tower that for a brief period in 1930 had been the tallest completed structure in the world. In Trump's 2012 personal financial statement (a copy of which Michael Cohen had provided to Congress after being arrested and prosecuted in 2018), Trump valued his interest in 40 Wall Street at over $527 million. But, according to what Carey told us in our telephone call, when it came to paying property taxes Trump had submitted a ridiculously "lowball" number. Trump had claimed to the tax authorities that the true value of his interest in 40 Wall Street was between $16 and $19 million. This figure was so low as to be absurd; the *New York Times* had reported some months earlier that the yearly rental income from 40 Wall Street had risen to over $40 million, and we later learned that Trump had reported net operating income figures for 40 Wall Street that were greater than $20 million per year. This meant that he told the tax authorities that the overall value of his interest in 40 Wall Street was less than what he was earning in a single year! Carey told us that Trump had personally signed forms attesting to the accuracy of the absurdly low valuation, and he said in our telephone call that Trump's tax filings "look[ed] like fraud." He and the district attorney were considering bringing criminal charges against Trump in a matter of weeks, not months.

But there was a logistical problem. At the end of 2020, the coronavirus pandemic was still raging, and that meant that grand juries were not convening to hear evidence. The DANY staff was working remotely, and the court staff was not empaneling new grand juries or requiring existing grand juries to meet. The presentation of felony charges to grand juries had come to a virtual standstill. Under the legal system in New York (and many other states), a prosecutor cannot bring felony criminal charges against anyone unless he or she presents evidence supporting the charges to a grand jury, which is a group of ordinary citizens that has the legal power to return indictments. Grand juries don't decide a person's guilt or innocence, but they do decide (typically by majority vote) whether they have heard enough evidence to charge a person with a crime. They don't need proof "beyond a reasonable doubt"; they decide only whether there is "probable cause," or enough evidence to show that a crime "probably" was committed and that a particular person "probably" committed that crime. If so, they return an indictment, which is a formal criminal charge that the accused person can defend in front of a trial jury that decides whether there is proof beyond a reasonable doubt.

Because no grand juries were available to hear evidence about Donald Trump, it was not possible for DANY to indict Donald Trump quickly. However, there was a possible workaround for this problem. Carey told us that he and Cy Vance were thinking about filing a felony complaint alleging that Trump had committed fraud in connection with the taxation of 40 Wall Street by undervaluing his property. A felony complaint is another way to begin a criminal case. A prosecutor can simply file sworn statements showing the court that there is "probable cause" to believe that a person has committed a crime. If the judge agrees, the person can be arrested and brought to court to be advised that a criminal complaint has been filed. A grand jury must eventually hear evidence in order to return an indictment—that is a requirement under the constitutions of New York State and the United States—but the judge can order a hearing to see if there is enough evidence of criminal conduct to justify keeping the charges outstanding pending the grand jury's consideration. In ordinary times, prosecutors in complicated investigations begin their cases by presenting evidence to grand juries and obtaining indictments. It is a more efficient way to proceed; the filing of a felony complaint before presenting evidence to a grand jury just adds a layer of unnecessary procedure to the case. But if no grand juries are available, a prosecutor can file a felony complaint and worry about the grand jury presentation later. If a felony complaint were filed against Donald Trump—who was still president of the United States as we were discussing these circumstances—that would be a dramatic step of cosmic significance. Carey and Cy wanted the outside counsel group to provide a reality check on whether this was a good idea.

As it turned out, the felony complaint idea never got off the ground. A few weeks later, Carey told us that New York City's Law Department had advised DANY that "everybody" submits lowball property valuations in the effort to lower property taxes on Manhattan office buildings. The lowball valuations are submitted "under penalty of perjury," but according to the Law Department the owner's initial valuation figures are not taken seriously, and are regarded as simply the first step in a series of negotiations. Since the city did not regard itself as having been defrauded by Trump's low valuation of 40 Wall Street, it was a no-harm, no-foul situation.

I had mixed reactions to this news. When I was chief of the Criminal Division for the United States Attorney's Office years earlier, I often heard from defense attorneys that their clients should not be prosecuted for some crime because "everybody does it," and it would be wrong to single out a particular wrongdoer. That argument never seemed persuasive to me. If a lot of people are committing the same crime, then perhaps the crime needs to be prosecuted vigorously to deter people from committing it. And, while it may seem unfair to come down more harshly on one wrongdoer than another, the criminal justice system never operates with precision. Who gets caught, and who gets prosecuted, is often the result of bad luck and circumstance. For Donald Trump there was the aggravating factor that he was not just the leader of the Trump Organization; he had urged the public to trust in his integrity by running for the presidency. I have always believed that people who occupy public positions of trust, and particularly those with law enforcement responsibilities, do particular damage to the fabric of society when the public learns that they have committed crimes. That inevitably leads to cynicism about politics and government. It reinforces the poisonous belief that public officials don't play by the rules, and that the citizenry is naive if they expect honest behavior from their leaders. So, even if a particular batch of criminal conduct is truly something that "everybody" does (which is almost never the case), someone who has been a senior public official can nevertheless be a good target for prosecution.

Here, though, the information that DANY got from the city's Law Department did not just mean that "everyone" was undervaluing their office buildings for tax purposes. It also meant that it would be well-nigh impossible to prove that Donald Trump had intended to mislead anyone by putting a ridiculously low figure on his tax form for 40 Wall Street, since apparently it was common knowledge that the tax authorities would disregard his number and arrive at a market value through a process in which nobody paid attention to what the taxpayer claimed in his initial filing. Although this seemed like a poor way for the city to conduct its business, bringing a criminal case based on a filing that nobody cared about or acted upon, and doing so as the opening gambit in a prosecution against a president, did not strike me, Carey, Cy, or anyone on the investigating team as a good idea.

We discussed the information we received from the Law Department about 40 Wall Street in a Zoom call that took place around 4 p.m. on the afternoon of January 6, 2021. Cy was on the call, as were Carey, I, and the other outside lawyers who were part of the advisory group.

At that moment, a mob of Trump supporters was overrunning the United States Capitol, bent on preventing the final tally of the electoral votes from the November 2020 election. I had been out walking our dog earlier in the afternoon when I started seeing the news alerts, and I returned home quickly to turn on the television. I was stunned to see that there had been a violent insurrection at the Capitol. I recall no discussion of the Capitol riot during our Zoom call that afternoon, perhaps a reflection of the irrelevance of politics to our discussions.

At around this time, I learned that the DANY investigative team, composed mainly of lawyers from the Major Economic Crimes Bureau, had identified several areas of inquiry into Trump's activities. The first area related to Trump's payment of hush money to adult actress Stephanie Clifford, also known as "Stormy" Daniels. The Stephanie Clifford saga had become a major scandal and part of the prosecution of Michael Cohen, Trump's personal lawyer. Clifford had claimed that she had had a sexual relationship with Trump, and she had threatened to expose the affair shortly before the 2016 presidential election. Cohen famously arranged to pay Clifford $130,000 in exchange for her agreement not to disclose the alleged affair. Cohen later revealed that Trump had reimbursed him for his payment to Clifford by means of phony invoices for "legal retainers." Cohen's payment of the hush money, and the circumstances of his reimbursement by Trump, had received a lot of attention during the district attorney's investigation, but there were many other avenues of interest.

A second area of inquiry was Trump's taxes. DANY had paid attention to a series of articles that the *New York Times* had published in the late summer and fall of 2020. Those articles analyzed data from Trump's tax returns that had been "leaked" to the *Times*. DANY did not yet have Trump's returns, but the articles raised issues involving potentially improper business expense deductions and the deductions of "consulting fees" across various business projects. Prosecutors frequently begin investigations after reading newspaper articles. In my earlier tenure as Criminal Division chief, Mary Jo White had been the United States attorney. She was an early riser and voracious reader. She often sent me newspaper clippings with tiny yellow Post-its reading, "What are we doing about this?" I knew that "nothing" would always be the wrong answer, and would make sure that one of our investigative units would take a look at the subject of the clipping. Those quick looks sometimes would blossom into investigations and prosecutions.

Third, DANY was interested in looking at Trump's relationship with Deutsche Bank. One issue was whether Trump had defrauded Deutsche Bank by getting financing through the use of overstated financial statements and asset valuations. This would later become an issue of overriding importance, but as of late 2020, DANY had simply noted that the issue was ripe for investigation, based in part on information that Michael Cohen had provided. The office also was looking at whether Trump had engaged in money laundering by depositing foreign assets into Deutsche Bank accounts that were maintained outside the United States.

There were other issues as well: the accuracy of materials that Trump had provided to the General Services Administration when he submitted a successful bid for the conversion of Washington, D.C.'s "Old Post Office" into a luxury hotel; the treatment of income from leasing communications equipment located on the top of the Trump International Hotel & Tower in Manhattan; the restructuring of a loan that Trump had received from Fortress Investment Group in connection with a Chicago skyscraper; potential insurance fraud; and the accuracy of the information that Trump had submitted to Ladder Capital Finance, an entity that had extended loans on various Trump properties.

My study of the materials led me to wonder whether the investigation was going anywhere. It seemed unfocused and sprawling. I also thought that the district attorney would need a "narrator" if he was going to build a credible criminal case. There were a lot of suspicious transactions and circumstances, but in a white-collar case it is difficult to persuade a jury that a defendant has committed a crime without a witness who can explain the wrongdoing and serve as a "tour guide" through the events and the documents.

Michael Cohen was a potential narrator, at least with respect to the payment of hush money to Stephanie Clifford, but he was a witness with a lot of baggage. As I will discuss in just a bit, DANY already had made a preliminary decision not to bring a criminal case against Donald Trump in connection with that payment. I did not yet know whether Cohen could provide a lot of detail on the other things that DANY was investigating. But, despite the issues with investigative sprawl and the lack of an obvious narrator, it was clear from even a cursory look at the case materials that Trump's chief financial officer, Allen Weisselberg, could be an important witness.

Weisselberg had worked for Trump for decades, and before that he had worked for Trump's father, Fred. He was a brood-

ing, bald, mustachioed gentleman in his seventies who seemed
to wear a perpetual frown on his face when photographed in
Trump's company. By the end of 2020, when I became involved
with the Trump investigation, he had been identified publicly
as Trump's right-hand man on all financial matters. In November 2020, Bloomberg had published a story about Weisselberg,
noting that he was the only non–family member appointed to
oversee the trust that Donald Trump had established to run his
business after his inauguration as president in January 2017.
The article cited the close and unusual ties between Trump,
Weisselberg, and members of Weisselberg's family. It cited information provided by Jennifer Weisselberg, who had been
married to Allen Weisselberg's son, Barry. The couple had divorced in 2018, and the divorce had been bitter. Jennifer Weisselberg told Bloomberg that Trump had provided her and her
husband with free housing.

Jennifer also had been chatting with DANY. In an October 2020 interview, she claimed that her former father-in-law
was desperately afraid of not pleasing Trump. He made it his
business to be in the office any time Trump was there, and he
would regularly fly down to Florida with Trump on weekends
so that he could attend to Trump's needs. Jennifer claimed that
Trump had compensated Allen Weisselberg in ways that allowed Weisselberg to avoid paying taxes, and that Weisselberg
knew a lot about all of Trump's deals. She said—prophetically,
as it turned out—that Weisselberg's whole self-worth depended on Trump liking him and making him feel worthy, so
he would "never" turn on Trump. As for Trump's view of Allen
Weisselberg, Jennifer claimed to have heard Trump tell Weisselberg that "you know what to do, my Jewish CPA . . . make
me happy, or else."

It was obvious to me, and to virtually anyone who had

looked closely at Donald Trump's business life, that Allen Weisselberg was a key potential witness. Trump had trusted him, and Weisselberg had intimate knowledge of Trump's financial dealings. If he had been involved in criminal conduct with Trump, he would be an ideal narrator in any case based on financial chicanery in Trump's business empire. In the coming months, we would build a criminal case against Allen Weisselberg, and use the leverage to try to "turn" him. But that came later. In the first weeks of my involvement with the Trump investigation, all I could do was highlight the need for a narrator and note that Weisselberg would be perfect for that role if he could be persuaded to audition for it.

In that regard, I was intrigued to learn that Weisselberg's main lawyer was Mary Mulligan. I knew Mary. She had been a fledgling federal prosecutor in Manhattan during my tenure as Criminal Division chief and had worked just down the hall from me. After I left the United States Attorney's Office, and Mary became a more senior prosecutor, I had a bunch of meetings with her as a potential adversary. She was investigating ExxonMobil, and I was one of ExxonMobil's defense lawyers. I regarded her as a straight shooter and was happy to see that she was working on Weisselberg's behalf, having now established herself as a private lawyer.

Those prior relationships matter. It's not that lawyers who know each other will do favors for each other; that has not been my experience. Rather, a prior relationship can help establish trust between opposing counsel. Lawyers who do not know each other, and who represent clients with opposing interests, do not instinctively like or trust each other. In fact, they often behave like dogs who encounter each other for the first time in the neighborhood dog park. They sniff around each other, looking for advantage, seeking dominance, ready to snarl at their new acquaintance if there is any display of untoward aggression. Lawyers who know each other, at least if they have had a positive relationship, act like dogs who have made each other's acquaintance before. They can communicate more easily, with less risk of misunderstanding and unnecessary displays of hostility. They will still stand their ground and represent their clients' interests, but with less posturing. So, when I learned that Mary was representing Allen Weisselberg, I mentally wagged my tail, and told folks at DANY that I would be happy to speak with her if and when that became appropriate.

By mid-January, from where I sat, DANY's investigation was not close to bringing a criminal prosecution. There was a long and unfocused laundry list of topics to investigate, no reliable cooperator other than Michael Cohen (a convicted perjurer), and DANY was still waiting to receive Trump's tax and accounting materials, notwithstanding its victory in the Supreme Court six months earlier. On the bright side, the moving force behind the investigation was Carey Dunne, a lawyer of great experience and ability. The decision whether to charge Trump ultimately would be up to District Attorney Cy Vance, who seemed like he was open to bringing charges if presented with a set of facts that would support them, but he was not a loud or a frequent speaker on the DANY Zoom calls I had attended. I had not yet met the others on the investigative team. To the extent I had heard them on Zoom calls, they seemed quiet and mainly in listening mode, perhaps reluctant to say too much in light of the senior people who were on the calls.

To this point, I had been serving as an "outside advisor." I did not have a big emotional investment in the investigation. I was essentially a voyeur, trying to add value when asked for my opinion. I was pleased to have a ringside seat to whatever might happen, but I had no responsibility to make anything happen. I was an interested observer, but not a protagonist.

On January 20, 2021, Donald Trump vacated the White House and flew to Florida, a private citizen once more. His departure from office meant that the thorny issues around investigating and prosecuting a sitting president would no longer hamper whatever action the district attorney might take. A few days later, I had a phone call that would change my relationship to the Trump investigation, and result in my taking a leading role as the investigation moved forward.

CHAPTER TWO

SWORN IN

I had not spoken with Carey for several weeks leading up to a phone call we had on the Saturday after Trump left office. I don't recall the details of that call, other than a discussion about the overall state of the investigation, but in retrospect Carey was conducting a job interview. After that call, he asked me if I would talk with him and the district attorney, Cy Vance, on Monday, January 25.

In our call Cy and Carey asked if I would agree to join the investigation as more than an outside advisor. They wanted me to be sworn in as a special assistant district attorney, which would allow me to make presentations to a grand jury and to appear in court on behalf of the People. The call began with a conversational gambit: as Cy put it, "We need more help, especially with respect to trying to develop a witness from within the Trump Organization. Do you know anybody who might have the expertise and the time?" I volunteered for the job and asked how much time I would be expected to commit to the investigation. Cy responded that they were hoping for a full-time commitment, but would accept whatever time I could spare, with no fixed expectation. Cy raised the issue of compensation, and I replied that I would not be looking for compensation, and I was ready, willing, and able to get started as soon as I could be sworn in.

After the telephone conversation, I went upstairs to tell my wife that I had agreed to be sworn in as a prosecutor in order to work on the Trump investigation. She was happy for me, but also asked in passing how much I would be paid. I replied in jest that the negotiations over salary had gone "great," because we had reached agreement that I would work on the case for nothing before I was even asked how much I was willing to pay the DA's office!

I was enthusiastic about working on the case and happy to work without pay. I already had retired and did not want to be a paid employee again. We did not need more money to support our lifestyle. My parents had been poor immigrants, who had come separately to America as children speaking no English. But their children had prospered. I became a successful lawyer. My older brother became a physician, and my younger sister became a university professor who spent many years in senior positions at the World Bank. Notwithstanding my earlier public service, I felt I still owed the country a debt of gratitude, and working without pay on an investigation involving a former president was a way of paying something back.

Doubtless there are cynics who will believe, notwithstanding whatever I say, that my enthusiasm came from not liking Trump, his politics, or his presidency. Trump himself later called me a "never Trumper." It is true that I had little regard for Trump or his business ethics. As a lawyer who had practiced for decades in New York City, I had long been familiar with his escapades. I had heard stories thirty-five years earlier from lawyers who had represented Trump in his business dealings, and I took from those stories that he was an unscrupulous wheeler-dealer. I had followed Trump's political ascent, his campaign for the Republican nomination in 2015 and 2016, and his victory over Hillary Clinton. Then I followed his presidency, the first impeachment proceeding, Michael Cohen's defection from Trump-world, and all the rest, including Trump's defeat by Joe Biden in the 2020 election and the events of January 6, 2021. I was not a fan.

But my enthusiasm to work on the investigation had nothing to do with my views about Trump's politics. The district attorney was conducting a law enforcement inquiry, not a political operation. It was "cops vs. robbers," not "Democrats vs. Republicans" or "liberals vs. conservatives."

What attracted me to the job was not politics but the opportunity to work on a case that was more exciting, meaningful, and interesting than virtually any case one could imagine. Litigators, and particularly criminal litigators, want to work on cases with the potential for drama. The human drama is what attracts us to criminal cases in the first place. From my very first law school class, an 8 a.m. session on introductory criminal law, criminal cases fascinated me. They were filled with emotion and moral complexities that mirrored the complexity of human behavior. Criminal cases hinge on subtle differences in conduct and intent that translate into vastly different legal consequences. Years earlier, I had been introduced to a very prominent Italian criminal defense lawyer. We sat next to each other at a dinner in Milan, but unfortunately I did not speak much Italian and he did not speak much English. Nevertheless, we tried to communicate about our respective criminal law practices. At one point I remarked to my dinner companion that the practice was all about "shades of gray," and his eyes lit up and he broke out in a big smile. "Yes," he said. "It is all 'chiaroscuro'"—the subtle artistic differences between light and dark. Criminal cases are portrayed in terms of "right" and "wrong," and "good vs. bad," or "innocence vs. guilt," but the truth is almost always vastly more complicated and more interesting. And what could be more interesting, more dramatic, and more filled with "shades of gray" than examining the conduct of a former president, a man of epic contradiction and complexity, whose behavior had inspired millions of people to admire him and millions of others to hate his guts?

I also thought that I could help, and perhaps I could make a difference. As my career as a criminal lawyer had progressed, I had avoided cases that seemed like pushovers for one side or another. As a defense attorney, that meant turning down representations that seemed hopeless. I did not want to be involved in matters where all I could do was "rearrange the deck chairs on the *Titanic*," an expression that many lawyers used to describe cases where we could make no conceivable difference. And as a prosecutor, I had spent my time handling cases that were challenging and difficult, in which I could get something done. This seemed like such a case.

From the materials I had seen, I had a sense that the Trump investigation might be floundering. There were lots of areas under inquiry, but none of them had progressed very far beyond noting the particular topic and summarizing what was known about that topic from public materials or from the limited fact-finding that the team had been able to do. It looked to me like the team needed to focus.

I had taught many young lawyers that the ability to focus is essential to success as a litigator. A central job of a litigator is to take an undifferentiated mass of stuff—documents, recollections, events, conversations, messages, and all the other detritus of human life—and pick out the pieces that fit together to create a picture that can be used to ask a court to do something. Armed with the substantive rules of law, and with an eye on the rules of evidence, the litigator's job is to discard all of the irrelevant junk and distill the mass of stuff down to something called a "case"—a collection of facts and events that fit together and that can be intelligibly presented in a courtroom. The lawyer has to know how the bits and pieces fit together, and to be able to discern the picture as it begins to come together, in order to serve the client's interests. Of course, what is useful depends on substantive legal principles, whom you represent, and the nature of your assignment.

As a prosecutor, you are trying to determine what actually happened, and whether the facts fit together into an accurate and recognizable picture of criminal behavior. If the picture does reveal serious criminal behavior, you have to go further and assemble the facts into a convincing (and admissible) portrayal of events that a jury can appreciate. It's like putting together a puzzle, but you don't know which pieces belong, and the pieces are scattered all over the place. And you are not given the image in advance; the puzzle box has no picture on it, and all the pieces are not necessarily contained in whatever "box," or case file, you are given. The pieces available to you may be part of an entirely different image, or they may belong to no image at all. The image that a prosecutor assembles must be an honest one; a prosecutor cannot ignore puzzle pieces that are missing or jam pieces into places they do not belong.

As a defense lawyer, you are often trying to do the opposite— scramble the pieces, change their shape, conceal a few of them (within the limits of ethics and the law), or just upset the whole table and scatter the pieces everywhere. Sometimes the defense lawyer is able to assemble his or her own collection of facts, and to present those materials as a competing picture (a defense case), but often the defense consists of scrambling the pieces that the prosecutor puts together and arguing to a court or jury that the prosecutor's picture is flawed, or incomplete, or unworthy of belief. In our system, the prosecutor bears the burden of proving the defendant's guilt beyond a reasonable doubt, so the defense has no obligation to present a pretty picture of its own. It is often enough to scramble or deface the prosecutor's picture of events, or to inject chaos or doubt so that the picture becomes unrecognizable or unattractive.

On the Trump case, I saw my job as helping the team to gather the puzzle pieces (that is, to assemble and follow the facts), fit them together, and look at the resulting images and interpret them. Were they real or illusory? Were they clear? How would people (especially judges and jurors) react to them? This was work that I had been doing, both as a prosecutor and as a defense attorney, for more than forty years. No false modesty: I knew I was good at it, and because of the high stakes involved in investigating a former president it was important that the work be done as professionally as possible. If it turned out that Trump had committed crimes, and there was evidence sufficient to charge and convict him, then building a compelling case seemed to me to be a worthy and exciting endeavor. And if there was no case, I could help the team avoid the perpetual wheel-spinning that might otherwise take place.

I also knew from the beginning that the job of sorting through a welter of unrelated details, documents, and miscellaneous facts is not the strength of most local prosecutors' offices. Local prosecutors typically get prepackaged "cases" from the police, or from a complaining victim. The prosecutors still have to present an attractive picture in the courtroom, but they are painting by the numbers. Often the image has been outlined and made recognizable as a case before the assistant district attorneys even open their files. And the images typically are not complicated. As one senior Manhattan homicide prosecutor told me, most of the cases fit a certain template: "Joe shot Pete, and Billy saw it happen."

DANY, unlike most local prosecuting offices, had brought some extremely complicated financial fraud cases in the past, including the prosecution of Dennis Kozlowski, the former chief executive officer of Tyco International, and the prosecution of the Bank of Credit and Commerce International, an international bank that had been involved in massive money laundering and other crimes. The office had a long history of pursuing white-collar investigations proactively; in fact, DANY is recognized as having one of the best cybercrime-fighting units in the world, armed with prosecutors who do their work across borders and often act as their own investigators. But the Trump investigation, with its many threads and political implications, was vastly more complex than anything DANY had handled within recent memory.

I was sworn in via Zoom on February 2, 2021. I was at home in the suburbs in front of my desktop computer, wearing a suit jacket and tie, along with sweatpants and sneakers that I hoped would remain invisible to the camera. Judy, my wife, stood out of camera range and eavesdropped on the very short ceremony. I agreed to support the constitutions of the United States and the State of New York, to support all applicable laws and ordinances, and to faithfully discharge the duties of a special assistant district attorney to the best of my ability.

This was the third time in my life that I had been sworn in as a prosecutor. The first time had been over forty years earlier, when at age twenty-seven I became an assistant United States attorney for the Southern District of New York. It was at the beginning of my career as a practicing lawyer. I had never stood up before a jury or questioned a witness in a courtroom. The second time was nineteen years later, when I was sworn in as chief of the Criminal Division in that same office. I was forty-six years old, an established lawyer in the middle of my career. I knew how the criminal justice system was supposed to work, and my job was to make sure it was working smoothly—that we were charging people who should be charged, declining prosecution where appropriate, and prosecuting our cases according to the law and the evidence, whether the defendants were terrorists, gangsters, drug dealers, killers, politicians, or executives. Now, more than twenty years along, I was at the end of my career. I had no need to burnish my resume or enhance my professional reputation. I just wanted to get on with the matter at hand.

A week or two later, the press found out that I had been added to the Trump team, and a small media frenzy ensued. My career was dissected, characterized, and mischaracterized in various newspapers and on TV talk shows. I was described as an "organized crime" prosecutor (only slightly true) and la-beled "the real deal," a "heavy hitter," etc. My family thought this was very funny. My wife made comments like, "Has the heavy hitter had time to feed the dog yet?" My four grown chil-dren chimed in with emails, including a clip from *My Cousin Vinny* where Mona Lisa Vito (played by Marisa Tomei) tells her fiancé, Vinny Gambini (played by Joe Pesci), that "you'll do a great job, *if* ya don't fuck it up!" There was a surreal moment when I came upstairs from my home office and found my wife watching *The Rachel Maddow Show* on MSNBC. My picture was on the screen, and Maddow was talking about my career as a prosecutor and later as a defense attorney. Maddow made much of my representation of Anthony "Bruno" Indelicato. She related that Indelicato was a convicted Mafia assassin who went by the nickname "Whack Whack." She said that he had been responsible for the infamous 1979 mob hit on Carmine "Lilo" Galante (then the acting boss of the Bonanno family) in Joe & Mary's Italian-American Restaurant in Brooklyn. I had indeed represented Bruno, and had been successful in getting his forty-year sentence for racketeering reduced to twenty years, but I had never heard the name "Whack Whack."

The press attention was an obstacle to getting things done as a prosecutor. There are lawyers who crave it, and who have "vanity walls" in their office to display their headlines, photos, and press clippings. That never appealed to me, and I shied away from publicity during my career. I refused countless requests to do television or radio interviews or to comment on cases with which I was involved. I had represented my share of high-profile clients, but I never understood the thrill of seeing or hearing my name in a story reporting on events with which I already was completely familiar. And I had learned a painful lesson many years earlier, when I represented the chief financial officer of a media company following the arrest of a young woman who had been charged with running a prostitution business. The woman had named my client as one of her benefactors and my client was anxious to keep his name out of the newspapers. I called a reporter who was working on a story about the woman's arrest, trying to convince him that the woman's uncorroborated naming of my client ought not result in his public shaming. But I did not watch my words; in fact, I tried to convince the reporter that he should not reference my client's name based on the mere word of some "bimbo," an offensive and sexist term I should never have used. The next day, I picked up the tabloid that had the story to see what had been printed about the woman's arrest. There was a front-page article naming my client as one of the woman's paramours. And there was a separate sidebar article, with the following headline: "CFO's lawyer: 'She's a bimbo.'" I was not happy; neither was my client. The whole episode helped remind me that reporters were not my friends, and I avoided conversations with the press as I worked on my cases.

Some years later, I was speaking with one of my daughters, who told me that my name and picture had been in the newspaper about some case. I asked her if she still had the newspaper. She told me that she had used the paper to clean up after a pet and had already thrown it out. Her comment struck me as reflecting a fundamental truth: the pleasing headline in today's paper will be used tomorrow to wrap fish, or worse, and be tossed in the garbage.

What especially concerned me about the press coverage of my appointment to the DANY Trump team was the impact on team morale and how I would be perceived by everyone working on the case. Prosecutors on complex cases work in teams. I had yet to meet the people on the team, and I was concerned that the press coverage would make it difficult to get along with folks who had been working on the case for a long time. I was both a Johnny-come-lately and much older than the assistant district attorneys who had been working on the case. I could have been the father of most of them, and the grandfather of some of them. And I had never worked at DANY—most of my work had been in federal and not state court. To make matters worse, everyone knew that I had spent years working in the United States Attorney's Office as a federal prosecutor.

The United States Attorney's Office in Manhattan and the New York County district attorney's office have always had a complex relationship. Local prosecutors have gone on to be federal prosecutors, and vice versa. Robert Morgenthau, a legendary district attorney in Manhattan, had previously served as United States attorney. The offices have overlapping jurisdiction in many cases, such as those involving drugs, guns, gang violence, and business frauds, and they sometimes form cooperative partnerships on particular investigations. Often, though, they compete with each other. The competition over who is going to handle a juicy criminal case—the feds or the locals—can be fierce and sometimes downright nasty. In my stint as Criminal Division chief for the feds, I had been involved in some epic battles with DANY. In one case, involving a very unlucky gangster, the feds had started an investigation and gotten approval from a federal judge to wiretap the gangster's telephone line. The local authorities also had begun an investigation and had gotten approval from a state judge to wiretap the same telephone line. In the middle was the telephone company, which had to decide which office should get the audio feed. We worked it out after many harsh words were exchanged. In another case, the United States Attorney's Office decided to commandeer an insider trading case that was being prosecuted by DANY. That dispute boiled over onto the front page of the *New York Times*, and diplomatic relations between the two offices effectively ceased for months. To make matters worse, federal prosecutors in the Southern District of New York, where I had cut my teeth, typically courted a reputation as the "A Team" in New York City—the legal equivalent of the New York Yankees. The local prosecutors were good, but the feds tended to treat them as a minor-league team, with some talented players but not in the same league.

With this backdrop, further complicated by the pandemic that was forcing everyone to work remotely, I was concerned about the publicity that attended my appointment to work on the Trump case. I was worried that I would be perceived as a "glory hound," steeped in arrogance after working as a federal prosecutor and as a well-known defense lawyer. Would I be seen as an officious meddler parachuting into a long-running investigation to tell everyone how to do their jobs? I desperately wanted to avoid this. I had not been recruited to lead the team, nor had I been put in charge of anything. I just wanted to get up to speed, learn about the case in detail, and help bring the scattered facts into focus. I sent Carey an email, saying I was worried that the members of the team might be "irked that this 'prominent' guy joins the team, gets a nice piece in the *Times*, and mouths off a lot about the case in meetings while we do the unglamorous work of drafting subpoenas, writing briefs, and keeping the investigation going."

Carey told me not to worry, but I sent an email to the team telling them that I had not contacted the press and had done nothing to solicit the media interest (all true). Recalling my conversation with my daughter, I said that if anyone on the team thought that using the newspaper to pick up dog poop was the highest and best use of the articles about me, I would take no offense. Cy read the email, and sent an email back, with a message that he would repeat many times over the ensuing year. He wrote that "[t]here are many twists and turns ahead. . . . I don't presume to know how this all ends, no matter how hard we work or how good we are. Outsiders will criticize us or praise us, no matter what. . . . [M]y job simply is to make sure that we go through an investigative process where at the end, win, lose or draw, I know we've done all we could as lawyers and prosecutors to make a case, if there is one to make."

Cy's email was prophetic. There were indeed many twists and turns ahead, and I came to understand—along with everyone else—that "to know how this all ends" may not be possible when it comes to applying the rule of law to Donald Trump.

CHAPTER THREE

THE "ZOMBIE" CASE

When I was sworn in as a prosecutor to join the Trump investigation, I had no particular instructions about what to do or where to start. I did not know how the Trump team was organized, or even how to find the bathroom. Fortunately, we were working remotely in the beginning of 2021, so finding the bathroom was not an immediate issue. Nevertheless, I had the disoriented feeling of being a stranger in a strange land.

I did know, from sporadic dealings with DANY over the years, that the culture in the office was conservative and resistant to change. One had only to walk through the halls to know that the place was not a swanky or sleek new operation. The halls reeked of tradition, with black-and-white photos of old white guys who had been office leaders, boxes of case files filling up every nook and cranny, bored police officers manning security stations, and bathrooms that had been old and uncomfortable for at least the last fifty years. The physical space was spread out across a number of different buildings, each containing a hodgepodge of hallways and offices, many of which were poorly lit and tired. If Humphrey Bogart, cast in his role as "Sam Spade, private eye," had been walking through the halls in a saggy raincoat and a fedora, he would not have looked out of place.

When Cy Vance became district attorney in January 2010, he was only the third person elected to that position in more than sixty-five years. Frank Hogan had served from 1942 to 1973, and Robert Morgenthau had served from 1975 until the end of 2009. As I was to learn, doing things as they had been done for decades was valued by the rank and file; creative thinking was distrusted and suspect if it involved unfamiliar ideas. The office was the legal equivalent of an old dog that had gone about its routine for years and years. Learning new tricks, or operating at the cutting edge of the criminal law, particularly in a high-profile investigation, was not a prized part of office culture.

The investigative team was rich with supervisors. Cy Vance himself was all over the case. He sat in on witness interviews and grand jury sessions, participated in update calls, and wanted to be kept abreast as we learned new facts. But he was not heavy-handed at all; if anything, he was overly deferential. He would sometimes finish an internal call by thanking his subordinates for allowing him to participate, which always surprised me because each of us was working in his name and under his authority.

Carey Dunne seemed to be the de facto leader of the overall effort, although as DANY's general counsel he continued to have many other responsibilities. Everyone knew that he and Cy were old colleagues, and Cy depended on Carey's judgment and advice. Chris Conroy, in his midfifties and a longtime veteran in the DA's office, was chief of the Investigation Division. He was not doing actual spadework on the case, but he had supervisory authority over the investigation, as did Julieta Lozano, who was chief of the Major Economic Crimes Bureau, which was the home bureau for the Trump investigation. The day-to-day work was being done by a team of four prosecutors assigned to the Major Economic Crimes Bureau.

The regular involvement of so many supervisors, and particularly the regular oversight of the district attorney and his close confidant Carey, was to be expected in an investigation that involved the sitting president of the United States when it began. But it was a departure from office tradition. Traditionally, the line prosecutors worked autonomously building their cases. When their cases were assembled, they would brief the supervisors and get permission to proceed. The expectation was that the supervisors would become heavily involved only toward the end of the investigation, when charges had to be authorized. In the Trump investigation, the supervisors were intimately involved in every decision, large and small. As the matter progressed, I wondered whether the close supervision had sapped the team's initiative and enthusiasm. We later had update calls and meetings where I encouraged everyone to speak, but I had mixed success.

After being sworn in, I got a data dump—case memos and interview notes that detailed a lot of the investigative work that had been done. At the outset, I dug into the payment of hush money to Stephanie Clifford. I started there because it was interesting and easy to understand. I had followed the whole story from the sidelines, and it involved allegations of sexual infidelity. As compared to delving into the valuation of an office building, or the propriety of tax deductions for donating conservation easements, it seemed like a good place to start. I was curious, as were many people, about the end of the federal investigation of the Stephanie Clifford saga. The federal prosecutors at the Southern District had charged Michael Cohen with committing a crime by making a hush money payment. The payment was not illegal in itself, but Cohen had paid Clifford so that she would not disclose her alleged affair with Trump on the eve of the 2016 election. The payment was made in late October 2016, and news of the alleged affair right before the election would have harmed Trump's campaign. Cohen made the payment to help Trump avoid the political damage that Clifford's allegation would have caused. That made the payment an illegal campaign contribution under federal law. In reciting their charges against Cohen the prosecutors had named Donald Trump as "Individual No. 1," the person whose campaign had benefited from the payment, and with whom Clifford had allegedly slept. Cohen claimed that Trump had directed him to make the payment and had approved his reimbursement for it. But there had been no prosecution of Donald Trump, and I wondered what had happened.

The materials I received did not explain why the federal prosecutors had not charged Trump with a crime, but I can venture some educated speculation. During Trump's presidency, the prosecutors in the Southern District of New York, as employees of the Justice Department, were barred by DOJ internal legal guidance from seeking an indictment of a sitting president. The DOJ internal guidance, contained in a 1973 memo that had been written by the DOJ's Office of Legal Counsel, was reaffirmed in 2000 in another Office of Legal Counsel memo. Together the two memos stated the DOJ's view of the law: a sitting president is constitutionally immune from indictment and criminal prosecution because prosecution would prevent the president from carrying out his responsibilities. Although the federal prosecutors in the Southern District of New York are famously independent, proud, and self-confident—sometimes referring to themselves as the "Sovereign" District of New York—hubris has its limits. The United States attorney would not have charged the president in defiance of official Justice Department policy, even though that policy had never been tested before a court.

The Manhattan federal prosecutors also had a problem with Michael Cohen, and he had a problem with them. Cohen had worked for Trump for years, and he was willing to cooperate and testify against Trump with regard to the hush money payment and other crimes. The federal prosecutors in Manhattan, however, had a protocol for dealing with potential cooperators that was much tougher than that of most other jurisdictions. They required a would-be cooperator to confess to any crime he had ever committed, anywhere, with anyone—not just crimes committed with the target of the investigation. To be a "cooperator," the person had to tell the prosecutors about everything illegal, whether or not the prosecutors already knew about it. Then, the would-be cooperator had to "take responsibility" for all of his criminal conduct. To "take responsibility," in the lexicon of the prosecutors, typically meant pleading guilty to all the crimes the cooperator had committed.

After pleading guilty to everything, the would-be cooperator then had to agree to cooperate fully, testifying and meeting with the prosecutors whenever necessary. The cooperator would not be sentenced until all the testimony and meetings were done, which could be years in the future. The payoff would be the government's agreement to recommend leniency to the sentencing judge. The judge, however, was not obliged to accept the government's recommendation; he or she could "throw the book" at the cooperator at the time of sentencing, even increasing the sentence to take into account the crimes that no one might have learned about but for the cooperator's baring of his soul in order to become a cooperator.

The Manhattan federal prosecutors had followed this protocol for decades. It was in place when I joined the SDNY in 1978, and it still represents SDNY dogma. The thinking is that, by requiring cooperators to admit to everything and to "take responsibility" for all of their bad acts, they will be more credible in the eyes of jurors and will not be seen as concealing or minimizing their criminal conduct.

The protocol, though, deters some witnesses who might otherwise be willing to testify for the government. In particular, it deters people like Michael Cohen—people who are willing to admit some wrongdoing, and to tell the truth about it, but who do not want to postpone their sentencing for years. The protocol also deters would-be cooperators who will not confess to conduct that the government does not know about, or conduct that implicates family or friends, or conduct that the potential cooperator denies or does not think was illegal. Cohen, by his own admission, had helped Donald Trump lie, cheat, and steal in myriad ways over the course of many years. Expecting him to dredge up every instance of wrongdoing, and to plead guilty to all of it, was perhaps too much. Also, Cohen had been involved in business deals away from Donald Trump, and the government had seized documents and electronic data from him and placed his business life under a microscope. There were transactions that the government thought were criminal and that Cohen maintained were innocent.

Disagreements like these make it impossible for a defendant to cooperate with federal prosecutors in Manhattan, because the government's protocol requires abject surrender of all defenses, agreement with the government's allegations of criminality, and throwing oneself on the mercy of the court. This works for many people; it did not work for Michael Cohen. Cohen did not want to wait, potentially for years, until he could be sentenced. He was willing to meet with the government and answer questions, but he wanted not to be kept dangling for years until his cooperation was finished and he could be sentenced. Cohen, therefore, did not enter into a cooperation agreement with the Southern District of New York.

By January 20, 2021, when Trump was no longer president, and Justice Department policy would have permitted his indictment and prosecution, Cohen had disclaimed his guilt with respect to some of the crimes to which he had already pleaded guilty, which disqualified him from "cooperating" with a federal prosecution of Donald Trump under the SDNY protocol for would-be cooperators. In any event, the point was moot; back in July 2019, the federal prosecutors had responded to a court inquiry by disclosing that they had ended their investigation of Michael Cohen's payment of hush money to women who claimed that they had had sex with Donald Trump.

The prosecutors at DANY had followed a different path. I learned that the district attorney's team had done a lot of work developing the facts surrounding the Clifford hush money payment. That investigation had started years earlier and had been part of what led DANY to subpoena Trump's tax and accounting records in the legal fracas that was resolved by the United States Supreme Court. Once the federal prosecutors acknowledged that they were finished looking at hush money payments, DANY's investigators had ramped up their efforts. In August and September 2019, they visited Cohen in federal prison, where he was serving his sentence, and asked Cohen about the Clifford facts.

By October 2019, the DANY team knew the details of the hush money scheme. Their focus was the manner in which Cohen had been reimbursed for the payment he made to Clifford. While Cohen had used his own money to make the $130,000 payment to Clifford to secure her silence about the alleged affair with Trump, Cohen said that Trump had agreed from the outset that Cohen would be reimbursed. The reimbursement involved camouflage: Cohen submitted phony invoices to the Trump Organization for "legal services rendered" under a fictional "retainer agreement." Each month, throughout 2017 (after Trump's inauguration as president), Cohen submitted an invoice referencing the "retainer agreement" and requesting payment for "services rendered" for that month. The Trump Organization maintained and processed each invoice for payment as "legal expenses." Cohen then received a check, hand-signed by Donald Trump. There had been no retainer agreement and no legal services; the documents were a disguise used to reimburse Cohen for money he had laid out on Trump's behalf.

Although DANY's investigators had pulled these facts together, they did not amount to much in legal terms. Paying hush money is not a crime under New York State law, even if the payment was made to help an electoral candidate. The payment to Clifford was a crime under federal election laws, but state prosecutors cannot charge people with federal crimes. Charges arising under federal law have to be brought by federal prosecutors; local prosecutors like the Manhattan district attorney can prosecute only violations of state or local laws.

The hush money and phony invoicing scheme had generated false business records, and New York State's Penal Law does make it a crime to falsify business records. But creating false business records is only a misdemeanor under New York law. (Misdemeanors are relatively minor crimes, for which the maximum jail sentence is less than one year. Prosecutors typically do not bring misdemeanor charges to address serious criminal conduct, believing that misdemeanor treatment in serious cases does not provide for adequate punishment, deterrence, or accountability.) Falsifying business records can be prosecuted as a felony if the defendant created the records intending to commit or conceal "another crime." This statutory language, however, is ambiguous. Does the reference to "another crime" include *federal* crimes, or just *state* crimes? This was an important legal question in the context of the hush money investigation, because Cohen (with the agreement of Trump and others at the Trump Organization) had used phony documents and invoices to commit and conceal a federal election law violation, but there appeared to be no comparable state crime in play. So, to charge Trump with something other than a misdemeanor, DANY would have to argue that the intent to commit or conceal a federal crime had converted the falsification of the records into a felony. No appellate court in New York had ever upheld (or rejected) this interpretation of the law.

While I was not present for the discussions that took place within DANY in the fall of 2019, I later learned that this gnarly legal question had gotten a lot of attention. DANY lawyers had looked at it, and they had commissioned an outside law firm to research the issue. But the issue had never been litigated, and there were good arguments to be made on both sides of it. The legal question was a "toss up," and no one could predict with certainty how an appellate court might eventually rule. This meant that if DANY brought a criminal case based on the hush money payment and the related phony invoices, there was a big risk that felony charges would be dismissed before a jury could even consider them. The prosecution might be left to go forward with only misdemeanor charges.

I doubt very much that Cy Vance seriously considered bringing any criminal charges—felonies or misdemeanors— against a sitting president in the fall of 2019. Though it has never been attempted, it is highly unlikely that a local prosecutor could pursue a criminal case against a sitting president. The Supreme Court would decide later that presidents do not have constitutional immunity from providing information called for by subpoenas, but allowing a sitting president to be charged, arraigned, tried, convicted, and potentially jailed by local authorities is something else entirely.

In any case, the district attorney had decided toward the end of 2019 that no charges would then be brought against anyone in connection with the hush money paid to Stephanie Clifford or the phony invoicing scheme by which Michael

Cohen had been reimbursed for the money he had laid out. That part of the Trump investigation was lying dormant, if not completely dead.

I looked closely at the facts after being sworn in as a Manhattan prosecutor in January 2021. By that time, of course, Donald Trump was no longer a sitting president. Joe Biden took office on January 20, 2021, notwithstanding Trump's yelling, kicking, and screaming over the results of the 2020 election. The hush money facts, and particularly the details of the dealings between Michael Cohen and Clifford and her lawyer, seemed really smelly to me. Clifford's manager, Gina Rodriguez, had contacted Dylan Howard, an entertainment journalist and editor in chief of the *National Enquirer* tabloid, telling Howard that Clifford was willing to publicize her story about having had sex with Donald Trump. Howard contacted his boss, David Pecker, the CEO of American Media, which at the time owned the *National Enquirer*. Howard told Pecker that Clifford's story was true, and that American Media needed to buy the story so that it would not come to light. Pecker told Howard that he did not want to buy the story from a porn star, and he and Howard then contacted Michael Cohen to see if Cohen would deal with Clifford directly on Donald Trump's behalf. Cohen got in contact with Clifford's lawyer, Keith Davidson, whom he knew from prior dealings.

Cohen and Davidson agreed to concoct a written settlement agreement between people identified as "David Dennison" and "Peggy Peterson." Peterson, in exchange for a payment of $130,000 from a company called Essential Consultants, would release her "claims" against Dennison and agree not to disclose her claims to anyone. "Peggy Peterson" was a pseudonym for Stephanie Clifford. "David Dennison" was a pseudonym for Donald Trump. The true names of the parties were identified in a side letter that was never intended to see the light of day. "Peterson," aka Clifford, had no real "claims" against "Dennison," aka Trump, but the nondisclosure agreement was structured as a "settlement agreement" and release of claims to dress up what it really was—an agreement to pay hush money. Essential Consultants was a company that Michael Cohen formed in order to make the payment to Clifford from an entity that did not have Donald Trump's name associated with it. Cohen had delayed sending the payment to Davidson, Clifford's lawyer. This had prompted Davidson to get word to Cohen, through Howard and Pecker at American Media, that Clifford was going to tell her story. This was something that "could look awfully bad for everyone," according to an email that was sent to Cohen. Cohen, after explaining that the delay was because it was hard to get money out of Donald Trump, set up a home equity line of credit on his own home. He borrowed money from the line of credit, deposited the money into a bank account he had set up in the name of Essential Consultants, and wired the money to Clifford's lawyer.

When I looked at these facts, along with the false invoices for the monthly "retainer" payments that had been used to reimburse Cohen, the whole situation reeked of deception to me. The use of pseudonyms, an agreement to settle nonexistent "claims," a secret side letter, the phony invoices—all of these things were devices to keep Donald Trump's name away from the hush money payment, even though he had dispatched Cohen to take care of the problem by paying Clifford.

Although DANY had not brought charges based on these facts in the fall of 2019, when Trump was president, I thought we needed to revisit that decision in early 2021. We therefore looked again to see whether the facts would support a felony prosecution for falsifying business records. We requested another thorough outside review of the legal question that DANY had considered previously: Could we charge Donald Trump with falsifying business records (the documents used to pay Clifford and reimburse Michael Cohen for non-existent "legal services") with the intent to commit or conceal a federal election law violation? Once again, the analysis could not answer this question because there was simply no clear answer to be had; to get an answer, we would need a court ruling. This meant that there was no way to avoid the substantial risk that felony charges would be dismissed, leaving us only with misdemeanor charges. At this early point in the investigation we did not want to wind up litigating only a misdemeanor charge against Donald Trump. We were actively investigating a host of other more serious felony charges unrelated to the payment of hush money, and bringing a possible misdemeanor case against the former president before doing more investigation would have been premature and imprudent.

Because a false business record charge might not hold up as a felony case, we considered whether there were other felony charges that could be brought in connection with the payment that Cohen had made to Clifford and the ensuing coverup. I knew from experience that disguising payments, and concealing their true purpose, were hallmarks of the crime of money laundering. I consulted New York's money-laundering statute. That section of the Penal Law makes it a crime to engage in a financial transaction that is designed to "conceal or disguise" the "source" or the true "ownership" of criminal proceeds. Money laundering is a felony.

At first blush, the statute seemed to mesh perfectly with the facts. The whole point of the contrived "settlement agreement" with Clifford and the phony Cohen invoices was to conceal that the hush money ultimately came from Donald Trump. The deal was structured to "conceal" and "disguise" Trump's identity as the true source of the payment. Michael Cohen, acting as Trump's intermediary, had "laundered" the money used to pay Clifford by entering into the contrived settlement agreement and using his line of credit and newly formed company, knowing that Trump would reimburse him. Trump, not Cohen, was the actual source of the money.

The only remaining legal issue seemed to be whether the money paid to Clifford was "proceeds" of criminal activity. It's perfectly legal to disguise the source of a plain-vanilla financial transaction. I can buy a car with money given to me by my brother but tell the dealership that the money came from my business. But I cannot do that with "criminal proceeds." So, if my brother actually got the money by robbing a bank, and I bought the car for him so that he could spend some of his ill-gotten gains, that's money laundering—conducting a financial transaction (paying for a car) with the intent to conceal that the money is dirty because it is proceeds of a bank robbery.

So, was the money paid to Clifford in fact "dirty" money, which represented the proceeds of criminal activity? I thought it might be. Demands to pay hush money often amount to extortion. Extortion is a crime that consists of obtaining money through force or threats. It is a crime in all fifty states, including New York. In New York, the crime is called larceny by extortion. It is committed when someone gets money by instilling in another person a fear that, unless the money is paid, someone will "publicize an asserted fact, whether true or false, tending to subject some person to hatred, contempt, or ridicule."

It seemed likely to me that Stephanie Clifford had committed the crime of extortion. She had instilled in Trump and Cohen the fear that, unless she got paid, she would publicize her alleged sexual tryst with Donald Trump. Exposing the tryst would subject Trump, at a minimum, to "contempt" and "ridicule." Indeed, the people close to Trump who knew that Clifford was threatening to tell her story thought it might cost

Trump the election. If the hush money had been paid in response to extortion, I thought it might qualify as criminal proceeds, that is, "dirty money," and concealing its source might be punishable as money laundering.

Threats to expose intimate relationships in exchange for money are often the backdrop for extortion charges. In 1997, federal prosecutors had convicted a woman named Autumn Jackson of extortion after she demanded money from Bill Cosby (then known as a comedian and not a sexual predator) in exchange for keeping silent about her claim that he was actually her father. If Clifford had gotten money by threatening to tell the world that she had slept with Donald Trump, that sounded like extortion to me. And if it was extortion, then maybe the hush money she received could be regarded as criminal proceeds, so action taken to conceal Trump's identity as the source of the money was chargeable as money laundering.

Viewing the hush money facts as a laundering of extortion proceeds was a new idea, and I got enthusiastic about it. I floated the idea with Carey, and later shared my thinking with the investigative team. The return to life of the hush money facts as a potential basis for prosecution sparked a nickname for this part of the investigation: the hush money inquiry came to be known as the "zombie" case, because it was alive, and then it was dead, and now it had sprung back to life.

Combing through Donald Trump's public statements, I found a tweet in which he said that the point of the agreement with Stephanie Clifford had been to stop her "extortionist accusations." Trump's use of the word *extortionist* seemed very helpful to the theory I was trying to develop. But to probe matters further, it would be necessary to speak with Michael Cohen.

CHAPTER FOUR

MEETING
MICHAEL COHEN

I had not met Michael Cohen before February 2021, but like millions of Americans, I felt like I knew him from reading about him and seeing him on television. Cohen had been a fierce defender of Donald Trump, having famously said he would "take a bullet" for his boss. But, after the FBI executed search warrants and seized evidence from him, Cohen had "flipped" from Trump's most ardent supporter to his most outspoken foe. He had testified against Trump in February 2019, in an appearance before the House Oversight Committee. That testimony, which was carried live on television, had been dramatic: Cohen described Trump as a "racist," a "con man," and a "cheat," and provided information in support of each of those labels.

As I prepared to interview Cohen for the first time, I thought about his legal situation, which was unusual. Ordinarily, witnesses who have committed crimes with others—so-called "accomplice" witnesses—are cooperative only because they have been charged with crimes themselves. They usually are awaiting sentencing, and they are looking for leniency. The prospect of being sentenced in the future hangs over cooperating witnesses like the Sword of Damocles and gives them a motive to give information to prosecutors and testify against their former confederates.

But Cohen was not the ordinary "accomplice" witness. He already had been sentenced in cases brought by the federal authorities. He had been charged with perjury by the special counsel, Robert Mueller, for lying to Congress in August 2017 with regard to Trump's involvement with a real estate project in Moscow, and he had been charged by federal prosecutors in New York for his role in the Stephanie Clifford affair and other offenses, including tax evasion. He had pleaded guilty, and he had been sentenced on all of the federal charges in December 2018. Because Cohen already had been sentenced, there was no "sword" dangling over his head to give him a reason to cooperate with DANY.

Unlike most "accomplice" witnesses, however, Cohen didn't need the dangling sword to prompt him to cooperate. He said he wanted to make sure that Donald Trump was prosecuted and held accountable for his crimes. He was an accomplice who did not have to be pressured, cajoled, or coaxed into answering questions.

As our investigation went on, Cohen was always ready to make himself available and to answer any question he was asked. He was not only willing to cooperate, but eager to do so. He would contact me from time to time, making sure we understood that he was available and asking when we might need to speak with him again.

But that would all come later. My first interviews of Cohen took place over Zoom on February 18 and February 26. Cohen was on home confinement at this point, having been released from prison because of the pandemic. He sat before his computer in his apartment—a familiar face in a box on a screen, surrounded by other boxes containing the faces of the members of the investigative team and Cohen's lawyer. I introduced myself and started asking questions. My focus was on the hush money facts, and particularly whether Cohen and Trump believed that Clifford was extorting them. If so, the payment to her might qualify as the proceeds of crime, which Cohen and Trump had conspired to "launder" by concealing the fact that the money was coming from Trump. My theory got a shot in the arm when I asked Cohen whether he and Trump spoke about Clifford's demand for money as extortion. He said that was not the word they used. I asked what words did they use, and his answer was that Trump referred to it as "fucking blackmail." That was more than sufficient for my purposes.

In our first conversation, Cohen impressed me as smart but manipulative. He struck me as a somewhat feral creature. Most importantly, I thought he was telling the truth. I had dealt with many cooperators over the years. Cohen reminded me of Barry Lipsky, a drug dealer turned cooperator who had testified for me in a narcotics trial that had taken place forty years earlier, when I was a young federal prosecutor. Cohen even had the same jowly look that I recalled about Lipsky. Both were street-smart survivors and wannabe gangsters with good memories, who not only turned on their criminal confederates but did so with gusto. Cohen, like Lipsky, wanted to be liked, and he craved attention. Lipsky, like Cohen, made no excuses for his own crimes and answered questions freely and in a straightforward fashion. I thought Lipsky had been a psychopath. He had strangled a young model, Patsy Parks, as he sat behind her in a car driven by Vinnie Pacelli Jr., a heroin dealer. I used Lipsky to convict Pacelli's business partner, a drug dealer named Abbe Perez.

Despite their similarities, Cohen was no psychopathic

killer, and he had a more complicated psyche. In our later conversations, he described to me an incident in which he had
been shopping with his daughter in a jewelry store on Forty-
Seventh Street, in Manhattan's Diamond District. His daughter
bent down and picked up a large, loose diamond that had been
lying unnoticed on the floor. She gave the diamond to Cohen,
who immediately told a store employee what his daughter had
found on the floor. At one point, his daughter asked why he had
turned over the diamond so quickly, when he easily could have
put it in his pocket. According to Cohen, he told his daughter
that he had always tried to raise her to know the difference
between right and wrong, and he had given up the jewel because that was the right thing to do. The story illustrated to
me the complexity of Cohen's character and the infinite variet-
ies of human behavior. The same man who had tried to teach
his daughter the difference between right and wrong had lied,
cheated, and connived with Donald Trump for many years,
and now he was sitting with prosecutors volunteering to tell
them all about it.

It was apparent after my first interview of Michael Cohen
that we had gotten along. The decades I had spent as a defense
attorney had made it easier to talk to Cohen. Prosecutors, and
particularly career prosecutors who have no experience representing people in trouble, can sometimes be too wooden
or even moralistic and judgmental in speaking with people
who have committed crimes. I felt like I had known guys like
Cohen all of my professional life. I had represented more than
a few similar people, including lawyers who had broken the
law. One former client, an attorney who had been a law secretary to a state court judge, had gotten into trouble by telling
an old friend that he could "fix" a case for him. The friend had
been caught passing counterfeit money, and my client told him

that he knew the judge who had the friend's case, and he could bribe the judge so the friend would not go to prison. The friend gave him ten thousand dollars for the judge, but my client just put the money in his pocket. Unbeknownst to my client, his "friend" was an informant, and the whole transaction had been tape-recorded by the FBI. The worst part of the tapes was my client's description of what happened when the judge for whom he worked died suddenly. The informant asked my client if he had to find another job right away. My client said he still could work for the dead judge for a few weeks longer. He said his judge had not spoken a lot when the judge was on the bench, so my client figured he could just "stuff him like Trigger" (Trigger was the name of Roy Rogers's horse, which had been stuffed and preserved after the horse died), prop the judge up on the bench, and move his arms once in a while. According to my client, it might take some time before anyone realized that the judge was dead. Of course, this was a joke, but it did not sound that funny when the government played the "Trigger" tape in open court during my client's trial. The presiding judge was particularly unamused, but my client was acquitted.

Having dealt with and represented an assortment of crooked lawyers, con men, and other miscreants over the years, it was not a chore to speak with Michael Cohen. Lawyers who try cases, or who handle criminal cases, need to develop a rapport with people who might testify for them. It is not rocket science, but it requires the ability to talk to people without passing judgment on them, keeping in mind the many shades of gray that color human behavior. Cohen's lawyer later called to tell me that Cohen "liked me," and we had "bonded." I am not ashamed to admit that I kind of liked Cohen as well. He was quick and eager to please. He was responsive. He had a sense of humor and understood irony. He had his own agenda, but when he focused on answering questions, and not volunteering information or exaggerating his own importance, he struck me as someone who would be convincing on the witness stand. I thought he was telling the truth. Of course, jurors would know that Cohen was furious with Donald Trump, and wanted to see him convicted. But I thought that Cohen's anger could be explained to jurors: He was angry with Trump because Trump had seduced Cohen into his criminal orbit, and Cohen had been the only one of Trump's enablers to have gone to prison. Cohen was angry with himself for allowing himself to be seduced by Trump. He also felt betrayed by Trump, who had distanced himself from Cohen after the investigations had started. Cohen's anger could be explained, and it did not make him incapable of telling the truth.

In our second Zoom interview, Cohen related a conversation with Trump that had taken place in the Oval Office of the White House. I had been asking him about events that occurred after the press had learned about his payment of $130,000 to Stephanie Clifford. That happened in January 2018, when the *Wall Street Journal* broke the Trump-Cohen-Clifford payment story. A month later, Cohen was peddling the lie that he had used his own money to pay Clifford and had never been reimbursed by the Trump Organization, "either directly or indirectly." Supposedly, Cohen had paid Clifford with his own money out of the goodness of his heart, to protect Trump (and Trump's marriage) from the adverse publicity that Clifford's allegations would have caused. Cohen had given this account to Maggie Haberman at the *New York Times*. According to Cohen, Haberman thought that Cohen's story was ridiculous, but she dutifully reported Cohen's claim that he had paid Clifford out of his own pocket and had never been reimbursed. Of course, the story was absurd. Cohen paid Clifford only because Trump and his CFO, Allen Weisselberg, had promised to repay Cohen, and in fact Cohen had been repaid. Trump, having first denied that he knew anything about Cohen's payment to Clifford, later acknowledged through his new lawyer, Rudy Giuliani, that Cohen had been reimbursed, but he argued that no campaign money had been used to pay Clifford or to reimburse Cohen.

I was interested in the brief window of time that Cohen had been telling the world, falsely, that he had used his own money with no expectation of reimbursement. I thought that this story was laughable—lawyers don't pony up six-figure sums out of their own pocket to benefit their clients, particularly clients who are self-professed multibillionaires. I thought it was likely that Cohen had given this ludicrous and false story to the *New York Times* only after having cleared it in advance with Donald Trump. I asked Cohen whether he had discussed with Trump what he was going to say about using his own money. He said that he had done so. I asked whether Trump had agreed with Cohen that Cohen should put out the false story. Cohen said he would not put it that way. I asked how he would put it. Cohen replied that Trump had not simply *agreed* that Cohen would put out the phony "I reached into my own pocket" story, but had *ordered* him to tell people he had used his own money and had not been reimbursed. Cohen said that the order to tell this lie had come from the president while both were in the Oval Office, where Cohen also had received signed reimbursement checks from the president.

Cohen's account of the conversation he had with Trump in the Oval Office upset me. It was distressing that such a tawdry exchange had taken place in the Oval Office, which I thought of as the *sanctum sanctorum* of American government. Maybe I was naive—after all, I had vivid memories of the Watergate scandal, which unfolded as I left law school and became a law clerk. I certainly remembered the criminal conversations that had taken place in the Nixon White House, but I was still disturbed when Cohen described Trump sitting in the Oval Office and directing him to put out a cock-and-bull story to protect the president's reputation. I was angry that the nation's self-described "chief law enforcement officer" had directed someone to tell lies to the public to conceal his dealings with a porn star.

As a lawyer, though, I knew that the conversation was important because it was easy to corroborate. Corroboration—evidence that confirms a witness is telling the truth and supports the witness's testimony—is the name of the game when a cooperator gives testimony at a criminal trial. Trials that feature cooperator testimony are all about corroboration. Most cooperators, like Michael Cohen, have testimonial "baggage" that cuts against their credibility. Virtually always they have committed criminal acts, and defense lawyers argue that the witnesses' crimes make them unreliable. Prosecutors inevitably respond by saying that they are not asking the jury to believe a cooperating witness just on the witness's word; they should believe the witness because his testimony makes sense and, most importantly, because there is supporting evidence.

Cohen's testimony that Trump had told him to lie about the hush money, and to tell everyone that he had fronted his own money without expecting or receiving reimbursement, could be corroborated by proving that Trump had been spouting the same lie at the same time. Trump had told reporters in early April 2018 that he had not known about Cohen's payment to Clifford and that he did not know where Cohen had gotten the money. That statement was videotaped as Trump spoke with reporters at the threshold of Air Force One. Later, Rudy Giuliani admitted on Trump's behalf that Trump had reimbursed

Cohen's payment to Clifford. Giuliani's admission came right after Cohen's premises had been searched, when it had become clear that the reimbursement could no longer be kept secret. So, when Cohen was claiming that he used his own money, Trump had claimed to be ignorant of the payment. Later, when Cohen admitted that Trump had reimbursed him, Trump likewise changed his story. The sequence of events lent credence to Cohen's statement that he and Trump had coordinated on Cohen's short-lived "I did it all myself" story.

There was other proof as well. Cohen had not only told the phony story to the media; he had recited the same phony story to First Lady Melania Trump at Donald Trump's direction. Cohen recounted an episode that had taken place right when he had first given the "I did it all myself" story to Haberman at the *Times*. Trump put Cohen on the telephone to speak to Melania so that Cohen could tell her the same false cover story about using his own money. During the phone call with Melania, Trump interrupted Cohen to ask, incredulously, whether Cohen was telling the Trumps that he had used his own money to pay Clifford, with no expectation of reimbursement, to protect the Trump campaign, his marriage, and his reputation. Cohen dutifully lied, saying that he had done so. There was another witness to the conversation—a business friend whose identity Cohen provided to us. The business friend had been riding in a car to New Jersey's Teterboro Airport with Cohen when the conversation with Trump and Melania had occurred, and he had heard enough of the conversation to know what had happened. So, if necessary, we could get records to show exactly when the conversation took place, and we had a potential witness to the conversation who had no reason to lie about what he had heard.

In short, I thought Cohen was telling the truth about the

Clifford payment and the attempt to cover it up. In my mind, Cohen could be corroborated, and he could be a compelling witness. Cy Vance agreed. He had listened to both of my interviews of Cohen and sent me an email. The email said: ". . . I think with the right examiner (you) and preparation, [Cohen] would be a believable witness, and actually a powerful one. Cross[-examination] may be very tough, but jury selection can take a lot of the sting out of the anticipated attacks at trial and, importantly, those lies he has told have, for the most part, been at the president's direction."

The bottom line for me was that the "zombie" case was very strong. The basic facts—that Clifford claimed she had slept with Trump, that she had wanted money to keep her mouth shut, that Cohen had agreed to pay her and had made the payment, that the payment and the agreement with Clifford had been disguised to keep Trump's identity secret, that Trump had then signed checks to reimburse Cohen for the money paid to Clifford, and that the reimbursement had involved phony invoices for "legal retainers"—were readily provable. Cohen could tell this story, and each piece of it could be corroborated by other witnesses and documents. Now we also had evidence that Trump had told Cohen in the Oval Office to tell the world the laughable and short-lived story that Cohen had paid Clifford with his own money with no expectation or agreement about reimbursement. It struck me as very powerful evidence of wrongdoing. But was it a crime under New York law?

CHAPTER FIVE

THE "ZOMBIE" CASE RETURNS TO THE GRAVE

On February 28, 2021, I sent a memo to the district attorney summarizing where we were on the "zombie" case. The memo recommended further investigative steps but opined that Trump might have criminal exposure for aiding and abetting money laundering and conspiracy to commit money laundering. The conspiracy charge would embrace the cover-up to conceal Trump's involvement, including the phony story hatched in the Oval Office conversation that Michael Cohen had described.

Legally, the money-laundering charges held together only if the hush money was "dirty money," that is, the proceeds of a crime. I thought that the hush money could be charged as the proceeds of Clifford's extortion of Donald Trump. Admittedly, this was a somewhat awkward construct. Step one would be to prove that Trump was, in effect, a blackmail victim. We would be claiming that Clifford had committed larceny by extortion when she threatened to publicize her alleged tryst unless Trump paid her money. We did not actually have to bring a criminal case against Clifford (or her lawyer), but we would have to allege that Trump had been extorted. If we established the extortion, we could go on to step two: charging Trump with money laundering because he had worked with Cohen to conceal his identity as the source of the extorted funds. It was a creative legal theory, neither intuitive nor obvious. The district attorney raised his eyebrows at the notion that we would be claiming that Donald Trump was a victim of blackmail, but he was intrigued by the idea.

At this point, however, my creative theorizing smacked into DANY's cautious and conservative culture, as it would several times during my tenure. Some of my new colleagues balked at the notion that Clifford's demand for hush money qualified as extortion. I was told that the extortion cases that the office had brought in the past had involved threats of physical violence, and explicit demands to pay money "or else" something very bad would happen to the victim. By contrast, Clifford had retained a lawyer and had been shopping her story to the media when Michael Cohen reached out to her with an offer to "purchase" her silence. This so-called "extortion" had been very soft and unthreatening, and therefore might not constitute a crime at all, or so the pushback went.

To me, the reservations that my new colleagues were expressing had no substance. Of course, extortion and blackmail cases often revolve around violence and physical threats. Classic extortion cases involve loan-sharking and explicit threats to "break the knees" of the victim if he doesn't pay up. But extortion does not have to be hard-core to be illegal; soft-core extortion is also against the law, and involving lawyers and dressing up the conduct with a written nondisclosure agreement did not excuse the conduct in my mind. At bottom, the threat had been crystal clear: "If you don't pay me, I will tell everyone that we had sex." Under the New York Penal Law, this was a demand for money and an effort to instill a fear of public humiliation if the money was not paid. And New York law is quite explicit that it does not matter if Clifford did or did not have sex with Donald Trump. It is a crime under the Penal Law to get money by threatening to publicize an asserted fact "whether true or false."

Although I thought that a jury would likely find that extortion had taken place—Cohen said that Trump had referred to the whole thing as "fucking blackmail"—I did what prosecutors typically do when there is a difference of opinion about a charging decision. We would go look for more evidence.

We began the process of extracting more evidence from Clifford's lawyer, Keith Davidson. Davidson was a California lawyer who frequently represented clients who sought money from prominent individuals. We also made a request for information from the federal prosecutors in Manhattan who had investigated the Stephanie Clifford payment in connection with their prosecution of Michael Cohen. This put me in an odd position. As I have mentioned, dealings between DANY and the federal authorities at the Southern District of New York can be fraught. The offices generally cooperate with each other, but there is also a long history of competition, turf battles, and occasional outright warfare between them. Earlier in my career, I had been on the front lines of that competition on behalf of the feds. Now I was working for the district attorney and asking for information from the feds. The irony was duly noted, but eventually we did get materials from the federal authorities regarding their investigation of the Stephanie Clifford hush money events.

As things turned out, we never had to decide whether Clifford and her lawyer had committed the crime of extortion. I was doing legal research on the crimes of money laundering and larceny by extortion and came upon a new legal problem, which left me with a sinking feeling in my stomach. Under New York law, the crime of "larceny by extortion" is complete only when the perpetrator actually obtains money by making a threat. Until the money is received, there has been no larceny, because the essence of the crime is an illegal taking. Similarly, if you are mugged on the street, the crime of robbery occurs only when you hand over your wallet or your pocketbook—that is when your property has been illegally "obtained" by force.

In the Trump case, this meant that Clifford had not committed larceny by extortion until she or her lawyer received the $130,000 in hush money that Michael Cohen had agreed to pay on Trump's behalf. At that point, the crime of larceny by extortion was complete, and the hush money became "criminal proceeds" within the meaning of the money-laundering statute. But this was too late to support the money-laundering charge I had in mind. The money had to qualify as "criminal proceeds" when Cohen sent it; otherwise sending it was not money laundering. If the money became criminal proceeds only when received, the crime of money laundering had not taken place. Money laundering involves dealing in "dirty money." Legally, the hush money payment had not become dirty money until Clifford (or her lawyer) received it, so neither Cohen nor Trump had committed money laundering by sending it.

If this sequencing problem seems ridiculous and illogical, recall Charles Dickens's oft-cited aphorism that there are times when "the law is a ass—a idiot." I look at it a bit differently, though. The law is society's attempt to distinguish among human behavior's infinite shades of gray and to assign legal consequences to the difference between the shades. Of course, some laws try to draw exact dividing lines between what is legal and illegal, like definitions of "driving under the influence" that depend on scientific calculations of blood alcohol levels. But even the lines that are intended most clearly to distinguish between what is a crime and what is not, like the definition of murder, can become blurred when they are applied across a universe of infinitely varied circumstances. What about turning off the ventilator of a person who is "brain dead"? Is that murder? At what point along the continuum from fertilized egg to zygote to fetus does human life begin? Virtually all laws draw distinctions that can seem capricious depending on the circumstances to which they are applied.

Here, the definition of money laundering did not clearly apply to the circumstances of the hush money payment we were investigating. There were possible work-arounds, like alleging that Clifford had committed the offense of coercion, rather than larceny by extortion, or alleging that the money laundering had taken place when the funds were distributed from Clifford's lawyer to Clifford herself. But none of the work-arounds were appealing, and there was still the lingering problem that my new colleagues were dubious about whether Trump had been "extorted" in the first place, as opposed to simply being the highest bidder for the story that Clifford had threatened to make public.

The "zombie" case went back into the grave in March 2021. It would reemerge one more time at the end of the investigation, but for now it was dead and buried.

I had struck out in my first effort to focus the team on a particular set of facts, and my novel theory had whiffed. No harm had been done, but I may have reinforced the unspoken concern of some of the office's old-timers that I did not know New York criminal law, that I was too aggressive, and that I was looking for a "quick kill" that might not hold up in court.

In my mind, though, the fact that the extortion/money-laundering theory had not panned out as a technical legal matter took nothing away from the venal and sordid nature of the conduct and the former president's willingness to engage in it. He had been involved in a scheme to keep Clifford's account of her sexual interlude with him from seeing the light of day and had agreed to pay her lots of money to keep her mouth shut. In the late stages of the 2016 election campaign, while he was attacking his opponent's bona fides and encouraging his supporters to chant "lock her up," he was arranging a disguised payoff. Then, when the payment to Clifford was exposed, he sat in the Oval Office and participated in a cover-up, telling Michael Cohen to take the rap for the payoff even as he signed checks reimbursing Cohen for the money that had been paid to Clifford. I viewed it as serious criminal conduct, even though it seemed we could not thread the needle of New York's antiquated Penal Law to find an appropriate felony charge that was immune from legal challenge.

CHAPTER SIX

SCOTUS SPEAKS AT LAST

While I was digging around the "zombie" theory, many other things were happening. Most importantly, DANY was conducting a vigil with respect to orders coming down from the United States Supreme Court. The office was waiting for the final ruling in what had been a long-running, epic legal battle between the district attorney and Donald Trump. In the summer of 2019, long prior to my involvement, the investigative team had served a grand jury subpoena on Mazars USA, Donald Trump's accounting firm, seeking Trump's tax returns and accounting information. Trump's tax returns had long been the topic of extensive public interest, and Trump's refusal to make them available (unlike every major presidential candidate before him since Watergate) had been an issue in the 2016 presidential election.

Trump brought a lawsuit in federal court to stop the enforcement of the subpoena to the accounting firm and the lower courts ruled against him, rejecting his claim that a president enjoyed constitutional immunity from having his private affairs investigated by a local prosecutor. The case went to the Supreme Court, and Carey Dunne argued the case before the justices on May 12, 2020.

Arguing a case before the Supreme Court is a big deal for a

lawyer. In more than forty years of active practice as a litigator, I never had the opportunity to argue in front of the court, but I had listened to many arguments during my year as a Supreme Court law clerk. One of the many perks of being a law clerk for a justice was the ability to sit in the courtroom and write a note with a particularly nasty question to put to one of the lawyers. A page would take the note and hand it to the justice, who could ask the question if he or she thought it on point. Playing "stump the lawyer" was part of the joy of attending the arguments.

I had seen with my own eyes that lawyers do not win cases through their arguments, but it is easy to lose a case with a crappy one. The justices use the argument to probe for the limits and weaknesses in a party's legal position. A good advocate will reassure the justices inclined to support his or her position that the position is sound, shooting down potential problems and criticisms. But it is almost impossible to change the mind of a justice who is inclined to rule against your position. So, the mission is not to win votes in your favor, but to avoid losing them. Occasionally a justice might come to the argument without being disposed toward one side or another, but so much work gets done ahead of time that it is rare for a justice not to have some opinion about a case before hearing the argument. By the time the argument takes place, each justice will have read (or at least have had the opportunity to read) the extensive legal briefs that have been filed in the case and received a "bench memo" from the law clerks summarizing the arguments, the case law, and the pros and cons of the parties' positions.

Lawyers getting ready to present arguments to the Supreme Court usually prepare for many hours, days, or weeks. They try to leave nothing to chance and to avoid surprises. They study the court's prior cases, as nothing is worse than having a justice ask, "What about our opinion in *Smith vs. Jones*?" and responding with an apologetic, "I'm sorry, your honor, but I am not familiar with that case." Lawyers for parties with common interests coordinate about who will argue what point, and typically they have rehearsals before moot courts, in which other lawyers play the parts of the justices and try to ask the questions that will come up at argument, so the lawyers can road-test their answers. Sometimes parties will hire former appellate judges to sit on moot courts, so they get questions from people who have spent years asking questions of lawyers at real oral arguments.

Carey Dunne, in keeping with his prudent, detailed approach to his work as a lawyer, prepared for his oral argument like an astronaut getting prepared for a voyage into space. He appeared before moot courts, prepared himself on the law, and rehearsed his answers to anticipated questions. He consulted with a brain trust of experienced Supreme Court advocates, to make sure he knew all the nuances of the argument logistics and could predict the likely concerns of each justice.

Carey even prepared for a power failure. Because of the pandemic, the argument took place over the telephone, rather than in person in Washington, D.C. Carey was calling in from his home in New York City, and he parked his car immediately outside his house so that, if the electricity failed, he could run out to his car, plug in his cell phone, and do the argument from his driver's seat. He even disabled his doorbell and removed the batteries from his smoke and fire detectors, lest his appearance be interrupted by a shrieking alarm. His dog, needless to say, was banished from the premises.

Though the Supreme Court argument took place long before I started to work on the Trump investigation, I later listened to a recording of the proceedings. Carey's argument was brilliant. He effectively answered the justices' questions, and his style and demeanor were pitch-perfect. One of Trump's main arguments was that presidents should not be subject to the investigative whims of state and local prosecutors, because there were 2,300 of them in the United States, each of whom could mount a vicious political attack against the president in the guise of a criminal investigation. Carey, however, came across as the essence of sweet reason. His modulated and respectful tone surely helped convince the justices that he would never be part of a political witch hunt, even if a witch jumped up in the middle of his argument and bit him in the ankle.

On July 9, 2020, right before taking its customary summer break, the Supreme Court issued its opinion rejecting Trump's claim that his status as president gave him absolute constitutional immunity from subpoenas seeking information relating to potential criminal conduct. The decision was a landmark, which the *New York Times* described as "a major statement on the scope and limits of presidential power." But that did not mean that the district attorney would get Trump's financial records without further delay. The court allowed the president to go back to the lower courts to present objections to the breadth of the challenged subpoena apart from the rejected claim of constitutional immunity.

Trump raised new claims in the lower courts that the subpoena to Mazars was too broad and had been issued in bad faith. The lower courts rejected these claims as well, but Trump had the right to try to persuade the Supreme Court to hear them. The district attorney agreed to take no steps to enforce its subpoena until Trump could ask the Supreme Court to stay the enforcement of the subpoena and the Supreme Court had ruled on that stay application. Undoubtedly, Carey and his colleagues thought that the Supreme Court would make short work of Trump's latest attempt to prevent production of his financial records. His claims were garden-variety subpoena objections, the lower courts had rejected them, and there was no reason why the Supreme Court should want to get involved again. The Supreme Court's docket is almost entirely discretionary; with few exceptions, it hears only those cases that at least four justices want to consider, and Trump had lost the first time around by a 7–2 vote.

Unfortunately for the pace of the district attorney's investigation, the Supreme Court decided to sit on Trump's request for a further stay of subpoena enforcement. Trump made his stay application in October 2020, and the Supreme Court did not rule on it for months. No one at DANY, and none of the outside lawyers who were Supreme Court experts, could say why the court did not rule on Trump's stay application. Was it because they were waiting until he was no longer president? Were they waiting for him to file another formal petition for review? Had the stay application gotten lost in the shuffle?

When I was sworn in as a DANY prosecutor in early February 2021, I could not help decipher what was happening at the court. My tenure as a Supreme Court law clerk had been decades earlier, and the court was a different institution in those days. There was very little security back before the "war on terror." The law clerks had enjoyed the run of the building. My wife and I had even snuck into the courtroom one weekend, hopped up the stairs to the bench, and twirled around in the chief justice's chair. A relative (who happened to be a professional photographer) took a few pictures as we sat in the justices' chairs, just horsing around. But I had clerked in a much more relaxed and less partisan era, when no one paid much attention to which president had appointed which justice, and the justices were less consumed with ideological warfare. The court was more humble then. As the saying went among the justices, at least in those days, "We are not last because we are right; we are right because we are last."

Finally, on February 22, 2021, the Supreme Court denied Trump's stay application. The DANY team had convened on a Zoom call that morning, knowing that the Supreme Court was due to announce decisions on some of its pending matters. We were hoping that our case would be on the decision list, though there was no guarantee that it would be, and there had been other "decision days" when our case had not been mentioned. This time, though, our crossed fingers brought good luck. The court's order list announced that Trump's stay application was denied. There was no opinion—just the word *denied*. There were cheers on the Zoom call, congratulations all around, and kudos to Carey for his efforts. Trump's arguments, procedural ploys, and litigation tactics had now run their course, and after an eighteen-month delay, his accountants would have to turn over his tax returns and personal financial records.

That afternoon, DANY dispatched an investigator to re-trieve the materials. The press had been following the events and reported that the long-hidden materials would now be arriving at DANY. Because the materials, including the tax re-turns, were so super-sensitive, the office was paranoid about a leak or a hack involving the returns. Some of the Supreme Court justices had questioned Carey about the likelihood of a leak, and he had deflected their concerns. It would be horri-ble if the tax returns now became available because DANY did not attend to their security. So, upon our receipt of them, the materials were basically locked in a vault where no one could see them. DANY's security experts consulted with New York City's Cyber Command, an agency that worked with the po-lice department and the Office of Emergency Management to repel attacks on the security of the city's electronic data. It all meant that there would be a further delay before anyone could access the data that the office had fought so long and so hard to obtain. Ultimately, we could peruse the data by using certain stand-alone computers located in a clean room, with no internet access, open only to persons with approved access credentials. This made it extremely cumbersome to work with the documents, particularly as the pandemic was still raging, and most people (including me) were working from home. Eventually we loosened up the protocols, but the problem of getting easy access to the materials continued for months.

CHAPTER SEVEN

WORKING WITH THE ATTORNEY GENERAL

W e did not know, as we celebrated the final victory in the Supreme Court, that New York's attorney general, Letitia James, had already gotten a lot of the personal accounting information that DANY had been fighting to receive. I never learned exactly how the attorney general's investigators managed to do it, but while DANY was litigating over its subpoena and waiting for a final order from the Supreme Court, James's people were reviewing Trump's financial statements and getting information about how they were prepared and used. They did not have Trump's tax returns, but they had enough material to take testimony from witnesses about how Trump had valued his real estate and other holdings. This work later became extremely important to the district attorney's proposed prosecution of Donald Trump. But during 2019 and 2020, while James's lawyers were beavering away, DANY knew virtually nothing about what they were doing.

In retrospect, everything might have been different if the district attorney and the attorney general had been actively working together during 2019 and 2020. But it is not surprising that they were working separately. While people tend to view all law enforcement agencies as monolithic, they are not. In New York, the attorney general has limited criminal jurisdiction, but broad civil jurisdiction to pursue improper business practices. The district attorney basically brings criminal cases. They also have different investigative tools at their disposal. The district attorney uses grand juries to get testimony and gather evidence, while the attorney general can make use of administrative subpoenas and civil depositions. The tools cannot be used interchangeably. Except in limited circumstances, a criminal prosecutor cannot simply provide grand jury information to the state's attorney general. And the attorney general cannot use her civil authority to take depositions with the sole purpose of giving the testimony to a prosecutor.

Beyond the differences in function and tools, law enforcement is a competitive business. Even in routine cases, there is so much overlapping jurisdiction that investigators make choices about where to bring their cases. There is no big "clearinghouse" that parcels out law enforcement assignments. New York City's Fulton Fish Market has functioned for decades as the central hub for the wholesale distribution of fresh fish and seafood; fish markets and restaurants from all over the local area go there to get what they need. But there is no Fulton Fish Market for law enforcement. If Joe the drug dealer brings a kilogram of heroin from the Bronx to Brooklyn to sell to an undercover agent, and gets arrested, that case can be handled by the United States attorney for the Eastern District of New York, the United States attorney for the Southern District of New York, the Bronx County district attorney, the Kings County district attorney, the Organized Crime Drug Enforcement Task Force, or the city's special narcotics prosecutor. Prosecutors want the "juicy" cases, so they curry favor with arresting officers, sometimes promising that their case will get special attention, or be assigned to the best lawyer, if the case is brought to one office versus another. In certain cases, the attorney general can play a role, along with a hodgepodge of other agencies, depending on the subject matter. Enforcing tax laws can involve the Internal Revenue Service, the New York State Department of Taxation and Finance, and the New York City Department of Finance.

In large, press-worthy investigations, the competition among law enforcement agencies can "jump ugly." DANY and the attorney general's office are like siblings. We love each other—sort of—but do not always play well together, particularly when we are both playing in the same sandbox.

Given the traditional rivalries that take place in high-profile investigations, I was not surprised to learn that there was some distrust between DANY and the attorney general's office with respect to their Trump investigations. Even before being formally sworn in, I had read about the attorney general's interest in pursuing Donald Trump. When Letitia James took office in January 2019, she promised to launch what the media called "sweeping investigations" of the president and his business affairs, and she had campaigned on her willingness to go after Trump. Carey let me know that he and Cy had some angst about working with James, given her aggressive public statements. I did not know James at all, but I knew that several of her predecessors had used the attorney general's office to advance their political aspirations. I worried that she might be another political animal more interested in touting her pursuit of Trump than in bringing serious cases. This turned out to be completely wrong; James's lawyers had been working quietly and effectively behind the scenes, and we simply did not know all that they had been doing.

Ironically, the catalyst that brought our investigations closer to each other was Trump's pardon of Steven Bannon on the last day of his presidency, January 20, 2021. Bannon had been the CEO of Trump's presidential campaign, and he served as the White House's "chief strategist" early in Trump's administration. Federal prosecutors in Manhattan had indicted Bannon, along with others, in August 2020. They charged him with a fraud scheme involving the "We Build the Wall" online funding campaign. The indictment alleged that the defendants had raised millions of dollars by soliciting donors to send money that would be used to build Trump's infamous "wall" along the southern border of the United States. The indictment charged that they didn't use the donations to build the wall but rather diverted the funds for their own personal use, basically stealing the donated money. This was a garden-variety fraud scheme, but Trump pardoned Bannon as he was leaving office. Presidential pardons do not extend to state crimes. So, when the pardon was announced, the district attorney and the attorney general both began to consider whether they could pick up the Bannon case.

A senior official in Letitia James's office contacted DANY to see if the two offices could work together on a Bannon prosecution. When I heard about the attorney general's desire to speak with our office about Bannon, I realized that we had to put aside the usual jealousy and mistrust and see if we could work together with James more broadly on the Trump investigation. I knew from experience that agencies sometimes do marry up and agree to work together on particular matters, though the marriages are typically fraught with issues, much like marriages between individual spouses. There are fights over money, over where cases will be brought, over who will work on them, over who will do what, and—above all—over how credit will be divided if and when a case is brought. Who is going to stand next to whom at the press conference? Who will speak first, etc.?

Notwithstanding the concern about James's public statements, I thought it would be foolish to stiff-arm the attorney
general's office. I sent an email to Carey on January 27, even
before being sworn in, urging him to find out more about the
attorney general's investigation. I wrote that "James continues
to be quite active in the press about her civil investigation, and
(as you noted) her public statements are very overtly political.
But perhaps it makes sense to meet with her folks to try to get
a sense whether they have gathered meaningful testimony and
documents that would give us a tangible advantage if materials
were shared with us. . . . If they actually have gathered some
significant evidence, then it would be worth the effort to figure
out how to get access to it."

As would so often be the case over the next year, Carey and
I saw eye to eye on this topic. He asked James's office to speak
with us about their investigation, and to James's credit, they
quickly agreed to share information. In mid-February 2021 we
had a detailed conference call that focused on Trump's sprawling Westchester County estate, known as Seven Springs. This
call was the first of many we had with the lawyers in the office
of the attorney general. Those lawyers were extremely forthcoming, intelligent, and cooperative. They answered our many
questions and provided us with documents and testimony that
helped us to understand where "the bodies were buried" in
Trump's financial statements. Of course, we did our own investigation as well, but the attorney general's staff had been way
ahead of us in reviewing the critical documents and speaking
to the critical witnesses. They shared their work and their conclusions without any of the jealousy and petty slights that so
often occur when competing law enforcement agencies try to
collaborate.

The information we received from the attorney general's office would become hugely important to the district attorney's investigation of Trump's financial statements that was just starting in early 2021. The briefings we received confirmed over time that our investigation was heading in the right direction and gave us a factual platform on which to build a criminal case. Recognizing the importance of the work the attorney general's lawyers had done, and the information they had gathered, we got court approval to provide additional investigative materials to the attorney general's office so that they could assist in our work. And assist us they did, not only sharing their analysis but also lending us two assistant attorney generals who were cross-designated as special assistant district attorneys to work directly with us.

Eventually, based on our investigation and the substantial information provided to us by the attorney general's office, we concluded that Trump's financial statements were held together by exaggeration and fabrication.

Seven Springs—the first property we discussed with the attorney general's office—is a case in point. As the attorney general later described in public filings, Trump's annual financial statements valued his Seven Springs property at $291 million in the years 2012–14. This whopping value was based on the fanciful notion that luxurious homes, each worth $35 million, could be built on the property and then sold. The underlying backup documents computed value as though the homes could be magically constructed and sold overnight, with no adjustment for the years it would take to build infrastructure (like roads), construct the mansions, get the necessary local approvals, and sell the mansions. The purported value also ignored the long history of Trump's failed efforts to develop the property. The plan to sell the luxurious homes came after years of efforts to develop Seven Springs as a golf course and an equestrian center. Proposed subdivision plans had run into problems like lack of road access (Trump lost a lawsuit he brought to gain road access), protected wetlands, steep terrain, and extensive rock outcroppings. Eventually, in 2015, after twenty years of failed development efforts, Trump donated the rights to develop Seven Springs in exchange for a $21 million tax deduction.

This donation took the form of a "conservation easement." A conservation easement is a legally binding agreement between a landowner and a charitable organization such as the Nature Conservancy. The landowner gives the organization the right to restrict the development and use of the land to achieve certain laudable goals, such as the preservation of open space, wildlife habitat, or agricultural land. The donation of a conservation easement entitles the landowner to a tax deduction for the value of the development rights that have been donated. Unfortunately, but predictably, landowners have used conservation easements to commit tax fraud by giving away development rights and claiming tax deductions on land that could not be developed, such as leftover floodplain and steep hillsides. Some owners commission appraisals of development rights that are wildly exaggerated in order to claim tax deductions to which they are not entitled. For this reason, the Internal Revenue Service has issued repeated warnings to taxpayers about abusive conservation easements, noting that it is aware of the potential for abuse and urging caution with respect to their use. Trump, we would come to learn, loved conservation easements, and used them or considered using them in connection with many of his properties.

With respect to Seven Springs, Trump claimed that he had given away development rights valued at over $20 million. The attorney general had been investigating whether this value was based on a legitimate appraisal or whether the appraisal rested on false data about the development potential of the property. But what struck me was not the size of the claimed tax deduction, but the absurdity of the value for Seven Springs that Trump had recorded in his financial statements. He had valued Seven Springs at $291 million, and the lion's share of that value—over $160 million, according to Trump's accounting backup—came from the right to build the luxurious homes that purportedly could be sold for $35 million each. Nobody, and certainly not Donald Trump, gives away development rights worth over $160 million in exchange for a tax deduction worth a small fraction of that amount. And there was this damning fact: in September 2014, well before Trump's 2014 financial statement was finalized, a property appraiser hired by the Trump Organization had done an analysis of the development value of Seven Springs. The appraiser had reported that the maximum potential value was $50 million. Yet Trump's financial statement reflected a property value of $291 million. The actual reasonable fair value of the property, as determined by experts retained by the district attorney's office, was $33 million.

As our investigation progressed, we learned that the massive overvaluation of Seven Springs was part of a pattern that extended to most of the assets that Trump listed on his financial statements, and that the fabricated values continued year after year. But that realization would come later. In the meantime, we would pursue another tidbit received from the attorney general's office. This tidbit, a small but hot ember when we received it, would grow into a flame that eventually became a criminal indictment against Allen Weisselberg, Trump's chief financial officer, and the Trump Organization itself.

CHAPTER EIGHT

ALLEN WEISSELBERG'S FREE APARTMENT

M any criminal cases, and most complicated white-collar cases, feature narrators who can tell jurors about the defendant's crimes because they played a part in committing them. Whether they are called "cooperators," "accomplices," "co-conspirators," "stool pigeons," or just "rats," they are regular cast members in the dramas that lawyers stage in criminal courtrooms. They are such regular players that defense lawyers and prosecutors have standard courtroom speeches about them. Defense lawyers refer to accomplice witnesses as "rats," and argue that they will say anything the prosecutor wants in order to spend less time in jail. Prosecutors for generations have argued to jurors that "if you want to know what goes on in the sewers, you have to ask the rats." Donald Trump, as the sitting president of the United States, called Michael Cohen a "rat" after Cohen started cooperating with the Justice Department. Having myself played a part in many criminal investigations, I can't recall one in which the prosecutors did not at least try to develop one or more cooperating witnesses, aka "rats." As a young federal prosecutor, I once sat with a troublesome cooperating witness in my office when a mouse ran across the floor.

My cooperator looked at me, saying, "Wow, you guys have a mouse problem!" I glared at him and remarked that most of our problems came from "rats."

Shortly before we had our first detailed call with the lawyers at the attorney general's office, Carey and I spoke about Allen Weisselberg's central importance in our investigation, and how we might go about convincing him to become a witness against Donald Trump. Of course, cooperators don't decide to become prosecution witnesses because they have sudden pangs of conscience or passing spasms of civic duty. They have to be "flipped," or "turned," which involves threatening to go after them, convict them, and send them away—that's just a fact of life in criminal investigations. So, as Carey and I discussed, if we were going to take a run at persuading Weisselberg to tell us what he knew about Trump's financial misdeeds, we needed to find out about any wrongdoing he himself had committed.

We suspected that there were skeletons in Weisselberg's closet, if only because he had worked closely with Trump for decades. But there were other indications that Weisselberg might have been personally involved in financial mischief. Allen's son, Barry Weisselberg, also worked for the Trump Organization, and Barry and his wife, Jennifer, had gone through a bitter divorce. Jennifer had been spilling her guts to the press about the Weisselberg family and their relationship with Trump, and she had met several times with DANY personnel prior to my arrival. In those meetings she had spoken about a "free apartment" that Trump had given her and Barry as a wedding present, and she had spoken generally about the relationship between Trump and Allen Weisselberg. Weisselberg, she said, had always been petrified of Trump, and she alluded to "murky" financial dealings between Trump and Weisselberg, whom she described as "very cheap."

Based on what Jennifer had said, and knowing that we needed to learn more about Weisselberg before pressing him to cooperate, Carey and I told the investigative team in February 2021 that we needed to focus on Weisselberg. We needed to go back to Cohen and interview him about Weisselberg, reinterview Jennifer Weisselberg, round up any public information about Allen Weisselberg, and do a deep dive into his personal finances to learn how he was compensated and how he spent his money.

Carey and I also discussed calling Weisselberg's lawyer to fire a warning shot over his bow. We could say that we might be coming after Weisselberg (without specifying what we had on him, which was very little at that point) in the hope that he would get scared and fall into our laps as a witness. I told Carey that it was not my practice to bluff. I said that on the basis of experience, knowing that bluffs usually are not effective. Many years earlier, I had represented a New York state senator in a corruption investigation, and the prosecutors in charge of the case wanted my client to cooperate against another public official. I met with the prosecutors, who told me some of the details of the potential case they had against my client. They intimated that they had told me about only the tip of the iceberg, and said they were "close" to having a compelling case. I called their bluff, saying that I needed to see the whole iceberg in order to advise my client, and being "close" to having a case was not the same as actually having one. It turned out that there was no rest of the iceberg.

Later, I heard about an episode in which a federal prosecutor had invited a potential cooperator to meet, and had set up an elaborate charade, creating a mock war room with file cabinets supposedly (but not actually) filled with incriminating evidence. The prosecutor had gone so far as to stage a fake telephone call, pretending to have received a call from his boss about the potential cooperator, and responding with, "Yes, I am with him now. Okay, but I think we should give him one last chance to help himself." The charade came crashing down when the prosecutor left the room for a moment, and the witness's lawyer tried to use the telephone to make a call, only to discover that the phone was a prop—it was not connected to anything! So, I had decided to follow a simple rule of thumb as a prosecutor: don't overstate the facts, and never bluff.

As it happened, there would be no need to bluff when it came to Allen Weisselberg, because he had indeed committed crimes worthy of prosecution. The first solid indication came the day after we had decided to look more closely at Weisselberg, and the same day as our first conference call with the attorney general's office about Seven Springs. That afternoon, representatives of the attorney general's office called to say that Weisselberg and his wife had been living rent-free in a luxury penthouse apartment on Manhattan's West Side from 2012 to 2017, without paying income taxes on the arrangement. The attorney general's folks had developed this information after their own separate interviews with Jennifer Weisselberg, who told them not only about the free apartment that Trump had provided her and her former husband as a wedding gift, but also about the free apartment that Trump had provided to her former father-in-law, Allen. The attorney general's investigators had already raised the free apartment as an issue with Weisselberg's lawyers, who had responded that Weisselberg believed that the free apartment was a fringe benefit of his work for the Trump Organization, on which he did not have to pay taxes. The attorney general's lawyers described this explanation as "laughable" and said that they were going to request a criminal referral from the New York State Department of Taxation and Finance.

When Carey told the team what he had learned from the attorney general's office about Weisselberg's free apartment, we realized immediately that the information might provide a basis for pursuing tax charges against the Trump Organization as well as Allen Weisselberg. I wrote to Carey that "the tax issues run to both the TO [the Trump Organization] and to AW [Allen Weisselberg]. AW presumably was obliged to report the imputed income from the free housing, and the TO was presumably obliged to issue a W-2 to him. It will be interesting to see how the TO handled the tax treatment on the corporate side. And, of course, also interesting to find out whether AW has filed amended returns, etc."

At the time, we knew little about how the Trump Organization had booked and reported Weisselberg's free housing. As we later learned, the housing wasn't really "free." The rent and utility expenses paid on the apartment amounted to more than $100,000 per year; Weisselberg was living in a penthouse, not a hovel. In the years prior to Donald Trump's presidency, the apartment was "free" to Weisselberg because the expenses were paid on his behalf by the Trump Organization and considered part of his annual compensation. We later determined that Weisselberg's W-2 statements did not disclose the payments made on his behalf, and the Trump Organization never reported having made the payments to the tax authorities. That later became a factor in the decision to indict the Trump Organization. But even before we knew these facts, we knew that the "free apartment" information could give us leverage to try to "flip" Weisselberg. We had something on him.

Weisselberg's failure to pay tax on his "free apartment" meant he had potential criminal exposure and gave DANY some leverage in dealing with him. It might make sense to forget about whatever tax crimes Weisselberg had committed in connection with his "free apartment" if he would cooperate against Trump. This tactic is one that divides prosecutors. Prosecutors don't like giving people a complete "pass" on crimes they have committed, even if they are willing to cooperate. As I have mentioned, this is a deal that my former federal colleagues in the Southern District of New York claim that they will never make. But I thought that it was a deal that we should consider for Weisselberg.

The problem was that it was not our deal to make, even if we all agreed that it was appropriate. The attorney general had developed the information that provided leverage over Weisselberg; she had done so before the district attorney, and she had already started a conversation with Weisselberg's lawyers. Additionally, she was seeking a criminal tax referral from the New York State Department of Taxation and Finance. This is a bureaucratic process by which the attorney general tells the Tax Department, in effect, "we have information that somebody has cheated on their state tax returns and might have committed criminal violations of the state tax law. We want you to look at the information. If you agree, send us the official copies of the person's tax returns and also give us a letter authorizing us to prosecute the person."

If the attorney general got a criminal referral, she would have the legal authority to bring a criminal case against Weisselberg independently from the district attorney. Under New York's byzantine system, local district attorneys can charge people with tax crimes without criminal referrals from the Tax Department. The attorney general cannot; she can bring cases to the district attorney, or she can seek a criminal referral to bring charges on her own. If the attorney general got a criminal referral as to Weisselberg, she did not have to work with our office. She could investigate the case, convene a grand jury, and charge him with crimes all by herself, leaving DANY out in the cold with respect to approaching Weisselberg to get him to cooperate.

The fact that the attorney general had gotten out ahead of the district attorney, and might go off on her own to prosecute Allen Weisselberg, turned me into something of a raving lunatic about the need for the two offices to work together. In my mind, the district attorney had to be directly involved in any dealings with Weisselberg, and the offices had to collaborate on their Trump investigations. I felt this way not because of any institutional loyalty to DANY. I had no such loyalty; I had never worked there, and I had not even set foot in that office for years. As of mid-February 2021, I had been an assistant district attorney for all of two weeks, and all of my work had been remote, sitting at home on my computer.

My concerns were twofold. First, notwithstanding the usual territoriality and suspicion that exists between offices headed by two separately elected political actors, it was indisputably in the public interest that the offices collaborate. We were investigating the president of the United States (though he had just begrudgingly left office). Trump and his lawyers could be expected to divide and conquer those investigating him, and to throw sand into the investigative gears at every opportunity. They already had been doing that, as we knew from our subpoena litigation and as the attorney general's office had experienced in trying to get documents from the Trump Organization.

Second, while the attorney general had clearly gotten out ahead of us in investigating the facts, she was conducting a civil investigation. At the end of the day, all she could do was bring a lawsuit against Donald Trump and the Trump Organization. If Trump had committed criminal conduct, it was the district attorney who could bring criminal charges. The attorney general could seek separate authority to bring some narrow tax charges against Allen Weisselberg, but Weisselberg's personal tax offenses, assuming they could be proved, were of little importance compared to his potential value as a cooperator against Trump. The district attorney needed to have his hand on the Weisselberg steering wheel, and it was critical that he and the attorney general both be traveling in the same direction.

To try to make sure that this happened, I sent an email to Cy, Carey, and the entire team, stressing that "we need to join forces with the NYAG, and create a true joint investigative effort." I argued that "there are smart people of sound judgment in their office and in ours," and opined that if we could work together in a sensible manner, "all of our efforts—including an approach to [Allen Weisselberg]—would gain a great deal of force. . . ."

As sensible as working closely together might seem in the abstract, in practice it seldom happens between agencies that have different leaders and agendas. But Cy and Carey agreed that we needed to make the effort and arranged to speak further with the attorney general and her staff. Cy called James directly to express the desire to work collaboratively, and she agreed, according to Cy, "with some enthusiasm."

I decided it would be useful to open a back channel and began speaking individually to Gary Fishman. Fishman had spent more than fifteen years in the Manhattan district attorney's office before moving over to the attorney general's office, where he had been working on the Trump investigation. He was a veteran white-collar prosecutor with a lot of experience in tax cases. He had a reputation for being aggressive and dogged in his approach to cases, and some of his former colleagues in the district attorney's office were not among his fans. But he was the lawyer who was sorting through Weisselberg's personal finances for the attorney general, and he knew everything there was to know about Weisselberg's apartment. He knew how to investigate financial crimes, and I was impressed with him. Gary and I agreed early on that it would serve our mutual interests to approach Weisselberg together, and to let his lawyer know that she could not divide and conquer her potential adversaries. Just as I was lobbying within the district attorney's office about the need to cooperate with the attorney general, I believe that he was lobbying within the attorney general's office that they should be comfortable working with us.

We never entered into a formal agreement with the attorney general's office, but we did form a useful and productive working relationship that endured for the next year. Together we pursued the facts relating to Weisselberg's apartment, and learned that there were other Trump executives whose rent was paid for by the Trump Organization. And the untaxed freebies were not limited to apartment rent. Some Trump executives, including Weisselberg, also got cars, cash, private school tuition, and other benefits that were not reported as compensation to the federal, state, or local tax authorities. Eventually, as I will describe, the facts developed jointly by the district attorney and the attorney general led to the indictment of the Trump Organization and Allen Weisselberg for tax fraud and related offenses.

Of course, we were working on our own leads, and looking at a bunch of different topics. In a complicated financial case, progress is seldom linear. You don't run one thing into the ground and then pick up something else. You work on many things at the same time. So, in February and March 2021, in addition to strategizing about making a case against Allen Weisselberg and looking closely at his personal finances and the "free apartment," we were taking a closer look at the Clifford hush money facts, trying to understand Trump's newly received tax returns, probing the Seven Springs conservation easement, and examining other issues, like Trump's relationship with Deutsche Bank. During that period, another topic began to loom larger and larger on my personal radar screen, one that would come to dominate my thinking and become our most important investigative focus: the legitimacy of Donald Trump's financial statements.

CHAPTER NINE

DIVING INTO THE FINANCIAL STATEMENTS

Eventually we would spend many months parsing Donald Trump's financial statements, traveling through the arteries and the veins of his real estate empire and ultimately into the capillaries. But the financial statements were not discussed during my first few weeks working on the investigation. Nor were they discussed in my first two interviews with Michael Cohen, which focused on the Stephanie Clifford hush money and the "zombie" case. Cohen had testified about Trump's financial statements when he appeared before the House Oversight Committee in February 2019, and DANY personnel had questioned him briefly about the financial statements during their jailhouse interviews later in 2019, but the district attorney's team had not spent significant time investigating those statements.

We began to pay more attention to the financial statements after getting a briefing from the lawyers working on the attorney general's Trump investigation on March 2, 2021. The DANY team had scheduled some upcoming interviews of bankers at Deutsche Bank, and we wanted to know what the attorney general's investigation had uncovered regarding

Trump's dealings with Deutsche Bank. It was common knowledge that Trump had gotten financing from Deutsche Bank, and there had been media speculation about whether Deutsche Bank had been irresponsible or reckless in doing business with a client whom the "mainstream" banking institutions in the United States—JPMorgan Chase, Citigroup, Bank of America, Wells Fargo, and the like—would not touch. There were also questions raised publicly about whether Deutsche Bank had facilitated money laundering by Donald Trump (an allegation that, so far as I know, turned out to be baseless). Deutsche Bank was cooperating with the investigations, but the investigative team had not yet sorted through Trump's accounting records or reviewed the loan files in detail.

When the attorney general's lawyers briefed us about their review of the Deutsche Bank files and their conversations with the bankers, the briefing showed once again that they were ahead of us in developing the facts. They had parsed Trump's financial statements, studied the worksheets behind those statements, begun to itemize how and why the statements were false, and were analyzing exactly what Deutsche Bank understood about Trump's finances.

This provoked a long conversation with Carey, in which we shared with each other our frustration about the status of DANY's investigation. We discussed the time it had taken to get the tax returns and accounting information, the problems with COVID and not having grand juries available to us, and also the cultural problem within the office that seemed to be impeding our progress. The team was used to working at its own deliberate pace, accommodating all requests for extra time to produce documents or schedule witness interviews, and working to identify only the most obvious, glaring legal violations they might find, if any. We also talked about the need to focus the team, and Carey mentioned Cy's growing impatience. Cy had not expressed his impatience to the team or said that he was concerned. But a week or two later we learned that there was a reason Cy was growing restive.

Hearing about the attorney general's work on Trump's financial statements prompted me to dig more deeply into them. Also, Carey and Cy asked me to get involved in our upcoming interviews of Deutsche Bank personnel. On March 3, 2021, I listened while one member of the team interviewed one of the bankers. The interview was broad-ranging but ineffectual, because we were not yet up to speed on Trump's financial statements and how they were falsified. I thought it made sense to wait to question other Deutsche Bank witnesses until we knew more about the financial statements so that we could ask focused questions about whether the bankers had been aware of particular fabricated values.

As I started to look into this area in early March 2021, I consulted the small library I had now accumulated. By this point, I had done a lot of reading about Trump and also about Michael Cohen. I had read Cohen's book, *Disloyal*, and another fifteen or so Trump-related books on my Kindle. I was working from home, and I was amazed at the amount of material I could scrounge from the public record just by tapping my keyboard. I immersed myself in what had been written about Trump's business empire and started to create little summaries for myself about each of his significant assets. I began a detailed study of Trump's yearly financial statements, thinking that they might become the fulcrum of a case against him if there was proof that they were false. Cohen had addressed this topic in his congressional testimony and had mentioned the financial statements in passing in his book, but we needed to flesh out what he knew and how his claims might be corroborated, so it was time to speak with him again.

We interviewed Cohen, again by Zoom, on March 10. I

led this interview, which turned out to be quite consequential. Cohen told us that he and Trump and Weisselberg had met often to phony up Trump's financial statements. The statements were revised annually and had to be submitted each year to banks that had extended financing on Trump's properties. Trump would dictate his bottom-line net worth and dispatch Cohen and Weisselberg to come up with asset values that would support the net worth figure that Trump wanted to show. In other words, the asset values were reverse-engineered to get to the total net worth figure that Trump had commanded. This is why his financial statements showed steady growth; Trump decided, arbitrarily, what his net worth would be, and he wanted each year's number to be bigger than the year before. At one point his growing net worth number became so inflated that Weisselberg warned him that he was creating a large potential estate tax liability—upon his death, the tax authorities could demand taxes commensurate with his inflated net worth. According to Cohen, Trump responded by telling Weisselberg that "I don't care, I'll be dead, and the kids will have to fend for themselves."

The takeaway from the interview was that Cohen had a lot more to say about the falsification of the financial statements than we had appreciated, and that Trump had been directly involved in their fabrication. We knew we needed a narrator but had not known until then that Cohen himself might be able to fill that need.

After listening to the attorney general's folks talking about their investigation, and after hearing what Cohen had to say about Trump's financial statements, I knew we had to drill down into those statements. We had to understand how each asset was valued and how the assets were grouped, and how the valuations and their calculation changed from asset to asset and year to year. This was a huge task. Trump had many assets of different types: cash, securities, homes, office buildings, hotels, airplanes, licensing deals, golf courses, his Mar-a-Lago estate in Palm Beach, Florida, the Miss Universe beauty pageant, and sundry other interests. And he had a new personal financial statement compiled every year. Understanding the numbers, the backup to the numbers, and the myriad details that went into the numbers was not glamorous work. It was all "green eyeshade" stuff. But it had to be done, asset by asset, year by year.

I set about to do it, not recognizing at first the enormity of the task. But at this early point in my tenure, I did not have the authority to assign tasks to others. I was not part of the office hierarchy and had no supervisory authority over anyone. I had just been added to the team with a general mandate to "help," and I was sensitive about bossing people around, which in any case is not something I like to do.

Also, I have always believed that lawyers should master the facts of every case in which they are involved. In complicated cases, this usually creates a dilemma. The senior lawyers on a litigation team have to make the decisions about how to handle the case, which requires a detailed and intimate knowledge of the facts and the documents. Unfortunately, they often lack the time to acquire that knowledge. The junior lawyers on the team—those who do have the time to trawl through documents, prepare chronologies, and the like—often lack the experience and perspective to recognize what is important and raise it up the chain of command. It is not exactly that the right hand does not know what the left hand is doing; it's more like the army generals are making decisions without knowing what's happening on the front lines, and the soldiers on the front lines know only what is behind the bushes immediately in front of them, without a strategic sense of the overall mission. Over the years, I came to believe that the only way to deal with the dilemma is through exchanging information, so the junior lawyers know what decisions are in the offing and can understand how their work fits into the overall strategy for the case. And the senior lawyers have to make the time to sort through the binders of "hot" documents and summary analyses that the junior lawyers have culled from the morass of available facts. It's an imperfect process, but the senior lawyer has to err on the side of getting into the weeds himself or herself; you just can't delegate "learning the case."

In the Trump investigation, I had the luxury of having only one case on my personal docket, so I decided to plunge into the task of learning everything I could about Trump's financial statements. I was working at home and in solitude, and it was somewhat lonely work examining spreadsheets and trying to figure out which of the thousands of financial details might be important. I would work for a few hours, walk the dog to break up the monotony, come back to the statements and spreadsheets and work for a few more hours, and walk the dog again. The dog was having the time of her life.

CHAPTER TEN

CY VANCE WILL NOT RUN FOR REELECTION

On March 11, 2021, in one of our frequent conversations, Carey Dunne told me that Cy Vance would be announcing on the next day that he would not be running for reelection, and so his tenure as Manhattan's district attorney would be over at the end of the year. This was already widely assumed, as he had not been raising money or acting like he would be seeking another term.

I was not Cy's confidant, and I don't know why he made the decision to step down. I was told later that it was a personal decision, and that he had promised his family years earlier that, unlike his two immediate predecessors, he would not be occupying the office for more than three decades. I do not think that the Trump investigation was foremost in his mind, because in March 2021 nobody had an idea how it would develop, and whether or when charges might be brought against Trump or anyone associated with him. Carey and I noted when we spoke that the Democratic primary election for district attorney would be held on June 24. Because Manhattan is an overwhelmingly Democratic community, the primary would effectively decide who would be taking Cy's place. Though the

general election would be held in November, there would be
a district-attorney-in-waiting as soon as the primary election
was over. The news of Cy's decision was interesting, but it had
no immediate impact on what I was doing. As Carey and I discussed, all we would do, and all we could do, was keep our
heads down and try to follow the facts.

Cy's decision was announced on March 12, and on that
day the *New Yorker* published a long article by investigative
reporter Jane Mayer with the provocative title, "Can Cyrus
Vance, Jr., Nail Trump?" The article referenced Cy's decision
not to seek another term and prompted tweets about whether
Cy had "given up" or was "bribed" or "intimidated." These
tweets, from everything I ever saw or heard, were ridiculously
wrong. We were just doing our work, in fits and starts, and
with no cooperation from the Trump Organization, which was
continuing its usual practice of obfuscation and delay. Following Cy's announcement, we had a team meeting via Zoom on
March 15. Cy attended. Everyone agreed that we should follow
up on Michael Cohen's information and drill into Trump's misrepresentations about the value of his assets and his net worth.
Cy called me at home the next evening, saying he would like to
make a charging decision before leaving office, and he thanked
me for focusing the team and concentrating our efforts.

CHAPTER ELEVEN

ENTERPRISE CORRUPTION

I spent the next several weeks continuing to study Trump's financial statements, known as Statements of Financial Condition (SOFCs). Part of that process was to speak again with Michael Cohen, which we did on March 19, this time in person. This was my first actual visit to the offices of the district attorney; because of the pandemic, I had been working remotely for weeks. Now, finally, I could meet my new colleagues in the flesh. When I met the lawyers on the team, they seemed so young to me. And I must have seemed so old to them—perhaps not a doddering fool, but certainly over the hill.

Whatever impression I made undoubtedly suffered when I realized at the end of the day that I had left my wallet at home. I had driven in from the suburbs and parked in a nearby commercial garage, and I had no cash or even a credit card to ransom my car. I had to ask one of my junior colleagues to loan me some cash. I asked for fifty dollars, but my colleague wisely realized that I would need more just to get my car out of hock and gave me a hundred. When I got home and told my wife what had happened, she looked askance at me, and asked how

I thought I could get to the bottom of Donald Trump's finances if I could not remember my own wallet in the morning!

My senility notwithstanding, it had been a good day. The Cohen interview, which Cy also attended, was revealing. We probed why Trump would want or need to portray himself as more wealthy than he was, as he was extremely wealthy by any yardstick. Cohen explained that Trump's identity and business model rested on impressing people about his fantastic financial success. Being seen as wealthier and more successful than virtually anyone else was hardwired into his narcissistic personality and the building of his empire. It enabled his success with his television show, *The Apprentice*, and also was important to his licensing deals. It gave him negotiating leverage, attracted deals, and helped with branding. It was also important for financing—Trump wanted to show such a huge net worth on his financial statements that bankers would not look too closely at the actual value of his properties.

Fantastic wealth and success also were a big part of Trump's marketing as a politician, according to Cohen. As rich as Trump may have been, it was always better to be perceived as even richer. In his mind, he was competing with other very wealthy people; there was literally no amount of wealth, and no ultimate net worth, that was enough for Donald Trump. No matter how much he had, it was better to have more. And he would do anything to be seen as having more, in ways large and small. This is why he wrangled all the time with media outlets like *Forbes* and the *Real Deal*, which regularly tried to get a handle on Trump's actual wealth.

Cohen recalled an incident when Trump sold a home in Palm Beach, Florida, to a Ukrainian businessman. The sale price was $95 million, but Trump wanted Cohen to call all the newspapers and tell them that the actual sales price was

$100 million. Why lie over $5 million? Just because $100 million sounded much bigger than $95 million, at least in Trump's mind. Cohen became involved in these conversations because Trump thought Cohen had a gift for dealing with the media and could be a spokesman for Trump's inflated wealth.

Trump's fixation with pumping up the value of his assets and his net worth translated directly into how his financial statements were prepared. Cohen elaborated on what he had told us in our last session with him—Trump would provide a net worth target and then it was up to Weisselberg, sometimes after discussion with Cohen, to fiddle with the value of each asset to make it all add up.

As a consequence, Cohen told us, every line on Trump's financial statements had subtleties that were part of the overall mission to come up with higher and higher values. For instance, the value of Trump's golf properties was not broken out on a club-by-club basis, because by grouping the values into one large number it would be harder for anyone to question the value of any specific golf course. The valuation of potential future deals was "ridiculous," according to Cohen, and it was easier to inflate the value of some assets (like Seven Springs) than others. Valuation methodologies might be changed from year to year because some methodologies would give more room for inflating the value of a particular asset. Or inflated figures might be used to increase the gross income, and hence the market value, of assets like Trump Tower, Trump's headquarters building in midtown Manhattan.

Cohen also told us that Trump was incredibly cheap and completely dishonest in many of his business dealings, including submitting inflated insurance claims. He described an incident in which a tornado had done some damage at one of Trump's golf courses. The course had a man-made pond on the property, and the insurance company was told that the tornado had ruined the pond lining, which would have to be replaced before the pond could be refilled, an expense that would cost hundreds of thousands of dollars. The insurance company, according to Cohen, paid $400,000 to fix the pond. In fact, an employee was sent down in scuba gear to patch the tears in the pond lining with a roll of waterproof Gorilla Tape. The employee patched up the pond lining in a few hours. While he was underwater, he gathered up the golf balls that had been hit into the pond. The retrieved golf balls were then sold in the pro shop as "Donald Trump Autographed Golf Balls." I asked Cohen if Trump had actually autographed the golf balls. He looked at me like I was a dunce, and replied, "Of course not," adding that the pro shop employees probably had hurt their wrists signing Trump's name so often.

Cohen emphasized that Trump paid attention to everything in his business empire that involved money, down to the smallest detail. At one point Trump's limo had sustained minor damage from being hit by a yellow cab. Trump demanded that the limo driver make sure that the damage was reimbursed. Cohen, who had connections in the taxicab business, wound up calling the yellow cab's garage to ask them just to pay the claim without an argument in order to placate the boss, who would not let it go.

Toward the end of our interview, Cohen spoke about "Trump University." Trump University was the name under which Donald Trump and some business associates had marketed a real estate training program. Part of the sales pitch was that Trump had made so much money buying and selling real estate that he was now prepared to share his moneymaking secrets with ordinary people. The materials and lessons commanded a high price—some students paid as much as $35,000 for a "Gold Elite" mentoring program—but the students were told that the high prices were set for their own benefit, to make sure that they took "personal responsibility" for doing the work that the program required.

Trump University closed in 2011, after its operations generated many complaints and much litigation from unhappy students. The business became an issue in the 2016 presidential campaign. Then–New York attorney general Eric Schneiderman brought a consumer fraud lawsuit against Trump and the Trump Organization, alleging that the training program had been an elaborate "bait-and-switch" scheme, involving teachers that Trump said he had selected and materials he claimed to have approved. He had done neither. Cohen confirmed that the whole thing had been a scam. The materials had no special value, and most of the students just lost their money. Cohen had been tasked with painting the attorney general as a political opportunist who had attacked Trump to further his gubernatorial aspirations, a play from Trump's standard playbook that he would reprise years later against Attorney General Letitia James.

Cohen's information was extremely valuable. We knew, of course, that he would have to be corroborated if he would be a testifying witness, but that was not an insurmountable challenge. By this point I had parsed Trump's financial statements. I had not mastered every detail, but I could see that we would be able to prove that asset values had been inflated just as Cohen had described. Even if Cohen did not know or recall every single fabrication or irregularity, we would be able to show that he was generally telling the truth about the financial statements.

But there was a downside to Cohen's eagerness to share intimate details of Trump's finances: Dealing with Cohen was like dealing with an explosive device. He could go off at any moment. He had already proved that it was difficult, if not completely impossible, to get him to stop talking to the press. After we had spoken with him about the "zombie" case and about Allen Weisselberg, he had gone on a press riff talking about how the district attorney's office was closing in on Weisselberg, that Weisselberg should cooperate, and generally extolling our investigation, complete with references to me, which I did not welcome.

I could and did exhort Cohen to keep away from the press, but the media attention was like catnip to him, and we had no means of keeping him away from the cameras. When he came in for his in-person interview on March 19, the press was waiting to take pictures of him arriving at our office. Cohen or his lawyer had likely alerted the media to his appointment with us. Explaining to Cohen why he had to stop talking about our investigation, and why his press interviews hurt our efforts and his credibility, was a task that occupied me for the entire time I worked on the case.

A few days after the Cohen interview, I read Donald Trump's deposition testimony from a lawsuit he had brought against Timothy L. O'Brien. O'Brien is a journalist and author who wrote a book called *TrumpNation: The Art of Being the Donald.* O'Brien claimed in his book that Trump had vastly overstated his wealth. Trump had sued O'Brien for libel, and that case had been dismissed in 2009. In 2007, however, Trump had given sworn testimony in the case that discussed his assets and financial statements. Even though the testimony was dated, much of it meshed with what Cohen had told us and would be helpful in a prosecution. For instance, Trump had testified that the asset values in his financial statements were "actually . . . quite conservative," a claim that was ridiculous on its face. He also testified that his net worth went up and down depending on his own "feelings." I would later cull out a large handful of sworn statements from the deposition that we could use in the criminal case we were building.

The biggest takeaway from the deposition transcript and videotape was that Donald Trump was an absolute train wreck of a witness. By this point, his affinity for lying was common knowledge, but some witnesses can lie effectively and convincingly when testifying. I have seen some liars who were so cool and articulate on the witness stand that butter would not melt in their mouths. Trump, though, was not just a pathological liar, but a hapless, arrogant, and horrible liar. For example, when asked if he had ever exaggerated the value of one of his properties, his answer was, "Not beyond reason." When asked what he considered to be "beyond reason," he answered, "I don't know. You'd have to give me a specific." The next question was, "Is $100 million beyond reason?" He answered, "It depends. . . . Property is very funny."

Witnesses who fence like this do not come across as credible in a courtroom. Trump was simply incapable of telling a straight story or answering questions in a plain and direct manner, without spin or editorial comment or argument with the lawyer asking him unfriendly questions. If we brought a case against him, the likelihood that he could testify in his own defense in a linear and straightforward manner, coming across as reasonable and credible, was zero. Under skillful cross-examination, even witnesses who are telling the truth can be made to seem like liars. Witnesses like Trump, who lie all the time and believe that they are smarter than everyone else, can usually be shredded on the witness stand. He would be the perfect case study for that old courtroom "chestnut": "Ladies and gentlemen, here's the telltale sign that lets you know whenever he's not telling the truth: his lips are moving!"

As we headed toward the end of March, I got a telephone call from the district attorney. Cy reiterated that he wanted to reach a charging decision before he left office at the end of the year. We discussed the need to streamline our efforts, and lamented the team's lack of trial experience, which made it more difficult for them to focus on the particular facts that mattered. We could not investigate Trump forever; we had to follow the facts, but that did not mean wandering aimlessly in a factual jungle. I told Cy that, from my perspective, everybody seemed to be investigating everything. And everywhere we were drilling we seemed to be striking oil in terms of potential criminality. Fraud on financial institutions, fraud on government contract authorities, tax fraud, insurance fraud, consumer fraud, a phony charity—there were so many areas to look at because neither Trump nor the Trump Organization seemed to care about stepping over legal lines.

While Trump and his enablers had no scruples about breaking the law, they were not heedless or reckless about getting caught. They knew how to cover their tracks with brush and loose dirt and seemed to have a canny sense of staying within scrambling distance of legal refuge, like squirrels who stay just close enough to trees to be able to climb away if a dog gives chase. Trump's financial statements were phony, but the underlying assets were real. He did not tout fictitious gold mines in Africa, as one of my clients had done. He claimed outsized deductions for giving away development rights to land that could not be developed, but he filed tax returns and employed accountants and appraisers to provide a veneer of credibility to his inflated numbers. He submitted exaggerated insurance claims, like the one for rebuilding his man-made pond, but only after there had been an actual tornado. He cheated the students who enrolled in Trump University, but there had been actual course materials, even if they were nothing like what had been promised. He surrounded himself with loyal confederates in the manner of a crime boss, and he never sent email.

Emails are incredibly useful to prosecutors in white-collar cases. We sometimes joked that the *e* stood for *evidence*. They are often written quickly, and they last forever. Trawling through email takes place in virtually every complex investigation. Trump's aversion to email was not because he was uncomfortable with the technology. I believe he did not want to leave a record of his daily thoughts and activities because he knew that would make it more difficult to prove criminal conduct. He was right.

In order to motivate the team, and to make sure we were working in a single, coordinated direction, I wrote up an outline of potential charges against Trump and the Trump Organization. The principal charge, around which all the others would revolve, was "enterprise corruption." "Enterprise corruption" is a New York State criminal offense under a law that was modeled on the federal RICO (an acronym for Racketeer Influenced and Corrupt Organizations) statute. The point of the federal law and its New York sibling was to give prosecutors a tool to go after businesses that engage in systematic and repeated criminal conduct. The paradigm target is an organized crime family operated by the Cosa Nostra, aka "The Mafia." But the laws also allow prosecutors to target legitimate businesses that engage in a pattern of criminal wrongdoing. The notion is that running a business that commits repeated crimes presents a danger that is greater than any of the individual crimes and calls for stiff punishment.

An enterprise corruption charge was an ideal vehicle for prosecuting Donald Trump and the Trump Organization. Of course, Trump had run a legitimate business empire for many years before becoming president. His empire was large, complex, and mainly successful (putting aside his dismal performance in Atlantic City). His holdings included office buildings, golf courses, hotels, and other assets, including licensing deals. But we had evidence that Trump had grown the business, and augmented his wealth, reputation, and power, through a pattern of criminal activity. The potential "pattern" crimes included defrauding persons and entities about his net worth and the value of his assets, underpaying his federal and state income taxes and property taxes, falsifying business records in order to conceal his agreement to pay hush money to women who claimed to have had extramarital affairs with him, operating Trump University as a consumer fraud, setting up a charitable foundation that was actually used as a personal slush fund, submitting fraudulent insurance claims, and other potential crimes.

The outline of potential charges I prepared did not claim that we had collected sufficient evidence to establish guilt on all of these charges, but all of the charges were "predicated," meaning that we had ample reason to investigate each of the crimes that together could comprise a pattern of criminal activity. We were not just conducting a wild goose chase or, as Trump would refer to it, a "witch hunt."

As to the financial statement fraud, we knew from the evidence that the attorney general had gathered, from what Cohen had told us, and from information about Trump's dealings with Deutsche Bank, that Trump had gotten loans by submitting financial statements that vastly overstated his net worth and the value of his assets. He also had submitted false financial statements to the General Services Administration when he presented a bid to convert the Old Post Office in Washington, D.C., into a luxury hotel.

As to the potential tax cheating charges, we knew that despite claiming that he was always making money hand over fist, Trump paid virtually nothing in income taxes. Whether or not the analysis of his income tax returns would ultimately yield proof of tax evasion, we already had substantial evidence of illegal conduct with respect to the Seven Springs conservation easement, and there were other donations of property and development rights that begged for further inquiry. In any case, there was reason to believe that Trump had been cheating on the payment of property taxes. As an example, documents later made public by the attorney general indicated that Trump had valued Trump National Golf Club Westchester in Ossining, New York, at more than $176 million, but he also had sued the town tax assessor, and had claimed in that litigation that the land value for property tax purposes was less than 10 percent of what he had claimed in his financial statements. Michael Cohen had told us that Trump manipulated the value of his holdings up and down, depending on circumstances. For banks, and for public consumption, the values were inflated, sometimes to levels that were absurd on their face. For the tax collector, property values were depressed to levels that were absurdly low.

We had abundant proof, from Michael Cohen and otherwise, of the hush money cover-up, and the "Trump University" scam had been detailed in a consumer fraud complaint filed by the attorney general. There had been no admission of wrongdoing, but Trump had paid $25 million to settle the case, and the attorney general's office would make available all of the underlying evidence to us for use in a criminal prosecution. The reference in my outline to the misuse of Trump's charitable foundation also had a solid basis in fact, as alleged in a lawsuit that a different New York attorney general had filed. The attorney general had cited "a pattern of persistent illegal conduct, occurring over more than a decade, that includes extensive unlawful political coordination with the Trump presidential campaign, repeated and willful self-dealing transactions to benefit Mr. Trump's personal and business interests, and violations of basic legal obligations for non-profit foundations." The attorney general's complaint had led to Trump's detailed admission of misconduct and the dissolution of the Trump Foundation.

The final component of the pattern of illegal conduct was insurance fraud. This was the least developed part of the case, and it would require us to corroborate what Michael Cohen had told us about occasions when Trump had cheated his insurers. There was the inflated tornado damage at one of Trump's golf courses, a fraudulent insurance claim that arose out of an elevator fire at 40 Wall Street, and even an inflated damage claim that resulted from a leak in Melania Trump's bathroom in the Trumps' gilded triplex penthouse atop Trump Tower.

If we could pull together the proof of the various crimes that would support a charge of enterprise corruption, there were formidable advantages such a charge would bring to a prosecution. First, there were the enhanced penalties. A person who participates in the affairs of an enterprise through a pattern of criminal activity commits a crime punishable by up to twenty-five years in prison, and a prison term of at least one year is the shortest permissible sentence. The law also allows for criminal forfeiture of the defendant's interest in the corrupt enterprise, which would place at risk all of Donald Trump's interest in the Trump Organization. If convicted, he could face complete financial ruination.

Second, bringing an enterprise corruption charge would allow the prosecutors to weave together a host of different criminal acts under one big tent. The proof as to some crimes might be less convincing than the proof as to other crimes, but all of the evidence taken together would reinforce the overall strength of the case. The whole might be more convincing than the sum of its parts, and the weakness of some parts of the case might not matter if other parts of the case were rock solid.

Third, an enterprise corruption charge would be in keeping with the reality of how Trump operated his business. Notwithstanding the success of Trump's business empire, there was a dark side to his prosperity. As we learned more and more about how he operated, we were developing evidence that he would break the law for financial advantage if he thought he could get away with it. As a businessman, Donald Trump was ruthless and avaricious; he would not think twice about walking away from financial commitments. Indeed, we learned that his staff would ask him to initial payment requests and invoices so that they had a piece of paper with his initials on it when he later wanted to renege on a financial commitment or berate an employee about having made a payment. He was also a bully who cultivated a reputation as a tough guy. He was cunning and, at times, charismatic. He demanded absolute loyalty and would go after anyone who crossed him. He seemed always to stay one step ahead of the law.

In my career as a lawyer, I had encountered only one other person who touched all of these bases: John Gotti, the head of the Gambino organized crime family and the so-called "Teflon Don." A few years ago, the *New York Times* ran an opinion piece called, "Who Said It: Trump or Gotti?" The piece provided seventeen quotes, and the reader could pick who said each quote, Trump or Gotti. Having met Gotti, having both represented and prosecuted members of his blood family and his "crime family," and having spent lots of time investigating Donald Trump, I thought I would ace the quiz when I recently retook it. But the similarity in how the two men spoke left me stumped.

To be sure, Donald Trump is not a common criminal, a cold-blooded killer, or a drug dealer. But the RICO and enterprise corruption statutes were made for circumstances in which a legitimate business augments its operations through ongoing and repeated criminal activity, which is what we were seeing as we gathered more and more facts. This helped convince me that an enterprise corruption charge against Trump would be appropriate.

When Cy Vance read my outline of a potential enterprise corruption charge he termed it "bold," but said he liked it. I sent the outline to the full team and we had a call to discuss it on March 29, 2021. The team seemed a bit subdued. There were references in the dialogue to this "new approach," which left me wondering, what had been the old approach?

Then we had an interesting exchange about including the Trump University scam as part of a possible case. One senior member of the investigating team observed that the fact pattern was not like the classic fraud cases that the district attorney traditionally pursued, because the students who enrolled in the training course actually did get "something," that is, books, printed materials, and lessons, and not absolutely nothing. Other team members voiced similar objections later in the investigation about prosecuting Trump for getting loans by submitting false financial statements to banks. Usually, those cases are brought when the borrower defaults on the loans, and the bank gets hit with a loss.

These objections reflected a profound underlying disagreement about when prosecutors should bring criminal cases. There is a point of view that prosecutors should never lose cases, because they have discretion about deciding to prosecute, and criminal prosecution should be reserved for "black-and-white" cases involving blatant fraud, where there is not any colorable defense. Less blatant frauds should be dealt with in other ways, including private lawsuits by aggrieved parties or civil enforcement actions.

My view was and is different. Of course, criminal prosecution is a drastic measure, and should be reserved for serious wrongdoing. But prosecutors who never lose cases, and who bring charges only when wrongdoing is both stark and easy to prove, are eligible for membership in what author Jesse Eisinger has dubbed "The Chickenshit Club" in his book of the same name. The Chickenshit Club is composed of prosecutors who are fearful of losing a case, and who have no desire to take risks. They bring only cases that are slam dunks, meaning that they can be lost only if a jury reaches an irrational result. Often, they lack experience as defense attorneys, which limits their ability to handicap their odds of an adverse verdict and makes them ill at ease if they have to try a case that has weaknesses.

While winning is important for prosecutors, winning isn't everything. As I will discuss later at some length, some cases need to be brought, notwithstanding the risk of loss, to vindicate the rule of law. Even leaving the supremacy of the rule of law to one side, good prosecutors consider not only the seriousness of the wrongdoing but also the track record of the potential defendant. Is the target someone who has made a mistake but has otherwise led a blameless life, or at least a more or less law-abiding life? If the target has committed crimes in the past, have measures short of criminal prosecution persuaded the target to conform his conduct to the law? And, even if the harm caused by a particular crime is modest, has the target generally been involved in antisocial behavior, such that the community needs to be protected from further misbehavior, or the target held to account for misdeeds that extend well beyond the particular crime at issue?

This last point brings into play the so-called "Al Capone" factor. Al Capone was a notorious gangster and businessman who had political influence, made donations to charities, and basked in public attention. He had a flamboyant lifestyle, enjoyed the company of beautiful women, and portrayed himself as a legitimate businessman while running Chicago's bootlegging business during Prohibition and orchestrating mob violence, including the infamous "Saint Valentine's Day Massacre." The feds eventually convicted him of tax evasion, which was surely among the least of his many crimes.

Even today, the Al Capone prosecution has its detractors. When I was a fledgling prosecutor in the late 1970s, I sometimes heard it said that prosecutors should target crimes, not criminals. The notion is that you pursue bad conduct, not bad people. In the abstract, this is a sound notion. But bad conduct can accumulate over time, and separate instances of bad conduct, each perhaps unworthy of prosecution viewed in isolation, can be judged as very serious conduct when viewed collectively. This is the premise of the RICO and enterprise corruption statutes. And, whether or not separate criminal acts can be combined into one great big crime, a person's history of unlawful behavior should be taken into account when deciding whether to prosecute, and how to punish. A core part of every criminal justice regime is that society must respond more harshly if someone breaks the law repeatedly.

As applied to Donald Trump, these abstract notions meant to me that we were warranted in throwing the book at him. Trump had become a master of breaking the law in ways that were difficult to reach. His conduct with respect to Trump University was an example. The fact pattern showed provable lies about what the students would receive (for example, lessons from instructors "handpicked" by Donald Trump, "everything they needed to know to make money in real estate," access to private funding sources, individualized "mentor" attention, and lessons on Trump's "very own" strategies and techniques for real estate investing), but they were also given "something" (pablum about real estate investing) so that Trump could point to a kernel of legitimacy when called upon to defend his deceptive conduct. The students who had lost thousands of dollars buying into Trump's hype had been hurt just as tangibly as victims who had fallen for more brazen frauds.

We were looking at instance after instance of suspected illegal conduct. Of course, they had to be provable, but if they were proved, their collective weight left no doubt in my mind that Trump deserved to be prosecuted. Measures short of criminal prosecution had been used against Trump, and he had dismissed them as trivial. He tweeted that he had paid $25 million to settle the civil claims against him in the Trump University litigation only because he had to focus on the country, and he did not want to go through a "long but winning trial." His settlement of the Trump Foundation civil claims, in which he paid a fine and agreed to a statement admitting wrongdoing, led to a tweet complaining of "politically motivated harassment" and a statement saying, "[a]ll they found was incredibly effective philanthropy and some small technical violations." Likewise, Trump had tweeted that the hush money payment to Stephanie Clifford was a "simple private transaction" correctly handled by his lawyer.

Looking at the totality of Trump's conduct over the years, I thought it was crystal clear that measures short of criminal prosecution meant nothing to him, and would not deter him in the slightest from engaging in other antisocial behavior. Indeed, the more successful he became, the more brazen was his behavior. He had "stiffed" many contractors and small business owners who had decided to advance services or products to the

Trump Organization because, after all, Donald Trump was so wealthy. Michael Cohen had told us that a big part of his job was telling small creditors who did business with Trump that they weren't going to get paid and forcing them to accept whatever modest sums Trump would give them. The enterprise corruption statute targeted just this kind of behavior: using a pattern of criminal activity to increase an entity's economic power, enabling it to inflict greater social harm.

Though the investigative team did not embrace a potential "enterprise corruption" charge with full-throated enthusiasm—it was a highly ambitious, complicated, and labor-intensive agenda—we began to gather the necessary facts. We had conference calls with the attorney general's office to speak with the lawyers who had been involved with the Trump Foundation investigation and the Trump University settlement. Those lawyers told us that both cases involved conduct that could have been charged criminally. Both were therefore worthy of further investigation and consideration as predicate acts for an enterprise corruption charge.

We also began ramping up the work that our outside consultant, FTI, was doing to parse Trump's tax returns and financial statements. FTI is a global consulting firm with thousands of employees and a leading practice in forensic and litigation consulting. It had tax experts and experts in the valuation of real estate, and DANY had hired FTI before my arrival. They were being paid out of a separate pot of funds that the office had received from a settlement with a large financial institution, but I never learned the details.

As we began to focus, delays and distractions arose. This is par for the course in complicated, high-profile investigations like this one. One of the distractions had to do with the press. At the end of March 2021, the *New York Times* ran a long article on our investigation, reporting that we had served subpoenas on Allen Weisselberg's banks for information on his personal finances. We knew that the issuance of the subpoenas had not been "leaked" by DANY, both because we canvassed our people and because we had some hearsay information that there had been a different source. Nevertheless, seeing this kind of information in the newspaper was troublesome. I received and responded to the inevitable letter from Weisselberg's lawyer, which complained about the "leaks" and insisted mistakenly that the district attorney's office had been responsible.

Press leaks in high-profile investigations are like cockroaches in apartment buildings. No matter how you try to prevent them, they make unwanted and aggravating appearances. As a personal matter, I had decided that I would not speak to the press at all during my tenure with the district attorney's office, and I never did. I did not return any of the countless emails or telephone calls I received asking for information. Carey and I agreed to ask everyone working on the case to report any media inquiries, so that the person making the inquiry could get an official response, which virtually always was to provide no information. But it is impossible to ensure that nobody working on the case ever lets anything slip or tells something to a friend who tells another friend who tells a reporter. Here, also, we were investigating a former president who had media ties and a gigantic press megaphone that he could and did employ at will, not to mention the folks at the Trump Organization and their lawyers. And the media was voracious and insatiable in its appetite to learn what might be happening in our investigation.

Contrary to what some may believe, experienced prosecutors do not want to see leaks in their investigations. We don't need the press to convey messages to witnesses or to ratchet up investigative pressure. We can do that ourselves. In the Trump investigation, for example, the media indulged in constant speculation about whether Weisselberg should or would cooperate with the district attorney's office. Having the media speculate was simply introducing clutter. When the moment was right, it was easy enough to call his lawyer to discuss the matter directly. And that moment was coming soon.

CHAPTER TWELVE

EUREKA!

As it turned out, the information we had received about Allen Weisselberg's free apartment proved to be a slice of a much larger pie. For many years, Weisselberg received hundreds of thousands of dollars of "off the books" compensation in the form of apartment rent, tuition payments for his grandchildren, cash, automobiles, and other benefits that should have been taxed but were not. He was able to evade taxes on these items because the Trump Organization's executive compensation regime was rigged so that certain executives got financial benefits that were concealed from federal, state, and local tax authorities.

Some of the underlying facts were developed in the grand jury, and I will have to leave those facts out of this story, because prosecutors are not allowed to disclose grand jury proceedings. However, most of the story took place away from the grand jury, and the important facts have since been made public.

On April 21, 2021, I was working at home. I was in front of my computer as usual, struggling with documents, adding up figures, and puzzling over spreadsheets and records having to do with Weisselberg's personal finances and compensation. Upon piecing the records together, I saw that the Trump Organization had been paying lots of money on Weisselberg's behalf—

payments for the rent on his Manhattan apartment, his utility bills (electricity, telephone, internet, and cable television), his monthly garage charges, tuition expenses for members of his family, lease expenses for automobiles for Weisselberg and his wife, and payments for other personal items like beds, televisions, carpeting, and furniture. Weisselberg even got some cash that he could use to hand out holiday tips.

The "eureka" moment came when I realized that there were internal spreadsheets that not only tracked these expenses but treated them as part of Weisselberg's annual compensation. Weisselberg was supposed to receive $940,000 in yearly compensation; that was the amount that Donald Trump had fixed for him in the years between 2011 and 2018. In order to make sure that Weisselberg was getting the right amount, there were spreadsheets that added the expenses paid on his behalf to his regularly paid salary. The internal spreadsheets indicated, however, that the Trump Organization did not report Weisselberg's total annual compensation to the tax authorities. The organization reported only the smaller amounts that he had received in his regular paychecks and end-of-year bonus checks. The other items that the Trump Organization had tracked as part of Weisselberg's compensation—the rental checks, the car payments, the tuition payments, and all the rest—never got reported to the tax man. In effect, the Trump Organization and Weisselberg had a deal by which he would get a regular salary and also have many of his living expenses paid for him. But the payment of his living expenses would be "off the books." The only part of his compensation that the federal, state, and local tax authorities would learn about was his regular salary. The other piece of his compensation would be kept secret.

One does not need to be an Internal Revenue Service agent or a forensic accountant to know that this is illegal. If it was proper, every working person in America would want a similar deal. Imagine being able to arrange with your employer to give you less in your paycheck, and use the money left out of your paycheck to pay your mortgage and your car payments. And let's imagine further that your employer would report paying you only what you got in your paycheck, while still deducting the payments to your bank or your car dealer as "housing expense" or "auto expense." Your employer would not be spending any more money and might even be paying less in the form of employer payroll taxes. You, however, would be getting a windfall, because you would pay taxes only on what you got in your paycheck, and you would pay no tax on the money used to pay your mortgage and your car payments. That's not the way our tax system works. The tax laws require employers to report all employee compensation, whether it is included in a paycheck or takes another form, like an envelope with cash. And you, as the employee, have to report all of your compensation, no matter what form it takes, such as a free apartment or a free car. There are some narrow exceptions for untaxed "fringe benefits," but those exceptions did not apply to the payments on Weisselberg's behalf.

As the documents fell into place, I realized that we had Weisselberg in our clutches. I had been staring at the spreadsheets for hours before the moment that the penny dropped. Those moments don't happen often. Sometimes, for defense lawyers, the moments happen in reverse, when you learn of a new fact that tells you immediately that your client's case is absolutely hopeless. Early in my career, my law partner had been representing a diamond dealer who had secretly sold some gems that had been entrusted to him on consignment. The case was defensible unless the Israeli diamond dealer to whom the client had sold the gems was willing to come to New York to testify against him. One day, we got word that not only was the diamond dealer coming to New York, but he had taped the conversation with our client. Uh-oh! Case closed.

I wasted no time in breaking the news about Weisselberg to Cy, Carey, and the whole team. Cy made a comment about "breaks" that change the course of investigations, and breaks being the product of hard work. We speculated about the conversations that might soon take place between Weisselberg and Trump, after Weisselberg found out that we would likely be charging him with tax crimes. Cy even wondered out loud if we could get a court order permitting us to intercept their conversations, but we did not have the legal basis to get such an order so it was just idle speculation.

The team was ebullient when it learned of the existence of the executive compensation scheme and moved quickly into high gear. We all realized that we had to finish gathering the facts and documents relating to Weisselberg's untaxed compensation, confront him and try to "turn" him, and then bring charges against him if he was not willing to cooperate. With all of the other investigative tasks that were on the agenda, Carey and I realized that we would need more help for the team.

Happily, Carey and I were able to persuade the large law firms for which we had once labored to provide us with associate help. A total of three talented associates were "seconded" to the district attorney's office by Davis Polk & Wardwell, where Carey had been a longtime partner, and the Paul Weiss firm, where I had been a partner before I retired. Having these associates join the Trump investigation was a "win/win" for them, as they stopped working on their firm matters to become special assistant district attorneys working on the Trump investigation while the law firms continued to pay their substantial salaries. Upon joining the investigative team, they became the most highly compensated employees in the office, earning more than Cy Vance.

Once we had a handle on how the executive compensation scheme worked and had assembled proof of the many expenses that had been paid on Weisselberg's behalf, we needed to speak to Weisselberg's personal tax preparer. This is a standard part of any tax fraud investigation. The subject's tax preparer can shed light on the subject's knowledge of tax law, the subject's involvement in the preparation of his tax returns, and any pertinent conversations between the subject and the tax preparer.

It was particularly important to speak with Weisselberg's tax preparer, because his tax preparer was Donald Bender, a certified public accountant at the Mazars accounting firm and the lead outside accountant for Donald Trump and the Trump Organization. This put Bender in the middle of our whole investigation. On the executive compensation scheme, he had prepared Weisselberg's tax returns. Had Weisselberg talked with him about the rental, tuition, and car payments that were made on his behalf? Had he given Weisselberg any advice about whether those items needed to be reported as taxable income? Or had the payments been concealed from him? Because Bender also was doing accounting for Trump and the Trump Organization, we had questions to ask him on the other side of the same tax issue. Had anyone at the Trump Organization spoken with Bender about the "off the books" compensation paid to Weisselberg and (as became clear) other senior executives? Had he given anyone advice about including these items on the W-2 forms that the company had to file with the tax authorities? Had he blessed the unorthodox arrangements that we were learning about? If no one had spoken to Bender on these topics, that would be a highly incriminating fact, since the Trump Organization looked to him for advice on all sorts of tax and accounting issues. Likewise, if Bender had been consulted and had warned people that they were doing something wrong, that also would be an incriminating piece of evidence. Bender also had been up to his neck in the preparation of Donald Trump's yearly financial statements. At some point, we would need to speak with him about those financial statements and what he knew about the inflated and fabricated asset values we were investigating.

At the outset, we were not sure that Bender would speak with us voluntarily. We were concerned that he would hire his own criminal defense attorney, who could advise him to clam up and tell us nothing. He had the right to say nothing, as anything he told us voluntarily could be used against him. If Bender refused to speak with us, we could compel him to testify in the grand jury, but under New York law witnesses who testify in the grand jury cannot be prosecuted for crimes that have anything to do with their testimony. They are automatically immunized from criminal prosecution. Prosecutors hate giving witnesses immunity "in the blind," before knowing what involvement the witness had in the matters under investigation. In the federal system, unlike in New York, prosecutors can bring witnesses before a grand jury and require them formally to invoke their Fifth Amendment rights and refuse to answer questions. Many witnesses, especially professionals like Bender who work for large companies, don't like invoking the Fifth Amendment, and sometimes they will decide to answer questions voluntarily to avoid doing that, particularly if their employers are urging them to cooperate with the investigation.

As it happened, Bender was willing to meet with us voluntarily. Interestingly, the lawyers for Mazars decided to tell Bender to meet with us and apparently did not advise him to get his own personal lawyer. Mazars had a strong reason to cooperate with our investigation. We had learned a few weeks earlier of a serious problem with their document production, which had led us to have some very direct and threatening conversations with them, including conversations with their general counsel, about the precarious legal situation in which the firm might find itself if it was not fully cooperative. The firm, to its credit, took those conversations to heart and made Bender available to us without a lot of hemming and hawing.

We spoke with Bender on May 5, 2021, via Zoom. Bender was a short, bald, bespectacled fellow. He struck me as extremely nervous, timid, and fidgety, and he presented himself more like a store clerk than the personal accountant to the former president. Bender knew a lot about accounting, but he came across as someone who could be counted upon not to rock any boats. During the questioning, we showed Bender the Trump Organization spreadsheets that tracked the payments on Weisselberg's behalf and treated them as unreported compensation. As we went through the facts with him, Bender realized that he had been used, and became emotional. Notwithstanding his role as Weisselberg's tax preparer, and his status as the Trump Organization's main outside accountant, no one had ever told him about the unreported compensation that Weisselberg and others had been receiving. He said that if he had been told about the practice, he would have asked his clients if they were "crazy." Furthermore, Bender had explained the tax rules about "free apartments" to Weisselberg when Weisselberg had asked him about the apartment that his son Barry had received, and Weisselberg therefore knew that the company's payment of rent on Weisselberg's behalf needed to be reported as income.

We also asked Bender about another unorthodox practice that the Trump Organization used to compensate senior executives. Each year, Trump would authorize the payment of end-of-year bonuses to his executives. Many of the bonuses were quite large—senior executives each might receive hundreds of thousands of dollars as their annual bonus. Oddly, though, some employees, including Weisselberg, got their bonus in the form of checks drawn on various Trump operating companies, and the checks would be reported not as regular paychecks but as "non-employee compensation," even though the recipients in fact were employees. In Weisselberg's case, getting bonus money that was reported as "non-employee compensation" allowed him to engage in a forbidden practice known as "double-dipping." He could put away money for his retirement in the company's regular pension and profit-sharing plan, and also pay into a separate retirement account (a Keogh account) that he had established. This allowed him to avoid paying income taxes on the money he stashed away in the separate account, but the gimmick was improper if the money he put away was just ordinary employee compensation. Bender had known about this practice, and had told Weisselberg that, "if it was me, I wouldn't do it."

The Bender interview meant that, notwithstanding his discomfort and weakness, he could be a significant witness. Bender had never blessed what Weisselberg and the Trump Organization were doing, and he had been largely kept in the dark about it, even though he was involved in preparing Weisselberg's tax returns and in the Trump Organization's wage and tax reporting. The potential criminal case against Weisselberg got another boost a day later, on May 6, when we learned of the alteration of documents relating to private school tuition payments that had been made on Weisselberg's behalf. Weisselberg had directed a staff member in Trump's accounting department to delete references to his name from accounting ledgers that recorded the payments, seemingly an effort to cover his tracks.

During the rest of May 2021, we concentrated on fleshing out the details of the illegal executive compensation scheme. Gary Fishman sent over some information from the attorney general's office about free apartments that had been provided to other Trump executives; as with Weisselberg, the free housing had not been reported to the tax authorities. In light of the evidence we had now developed, the attorney general agreed that she would defer to DANY with respect to bringing criminal charges against Weisselberg and the Trump Organization, and Fishman would be cross-designated to our office so he could work both as a special assistant district attorney and as an assistant attorney general.

Near the end of the month, we had another conversation with Bender, which left him virtually in tears. He told us that he was very upset about what he had learned from us with respect to the Trump Organization's executive compensation practices. He said he was disappointed in himself. He had tried to do a good job, but he never saw himself as becoming the accountant for a president; he thought he would be the accountant for grocery stores and beauty parlors. After Trump's election, Bender told Weisselberg that the business now had to be "squeaky clean," and "if you're doing anything, stop doing it." Not surprisingly, the Trump Organization's payments of rent, private school tuition, and other expenses on Weisselberg's behalf ended around the time of Trump's inauguration.

On top of gathering all of the necessary documents and fleshing out the facts surrounding the illegal compensation scheme, we started taking the steps necessary to file an indictment. In order to indict a case, the facts have to be presented to a grand jury. I had plenty of experience in presenting cases to federal grand juries and no experience with New York State grand juries, but their basic role is the same. In both state and federal court, a judge supervises the convening of a grand jury consisting of twenty-three ordinary citizens who respond to summonses for jury duty. The grand jurors listen to evidence presented to them by the prosecutors, with no judge or outsiders in attendance (except for the court reporter). When the prosecutors think the grand jurors have heard enough evidence, they prepare an indictment setting forth criminal charges against one or more defendants, and they ask the grand jurors to approve the indictment. The grand jury deliberates in secret, and if a majority of the grand jurors agree, the indictment is authorized. The grand jurors do not need proof beyond a reasonable doubt; they are told that criminal charges are appropriate if they find evidence showing that there is "probable cause" to believe that the defendants committed the crimes stated in the indictment. These basic rules govern the federal and the New York State grand jury processes.

In practice, however, there is a world of difference between a federal grand jury presentation and a state grand jury presentation. In federal court, prosecutors can present "hearsay" evidence. So, let's imagine that federal agents have been investigating a street-level narcotics dealer who has sold drugs to a police informant, with the transaction having been surveilled by agents who observed the dealer meeting and talking to the informant. As a federal prosecutor, I could (and sometimes did) indict that case without bringing the informant or even one of the surveillance agents to testify before the grand jury. In a pinch, I could have another agent read the investigative reports beforehand and simply tell the grand jury what had happened on the street when the drug sale took place. I did not need the testimony of an eyewitness. If I wanted the grand jury to see banking records, or business records, or telephone records, I didn't need a witness from the bank, the business, or the telephone company. I could call a paralegal who would testify that he or she was familiar with the investigation, and here are some records we got from whatever company supplied them. The paralegal could even explain what the records showed. Grand jury presentations can be lengthy and involved, but the ability to use hearsay streamlines the process.

In New York State grand juries, hearsay evidence is typically not allowed. To indict my street-level narcotics dealer, I would have to call the informant as a witness, and probably also make sure the grand jury understood that the informant was a criminal himself (if that's the case, as it usually is). To be on the safe side, I might call a surveillance agent to testify about what the agent saw on the street when the drug deal took place. All of this, along with some other procedures that have to be followed in state court, make the process much more involved than the federal process. It has been said that, because grand juries function under the control of the prosecutor, a grand jury can be persuaded to "indict a ham sandwich." That may be true, but in New York the prosecutor first has to go out and catch the pig with his or her bare hands!

I can't describe the grand jury process that led to the indictment of Allen Weisselberg and the Trump Organization, which by law must remain secret. What we were doing did not feel very "secret" at the time, however. The press certainly understood that we were beginning to focus on Weisselberg, and this led to constant speculation among the pundits, to whom we referred as the "talking feds." One evening, toward the end of May 2021, I watched a MSNBC roundtable featuring both Michael Cohen and Jennifer Weisselberg holding forth about our investigation, and about Allen Weisselberg's imminent legal peril on tax charges.

This press coverage was particularly unhelpful. I had spoken directly with Weisselberg's main defense lawyer, Mary Mulligan, to tell her that we had progressed in our investigation and were getting ready to charge her client. We had arranged for a meeting to take place on June 1, to be attended in person by Weisselberg, at which we would preview his criminal exposure. Mulligan knew, of course, that we were hoping to persuade Weisselberg to cooperate with our investigation. By late May 2021 it seemed like everybody watching television or reading the newspaper knew that, and the unrelenting media speculation about Weisselberg got in the way of the planned in-person meeting because Mulligan was concerned that the press effectively would be in attendance. By this point, many witnesses and lawyers knew that a grand jury was hearing evidence. I had no reason to think that anyone from DANY was speaking to the press, but the media was nevertheless having a field day speculating about what was going on.

Near the end of the month, Carey Dunne and I were standing on the sidewalk together and we had a long conversation about the overall state of the investigation and Carey's plans for the future after the end of the year. Cy's departure was beginning to loom over the case like a shadow. We discussed the prospect that the charges we were planning to bring against Weisselberg and the Trump Organization might be the only charges that would ever result from our investigation, because the effort required to bring and then prosecute the executive compensation scheme would take up too much "bandwidth" in the district attorney's office. We were still working on all of the other issues—the financial statements, the conservation easements, and so forth—but we were concerned that there might not be enough time, energy, and resources to bring a case against Trump, even if such a case could be made on the facts. This was a possibility that Solomon Shinerock, the senior assistant district attorney on the investigative team, had voiced a week or two earlier.

We decided that all we could do was keep investigating and see where that took us. There was no secret pact to "get" Donald Trump during that conversation or at any other point. Nor was there any conversation about politics, about the 2020 election, the "stop the steal" shenanigans, or whether Trump needed to be prosecuted because his behavior as president was repugnant to us or to others. The political implications of a prosecution were simply out of bounds, and irrelevant to our conversations. Everyone accepted that politics had nothing to do with the task at hand, which was to investigate the facts and decide whether those facts established that Trump, his company, or his associates had committed crimes within our jurisdiction.

We weren't being naive, and we were not blind to other Trump-related controversies, like the events of January 6, 2021. But we didn't have jurisdiction to look at those matters, so we just never talked about them except insofar as they were relevant to our tasks. I am sure we all had our private thoughts and opinions about Trump's politics, but none of that mattered, and we kept such thoughts to ourselves. What mattered were the facts and the law. This was not the result of putting on blinders; it's simply what occupies most prosecutors, who typically have more things to do than time to do them. Think of it this way—if we all had been cardiologists, trying to determine whether Trump had a heart condition, we would be learning all we could about his cardiac anatomy, his heart symptoms, and his test results. That is what we would talk about. His politics, or for that matter the appearance of his hair or body parts, would not have an impact on what we thought of his heart condition, or how we discussed his treatment. Similarly, neither his politics nor his postelection behavior had much to do with the weight of the evidence, or the question whether he had committed crimes within our jurisdiction.

Some people may not believe that we didn't discuss Trump's politics. Sadly, some of the disbelief stems from Trump's own conduct and rhetoric. In his world, legal decisions all derive from politics; he had no reluctance to politicize the Department of Justice, and his campaign rallies featured "Lock Her Up" as a slogan, reflecting his view that political enemies should be treated as criminals. But before Trump broke it, the norm was that politics should be divorced from law enforcement. Twenty years earlier, my partner Ted Wells and I had been representing New Jersey Democratic senator Bob Torricelli in a federal bribery investigation. Control of the United States Senate potentially hung in the balance, because the Democrats had a one-seat advantage in the Senate, and Torricelli's indictment could have resulted in a change in the Senate's political control. Though ultimately there were no charges, we had many long and heated conversations with the federal prosecutors in charge of the investigation. To my recollection the political ramifications of an indictment were never mentioned. If the president at the time, George W. Bush, had intervened in the investigation, there would have been hell to pay.

CHAPTER THIRTEEN

INDICTMENT

June 2021 was taken up with preparation for the indictment of Weisselberg and the Trump Organization, which became public on July 1. The first order of business was to see if the prospect of criminal charges might lead Weisselberg to flip and cooperate with our investigation.

We met via Zoom with Weisselberg and his lawyers on June 1. A meeting like this, attended in person by the target, is unusual; such meetings commonly take place just between the prosecutors and the defense lawyers. We wanted a meeting directly with Weisselberg so we could be sure that what we said would not be lost in translation. His lawyers also wanted the meeting, perhaps so that he could hear us directly and also because we might be more informative about the details of our case if we were making a direct pitch for Weisselberg's cooperation, which they knew would be the main item on the agenda.

I began by telling Weisselberg that we would be seeking his indictment within the next few weeks, and we wanted to give him and his lawyers the opportunity to tell us if our view of the facts or the law was mistaken. We also wanted to give him information so he could decide whether to cooperate with our investigation. I stressed that time was of the essence, and noted that before an indictment was returned, "nothing is carved in stone." This was an artful way of saying that we would consider not charging him with any crime at all if he were cooperative and truthful with us. It may have been a bit too artful, as I had to clarify later in a telephone call with the lawyers that a complete "pass" (that is, no prosecution at all) was within the realm of possibility, depending of course on the nature and quality of Weisselberg's cooperation. I also noted later, though, that we do not "rip up" indictments after they are filed, so Weisselberg had to decide now whether to cooperate, because later we would not be willing to forgo his prosecution. I went through the facts that would be contained in a criminal indictment, laying out the Trump Organization's practice of providing certain employees, including Weisselberg himself, benefits like rent-free apartments and leased cars without reporting those benefits as income to the tax authorities.

I did not mince words about what we were prepared to charge and prove. I told Weisselberg that we had found that the rent, utility, and garage expenses paid on his behalf totaled well over a million dollars, along with auto lease expenses of several hundred thousand dollars and private school tuition payments of over $350,000. We knew, of course, that Weisselberg had not disclosed this income to his tax preparer, and we also went through his improper receipt of "non-employee compensation," along with the fact that for many years Weisselberg had not paid taxes to New York City even though he was a city resident.

I also spoke about Weisselberg's son Barry, saying that we knew that Barry was a beneficiary of the employee compensation scheme, since he and his wife had lived rent-free for many years and his children had their private school tuition paid by Donald Trump. But I made it clear that, while Weisselberg might help his son if he cooperated, his decision not to cooperate would not be held against Barry, because we do not visit the sins of a father onto his sons.

I told Weisselberg that we were not bluffing, and that as a result of our prosecution he might go to jail. He might avoid a jail sentence, depending on what a judge would do if he were convicted, but nobody knew what would happen. I closed by saying that, if Weisselberg were prepared to tell us the un-varnished truth about his dealings with Donald Trump, that might give him a way to avoid indictment, conviction, and imprisonment.

Weisselberg sat there during my remarks as silent as a sphinx. He was listening intently, but—undoubtedly following his lawyers' instructions—he never said a word.

In our follow-up calls with Weisselberg's lawyers we were told that he was "actively considering" what to do, and the law-yers wanted details about the nature and extent of the coop-eration we thought Weisselberg could provide. Based on the conversations with counsel, I thought Weisselberg was about to flip, and I started mulling the work we would need to do in that case. But it was not to be. Two weeks after our June 1 meeting, the lawyers called to say that they had spoken extensively with him, but Weisselberg did not have the kind of information we were looking for and so could not cooperate with us.

I believed, and still believe, that Weisselberg had informa-tion to provide about criminal conduct committed by Donald Trump. Weisselberg had been intimately involved with the preparation of Trump's falsified financial statements, and we knew from Cohen and other witnesses that regular discussions about those statements had taken place behind closed doors between Weisselberg and Trump. The issue, as I saw it, was not that Weisselberg lacked incriminating information; he just decided not to share it.

We will likely never know how close we came, or why Weisselberg didn't flip. We heard a rumor that Trump had reached some "understanding" with Weisselberg, but we never got evidence that there had been a promised pot of gold. Maybe, after organizing his entire life around Trump for many decades, Weisselberg could not imagine a rupture from the man who had been the center of his universe. Some people simply cannot abide the notion of cooperating and cannot envision themselves cast in the role of a turncoat. Maybe Weisselberg was afraid of telling the truth about his own role in criminal conduct, or just afraid in general. I had represented cooperators, and also people for whom cooperation was anathema. It is a personal decision, not always reached by creating a spreadsheet of pros and cons.

Since we had tried and failed to secure Weisselberg's cooperation, we went ahead with the criminal case that we had built against him and the Trump Organization. In the extensive media coverage of the case, the pundits and the "talking feds" usually mischaracterized what had happened. Former prosecutors and "talking feds" filled the blogosphere by saying that we brought the criminal case to pressure Weisselberg into cooperating. This was just plain wrong. We didn't bring the criminal case to pressure Weisselberg; we brought it because we thought he had committed serious crimes. Before bringing the case, we let Weisselberg know what we were planning so that he could decide whether to cooperate, but we did not bring the case to persuade him to cooperate. Nor did we bring it to retaliate against him because he decided not to cooperate, or to try to change his mind. We accepted his decision to remain one of Donald Trump's lieutenants. And then we indicted him for the crimes he had committed, since he gave us no reason to veer from the direction in which the facts and the law had led us.

Would we have found those crimes, or even looked for them, if we had not been trying to get Weisselberg to flip? That's a hard question to answer, but it is beside the point. The point is that prosecutors look for evidence of serious wrongdoing. When they find it, they bring charges unless there is reason to hold back. It's not a lot more complicated than that.

Before asking the grand jury to return the indictment, we gave counsel for the Trump Organization and Weisselberg a last opportunity to present arguments why we should not go forward. This is a standard part of white-collar practice. No law or regulation requires that defense lawyers be given the chance to talk prosecutors out of bringing a case, but it makes sense for both sides. For the defense lawyers, it is an opportunity to present facts or legal principles that the prosecutors may have overlooked and to make policy arguments addressed to prosecutorial discretion. For prosecutors, hearing from defense lawyers allows them to think through any weaknesses in their case and make a final decision. They also want to listen to the defense lawyers to see if they need to fine-tune their strategy in light of what their adversaries are saying.

The conversations with counsel for the Trump Organization were memorable to me because they featured the participation of my former law partner Ron Fischetti. Several months earlier, Donald Trump had hired Ron to represent him in connection with the district attorney's investigation. The hiring took place not long after I had joined the investigation. Were the two events connected? That was a question asked by many, including some in the media, but I did not know how to answer it.

I had gotten to know Ron during my first stint as a federal prosecutor in the late 1970s, when we tried a drug distribution case against each other. When I left the U.S. Attorney's Office in 1982 and started teaching law at the Columbia Law School,

I began consulting with Ron on criminal cases. Eventually we decided to become law partners. I left my teaching job in 1984, and Ron and I formed a small criminal defense "boutique" known at one point as Fischetti & Pomerantz. We were partners for six years before I left to start a white-collar criminal practice at a much larger firm.

During our years together, Ron and I were fast friends. We tried cases with each other, and we defended lawyers, doctors, and accountants, as well as drug dealers, gangsters, killers, and con men. Our exploits during the years we were partners could fill the pages of a book like this one. But we had drifted apart over the years and were no longer in regular contact when Trump hired Ron to represent him. Ron was just short of his eighty-fifth birthday when Trump hired him. My colleagues in the district attorney's office asked me if, given his age, Ron had perhaps "lost something off his fastball." I replied that he never really relied on his fastball; even in his prime days as a lawyer he threw a lot of nasty curveballs and even a few spitballs.

Ron and I spoke for the first time about the Trump investigation when he called me at home. We reminisced a bit about the "old days" and some of the clients we had represented. I commented that he was now representing the former president of the United States, and I was actively investigating the former president's business affairs, which showed that anything could happen if you lived long enough. Then we got down to business. Ron said he needed first to make sure that Cy Vance knew that, contrary to some recent media piece, Trump had not called Cy a "political hack." According to Ron, the reporter had misquoted Trump, who had actually called Letitia James a "political hack." This was not a great note on which to begin. In any event, Ron wanted to have an in-person meeting at which he and an entourage of lawyers defending the Trump Organization could have a dialogue with the district attorney's office.

It was not clear to us why Ron Fischetti was getting involved. We had not seriously entertained the notion of charging Donald Trump personally in connection with the executive compensation scheme. There were reasons to think he had been complicit—he had surely known and approved the "free apartments" and many of the other benefits that had been bestowed on certain executives, and he had signed the checks used to pay the private school tuition for Weisselberg's family members. But we did not have a witness who would testify that Trump was involved. Also, we had no proof that Trump knew either that Weisselberg had underpaid his taxes or that the Trump Organization had failed to report the payment of personal expenses as income earned by the executives.

Nevertheless, we agreed to have a Zoom meeting at which Ron and the company's lawyers could present their arguments why the Trump Organization should not be indicted. The arguments they made had no substance. Ron began by insulting me and Carey, saying essentially that we were hypocrites because we had both worked for big law firms defending big corporations that had not been prosecuted for much worse crimes. He depicted our case as involving insignificant crimes and "isolated wrongdoing" that had not benefited the Trump Organization, and one of his colleagues drew an analogy to the financial institutions that had not been charged in connection with the 2008 financial crisis. They argued that any tax evasion had not been done on behalf of the company, missing the point that the company's illegal decision not to report all the compensation that Weisselberg and other executives received was what enabled them to underpay their taxes. They also alluded to the company's production of many documents, which prompted me to note that the Trump Organization had done everything within its power to delay and frustrate our investigation, including "slow walking" its document production and making sure that not a single employee spoke with us voluntarily.

Toward the end of the meeting, one of the defense lawyers started to argue that an indictment would be unfair because criminal charges might somehow implicate the company's outstanding bank loans. Companies facing potential indictment always make arguments addressed to the collateral consequences of being charged with a crime. I had made dozens of similar arguments to prosecutors and regulators on behalf of clients like Citigroup, Lehman Brothers, and Deutsche Bank, arguing that criminal sanctions for the conduct of low-level employees would mainly hurt innocent shareholders. Here the misconduct involved very senior employees; the main malefactor was the company's chief financial officer. And there were no innocent shareholders. The Trump Organization was effectively owned by one person: Donald J. Trump, and his lawyer had begun the meeting by noting that Trump regarded Weisselberg as a valued employee who would be staying with the company.

All told, as Carey and I discussed after the meeting, the case for prosecuting the Trump Organization was overwhelming. Some years earlier, the district attorney's office had made public a policy memorandum detailing a framework for deciding whether to indict a company. Virtually every factor cited in the memo as a relevant consideration pointed in favor of charging the Trump Organization. The first factor the memo listed was the organization's timely and voluntary disclosure of wrongdoing and its cooperation in the investigation. The Trump Organization scored a perfect zero on this point. It had not disclosed the illegal compensation scheme. Indeed, Donald Bender had told us that there had been discussions in 2017 about changing the company's practices, but no amended returns had been filed and nothing had been brought to the attention of the tax authorities. There had been no cooperation with the investigation, only intentional efforts to delay and frustrate our efforts. Another factor was the pervasiveness of wrongdoing within the organization, including the complicity in, or the condoning of, the wrongdoing by senior management. Here the wrongdoing had involved very senior management, and Trump's lawyer had begun the meeting by telling us that Trump was not cutting ties with Weisselberg but hugging him more closely. To make matters worse, the Trump Organization had a history of wrongdoing. Putting aside all of the people it had cheated and "stiffed" over the years, it had been involved in the Trump University scam, the misuse of the Trump Foundation, the payment of hush money to Stephanie Clifford, and of course we were hot on the trail of financial statement fraud. The adequacy of the company's "compliance programs"? There were none.

I had spent decades representing companies in which some wrongdoing had taken place. All companies are run by people, and people are imperfect. But the Trump Organization had little in common with the companies I had represented. It was little more than the alter ego of its owner, Donald Trump. Trump's mantra was to deny all wrongdoing and to stick his finger in the eye of anyone investigating his affairs. The company had no "checks and balances." It was a collection of hundreds of separate entities owned by Trump, created over time to minimize liability and accountability and to create opacity. Our meeting with defense counsel gave us no pause about indicting the Trump Organization. The lawyers had simply dumped gasoline on the fire.

We also had a final conversation with Weisselberg's lawyers, who at least made arguments that were respectable, if unconvincing. Their main point was that Weisselberg was being "run over" in our zeal to prosecute Donald Trump. They depicted their client as "roadkill," who would not have been charged in a different case. Perhaps his wrongdoing might never have been discovered in a different case, but once we found it, he had to be prosecuted. He was a trained finance professional, who understood the tax laws. He was very handsomely paid. He had access to accounting professionals. His tax cheating was substantial and had continued over many years. Neither I nor anyone on the investigative team had any reservations about bringing criminal charges against him. His more technical defenses revolved around the claim that he regarded the untaxed benefits he had received as "gifts" to him, which therefore were not taxable income. But the Trump Organization had tracked these supposed gifts on spreadsheets and treated them as part of Weisselberg's compensation. He could try to sell this argument to a jury, but we were not buying it.

Toward the end of the month, I wrote up the indictment containing the formal charges. We decided to issue what is known as a "speaking indictment"—an instrument that not only lists the charges but also explains them in some detail so that people reading it would understand the facts. We knew, of course, that many millions of people would be reading the indictment, or learning about it, in the coming few days. The office's rear guard—those standing up for orthodoxy in the district attorney's office, and for hewing to "the way we always do things"—nevertheless wanted some changes. We actually had a ridiculous discussion about numbering the paragraphs in the indictment. I was told that the office simply did not do it that way. We reached a compromise on this burning issue. A keen-eyed reader studying the indictment will discover that the paragraphs in the first half of the document are numbered, but there are no paragraph numbers in the second half.

The grand jury voted the indictment, and the defendants appeared before the court for arraignment on July 1, 2021. The Trump Organization appeared through counsel; Trump himself was not present because he was not charged as an individual. Allen Weisselberg had to appear in person, but we did not send police to arrest him. Decades earlier, then–United States attorney Rudy Giuliani had ignited a debate among criminal lawyers by sending agents to arrest Wall Street figures at their places of work, making them go through a staged "perp walk." Ironically, the wife of one of the arrestees described the public arrest as part of a "witch hunt." We decided that there was no need to arrest Weisselberg, a seventy-three-year-old accountant. We called his lawyers to tell them that Weisselberg had to surrender to face the charges and arranged for his quiet entrance into the courthouse.

An arraignment is usually a perfunctory proceeding. The presiding judge verifies that the defendants have been advised of the charges against them and the defendants enter not guilty pleas. The judge then sets a preliminary schedule and fixes conditions of release for individual defendants. The arraignment of the Trump Organization and Allen Weisselberg, however, was a three-ring circus. All the court personnel who had any conceivable reason to be in the courtroom made it their business to attend, and they were all dressed in their Sunday best. The press was everywhere. Media trucks massed outside the courthouse and getting into the courtroom required running a gauntlet of reporters and photographers. The reporters were shouting questions and the camera lights were flashing. I had been involved in other high-profile cases, but the media interest in the Trump investigation was at a different and higher level. I found out later that the *New York Times* had put the area around the courthouse under surveillance in the effort to figure out what had been going on in the grand jury, and which witnesses were testifying. People were delegated to find out the identity of "paisley bow tie guy" who was spotted walking one day with members of the investigative team. The *Times* eventually identified him by looking through photographs of unrelated gatherings attended by FTI personnel and seeing the telltale bow tie around the neck of Mark Dunec, a FTI real estate appraisal expert who was working with us on the financial statement investigation.

Carey Dunne spoke at the arraignment about the "sweeping and audacious" nature of the scheme charged in the indictment, which was a preemptive strike to deal with the vitriolic comments we were sure would come from Trump about our case. Trump did not disappoint. To no one's surprise, he put out a statement calling our investigation a "witch hunt." Days earlier, he issued a statement calling the prosecutors "rude"—this from a man who had been taped talking gleefully about grabbing women by their private parts! His statement also claimed that untaxed benefits like the ones that Weisselberg had received were "standard practice throughout the U.S. business community." This was complete nonsense. The practices not only were unorthodox, but similar off-the-books compensation schemes had been prosecuted time and again.

Some in the media questioned whether the charges against Weisselberg and the Trump Organization were the only charges we intended to bring, and some editorials opined that the crimes charged in the indictment were minor or even trivial. Of course, in the beginning of July we did not know what the future would bring, only that we would keep working and make decisions when we were further along in the investigation. We could have waited to bring the charges until the end of the investigation, but there seemed no point in doing that.

We brought the case as soon as it was ready to bring, and the timing had the ancillary benefit of letting opposing counsel know that, as I had told Allen Weisselberg to his face, we don't bluff. He had been warned on June 1 that he might be indicted within a month. Exactly a month later, he was being arraigned on our indictment. As for the severity of the charges, the indictment alleged that Weisselberg had evaded federal, state, and local taxes over a fifteen-year period. His tax savings totaled about $900,000. This figure may have been regarded as trivial in Trump's circles, but a lot of people in New York County did not make that much in a decade or even a lifetime.

Cy, consistent with his overall desire to be prudent and to keep a low profile about the investigation, did not tout the significance of the indictment in a press release. His statement to the press said only that "the work continues." I got a telephone call from him a few days later in which he thanked me for my labors over the last five months and forbade me from leaving the office, which I said I had no intention of doing. We talked about the need to refocus our efforts and decide which leads to follow. Shortly thereafter, Cy presented us with plain white T-shirts imprinted only with the words THE WORK CONTINUES. . . . It did indeed.

CHAPTER FOURTEEN

BOILING THE OCEAN

The main task for the rest of the summer and fall was to pursue the investigation of Donald Trump's financial statements—the SOFCs. We needed to burrow deeply into the SOFCs and decide whether they were false and whether they had been used to commit crimes. If we could prove that Trump had routinely misled people about the value of his business empire, the resulting charges could form the capstone of the enterprise corruption case that we had discussed months before.

We had started doing this work earlier, after getting information from the attorney general's office and speaking several times with Michael Cohen in March 2021. But I had underestimated the enormity of the task, and we all had been busy working on other aspects of the investigation. Now that the Trump Organization/Weisselberg indictment had been filed it was time to refocus on the SOFCs.

The task of understanding Trump's business interests, and how those interests were valued on his SOFCs, was enormously complicated. Apart from the sheer number of assets and years that we could examine, there were other complexities. Trump's financial statements included pages of notes and caveats. Understanding their significance meant we had to get schooled in the language of accountancy and the rules that apply to the preparation of personal financial statements. We had to understand why the values of certain properties were lumped together, and why a particular property might be listed and valued separately one year but grouped with other assets a year later. We also had to parse the exact nature of Trump's real estate interests. He owned some properties outright, but there were properties for which he held only a ground lease (for example, 40 Wall Street), and still others for which he had given away his rights to develop or reconfigure the property (for example, Mar-a-Lago).

We also had to grapple with the reality that very few of Trump's assets had values that we could look up in the newspaper or on the internet. Many of his properties, like his Seven Springs mansion in Westchester County or his penthouse apartment on the top of Trump Tower, were unique. There are many ways to assign values to real estate. We had to know the particular method that was used to value each of Trump's properties and determine whether that method was legitimate and in line with market practice or rigged simply to boost the property's reported value by tens or hundreds of millions of dollars.

We needed to understand what Trump's accountants knew and didn't know about any false valuations, and also determine what Trump's bankers knew or didn't know. Who had received the SOFCs, and for what purpose? Did the recipients think that the values were real? Had they relied on the financial statements?

Hanging over all of these complexities was a central question: What were Trump's assets really worth? It would not be enough to show that the manner in which Trump valued his properties was unusual, flawed, or even ridiculous. To consider criminal charges, we would have to show that the true values were much less than what appeared on the financial statements. Our valuation experts at FTI would have to look at Trump's properties, one by one and year by year, and tell us what the reasonable values actually were.

Assuming that we could prove that the financial statements routinely and massively overstated the value of Trump's assets, we had to be sure that the overstatement was intentional. And, critically, we had to determine whether Donald Trump intended to issue financial statements that he knew to be false. Showing criminal intent, or a culpable "state of mind," is central to virtually every white-collar prosecution. The criminal statutes that prohibit lying, cheating, and stealing all define "intent" crimes, meaning that the prosecution has to prove that the defendant intended to engage in criminal conduct. The exact formulation of the intent requirement differs slightly from crime to crime, but generally the prosecution must prove that the defendant acted knowingly and willfully; negligent or reckless conduct is not enough. Trials in white-collar cases typically turn on how jurors assess the defendant's state of mind. Usually, proof of intent is circumstantial, because sophisticated criminals rarely confess or create documentary evidence referring explicitly to a purpose to break the law.

In our case, if we could establish that the financial statements were routinely falsified, year after year in huge amounts, it seemed obvious that Trump had to have been involved and had to have known and intended that the SOFCs were false. The assets were all his; he had bought or built 100 percent of all but a few of them. They were his financial statements, prepared for his benefit and use, by people who did his bidding. He touted his great wealth at every opportunity and, as he reminded people all the time, he knew everything there was to know about real estate. He even pronounced himself a "stable genius." But in a criminal case prosecutors frequently have to prove the obvious. You can't just stand in front of a jury and say, "Of course he was involved." You need proof of specific statements and deeds to back up what might otherwise seem self-evident.

So, on top of becoming intimately familiar with Trump's assets, how they had been valued, and what they were actually worth, we had to study Trump's many prior statements about his assets and his wealth. There was his prior testimony, his thousands of "tweets," his press releases and public statements, papers from court cases, and the vast trove of materials in the public domain referring to what Trump had said about his wealth over the years. We had to "follow the facts," but we were drowning in facts. Carey had a wonderful expression whenever we talked about this work: he was concerned that we would be trying to "boil the ocean." At times it felt like we were doing just that.

Much of the work was painstaking and what many people would consider boring and dull. It was not cops-and-robbers drama. Among the lawyers on our investigative team, I took the laboring oar in sorting through the SOFC values and understanding how and why they were false. This involved spending hour after hour in front of my computer screen, working days, nights, and weekends studying the SOFCs, the accounting backup to the SOFCs, appraisal reports, tax protest documents, emails, real estate listings, and countless other pieces of information.

The work was time-consuming but I did not view it as drudgery. The picture that was emerging from the factual morass was becoming clearer as I studied each of Trump's major assets and how he had valued them. Truly, the devil was in the details, but each passing week brought the devil into sharper focus, so it felt like we were making progress. Also, I have always liked working with numbers. I was a math nerd as a child. In fourth grade I showed my teacher how I calculated the number of miles between our solar system and the nearest star, Alpha Centauri. I had read that the distance was about 4.5 light-years, and I tried to figure out the corresponding number of miles, based on the distance light could travel per second and the number of seconds contained in 4.5 years. My teacher asked me to show my work on the blackboard, whereupon I was "skipped" to fifth grade. As a teenager I spent many hours trying (and failing) to work out a proof of Fermat's last theorem, and I started out as a math major at Harvard College before realizing that the other math majors knew lots more than I did. As a lawyer, cases involving numbers did not scare me, and financial cases had been a huge chunk of my practice. I had helped represent Citigroup in the Enron scandal, and figuring out the complexities of the prepaid energy transactions at issue in that investigation had happily occupied me for many months.

In taking a deep dive into Trump's financial statements I was not starting from scratch. I had the considerable benefit of the work that the New York State attorney general's office already had done on these topics. We received extensive briefings from two smart lawyers there, Eric Haren and Kevin Wallace, who had spent many months studying the SOFCs, the accounting backup to the SOFCs, and related materials, and they provided us with documents and shared their analysis.

The attorney general also agreed to provide us with witness transcripts from depositions they had taken. The depositions were like a rich vein of ore from a gold mine. The transcripts had to be read and absorbed, which is time-consuming work, the forensic equivalent of crushing tons of rocks that contain valuable nuggets. Over time, and with effort, the nuggets emerged, but only if the reader was steeped in the details of how the SOFCs were prepared and read the transcripts against the backdrop of other information.

Here's an example: We discussed with the attorney general's lawyers the systematic overvaluation of Trump's golf courses. As we could see on the face of the financial statements that had been made public, the SOFCs did not list the value of individual golf courses. Michael Cohen had told us that the value of individual golf courses was not disclosed because, by providing only a total value for all of the golf courses lumped together, Trump made it hard to understand how any particular course had been valued. For 2013, the total value for all of Trump's "[c]lub facilities and related real estate" was a whopping $1.656 billion. Part of that $1.656 billion was the purported value of Trump's golf course in Jupiter, Florida. The attorney general's lawyers told us that Trump had bought the Jupiter golf course in December 2012 for $5 million, but it was reflected on the backup materials to the 2013 SOFC as being worth $62 million as of June 30, 2013.

How had a golf club Trump had bought for $5 million cash in December come to be worth $62 million just six months later? The answer emerged from the testimony of Jeffrey McConney, one of Trump's employees who was deposed by the attorney general several times in 2019 and 2020. Trump had paid $5 million to buy the Jupiter golf course in December 2012, but he also had taken on more than $40 million in possible liability to the members of the golf club. The liability existed because the members of the club had paid membership deposits that might be refundable when the members resigned from the golf club. Trump's financial statements said that he had decided to value this liability at zero, because he would be holding the deposits for a long time and a resigning member would most likely be replaced by a new member. A careful study of McConney's testimony revealed that the liability that Trump had valued at zero had been used to boost the club's purported value to $62 million. Trump had decided to value the Jupiter golf course based on the value of its fixed assets. Golf courses are never valued in the marketplace on the basis of fixed assets. Putting that to one side, the same liability that the SOFC said was valued at zero was valued at over $40 million to calculate the amount of Jupiter's fixed assets. The inconsistent treatment of the liability was hidden from view. Then, to make matters worse, the club's inflated fixed-asset value was bumped up by an additional 30 percent, so the total purported value of the golf course became $62 million. The 30 percent value increase was because Trump added "his feel and touch" to the golf courses, according to McConney. In substance, the 30 percent bump was an addition because of the supposed value of Trump's brand, even though the notes to the financial statements said that brand value had not been included.

The bottom line was that the numbers on Trump's 2013 financial statement included a purported value for the Jupiter golf course of $62 million. Trump had paid only $5 million to buy it just a few months earlier, and he later sued the Palm Beach County tax authorities, arguing that they should have respected the fact that he bought the property in an arm's-length transaction for only $5 million. As Michael Cohen had testified, Trump was claiming a low value when dealing with the tax assessor but using a vastly higher value in the financial statement that was given to his bankers.

Toward the end of the summer and into the fall of 2021, we were making substantial progress. From all of the evidence, including the information that the attorney general's office provided, what Michael Cohen had told us, and what we learned from our own review of the SOFCs and the backup for the asset values on the SOFCs, we could see that the values in the SOFCs had been overstated by billions of dollars each year. We also could see that the overstatements had continued for many years, and they could not be explained simply as disagreements over value, "exaggeration," or "optimism" about what certain properties were worth.

Another good example involves the triplex apartment on the top of Trump Tower. Donald Trump and his family lived there before moving to the White House in January 2017. Trump's SOFCs for 2015 and 2016 reported the value of the apartment at $327 million, an amount much higher than the price anyone has *ever* paid for a private residence in the United States, from the beginning of the country through 2021. Even the megamansion in Los Angeles known as "The One" was listed for sale in 2022 at a mere $295 million asking price. That home, which comprises a cozy 105,000 square feet, reportedly contains 21 bedrooms, 42 bathrooms, a spa, a beauty salon, a bowling alley, a home theater with seating for 40, an outdoor running track, and a 30-car garage, all situated on four acres with views of the Pacific Ocean. Though listed for $295 million, the home sold for $126 million in March 2022. Trump's apartment, opulent though it was, could have fit into a small corner of "The One."

The accounting backup for the valuation of Trump's triplex reflected that its value of over $300 million was based largely on its reported size of 30,000 square feet. But the apartment did not contain 30,000 square feet. In May 2017, an article appeared in *Forbes* titled, "Donald Trump Has Been Lying About the Size of His Penthouse." The article reported that the actual size of the Trump triplex was only just shy of 11,000 square feet. Following the publication of the article, Trump's 2017 financial statement quietly slashed the value of the triplex by several hundred million dollars, and the backup information restated the size of the apartment from 30,000 to 10,996 square feet. As the *Forbes* article reported, Trump himself had previously claimed that the apartment contained 33,000 square feet. Did Trump know the difference between 33,000 square feet and the apartment's actual size of 10,996 square feet? His business was buying and selling real estate, and he had built and sold thousands of apartments over the years. He was a real estate "genius." He had the triplex apartment designed and renovated to his specifications. And he lived in it for many years. I asked Michael Cohen, who had been in the apartment many times, whether Trump knew that the apartment did not really contain 33,000 square feet. He laughed at me. Our experts later pegged the actual reasonable value of the triplex at roughly $60 million, meaning that for some years the SOFCs had overstated the value of the triplex by more than 500 percent.

As the weeks passed, and as we boiled more of the ocean, it became increasingly clear that the SOFCs vastly overstated the value of many of Trump's assets. However, this was only part of the puzzle we were putting together. We needed a fix on the actual values of the listed assets, and we needed to understand how the financial statements had been used.

The full DANY investigative team started working to answer these questions. We asked our consulting firm, FTI, to prepare exhaustive, property-by-property and year-by-year analyses of the actual values of Trump's main assets. Much of the analysis was done by Mark Dunec (the "paisley bow tie guy" whose identity the *New York Times* had worked to determine). Eventually, the lawyers on the team also prepared property-by-property analyses and binders, incorporating FTI's work, identifying key documents bearing on valuation, and marshaling the information from witnesses.

Our conclusion from all of this work was that Trump's financial statements had overstated the value of his assets by massive amounts. The analysis focused on the years between 2011 and 2017. In every one of those years, the SOFCs represented the value of his assets in amounts that were billions of dollars higher than they actually were worth, according to our experts. And the overstatements were pervasive. For each year, our analysts looked at assets comprising about 90 percent of the total asset value that Trump had referenced in his financial statements. The overvaluations cut across virtually all his assets, and meant that he had reported asset values that, on average, were about double what they were actually worth. In short, there was a pattern of overstatement that extended to most of Trump's assets. The pattern continued year after year; the assets and amounts shifted, but the pattern was unmistakable. The overstatements had to have been intentional, which of course is what Michael Cohen had told us.

As we got more clarity about the inflation of the SOFCs, and better understood the details, the investigative team worked to identify the people and institutions who had received the false financial statements. We started interviewing witnesses who could tell us in detail what importance they attached to the SOFCs. We also got back in touch with Trump's accountants—Mazars and Donald Bender. Mazars had issued the financial statements on its letterhead, based on information received from Trump and the people acting on his behalf, including Allen Weisselberg. We needed to find out what Bender knew about the falsification of the values in the financial statements. We had to determine whether significant information relating to asset value been concealed from him and whether he had helped to come up with the inflated values.

As this work was going on, I was bombarding the team with a never-ending stream of emails. Are we sure we have

all the appraisals that were done on Trump's properties? Have
we rounded up all the property tax litigation that the Trump
Organization brought? Have we looked at all the emails that
discuss property valuation? Have we compared net operating
income figures that were used to arrive at property valuations
with income figures on tax returns, or data that the Trump Organization had given to appraisers and tax assessors? I was a
combination cheerleader, teacher, taskmaster, nuisance, and
overall pain in the ass as we made progress boiling through the
endless ocean of facts. I had become the team's "numbers guy,"
although my wife reminded me that my mother never thought
I could balance a checkbook!

The SOFC investigation was complicated, sprawling, challenging, and time-consuming. It also was far from the only
thing that we were doing. We were having constant fights with
the lawyers for the Trump Organization over the adequacy of
their document production. Because those fights involved litigation that was sealed by the court, I cannot speak about the
details except to say that our efforts were the legal equivalent of
trench warfare. Everything was a fight.

Members of the team also had to shoulder the burden of
producing discovery material to the defense lawyers for the
Trump Organization and for Allen Weisselberg in the case we
had indicted. New York had recently amended its criminal discovery rules to make them much more expansive. As a consequence, members of the team spent many days making sure
that the prosecution was living up to its obligations and producing the necessary documents and information. This, too,
became a time-consuming and contentious exercise.

The team also was pursuing investigative avenues apart from
the financial statements. We were aware that the Trump chil-

dren had a separate consulting business and checked to see whether that business was legitimate. We found no evidence convincing us to the contrary. We were also continuing to investigate the role of other Trump executives in the executive compensation scheme and following up on a host of other leads.

Life also intruded. I had cancer scans and an appointment with my oncologist in mid-July. The scans always produced some angst, but the radiology reports were clear. Then, on September 1, 2021, Hurricane Ida hit the greater New York area. The epic rainfall caused lots of flooding in our neighborhood. My wife and I watched with dismay as the water level rose around our home, and finally water began pouring into the house. At one point a small stream started flowing through the lower area of the house, where I did all my work. As the water got higher and higher, my wife (in her nightgown) and I were scurrying around my home office to rescue all of my Trump files from the flood and carry them upstairs to safety.

As the summer and Labor Day passed by, I realized that an enterprise corruption charge was not going to happen. The financial statement investigation had become all-consuming. The task of building out the proof on the whole pattern of enterprise corruption was simply too ambitious for the human and investigative bandwidth we had. We were not a special counsel office like the one that Robert Mueller had put together. Mueller had recruited the best and the brightest from across the Department of Justice. We were a local prosecutor's office, with limited jurisdiction and a reluctance to bring sensational cases that did not fit comfortably within the office's usual work. We had a handful of regular assistant district attorneys working on the case, supplemented by some young associates on loan from their law firms, and me—an old lawyer emerged from retirement and mostly working from home. We had two lawyers cross-designated to DANY from the attorney general's office, but they also had to attend to their preexisting obligations, as did Carey Dunne. Carey was keeping a close eye on the investigation; however, he also had a full portfolio of other responsibilities in his job as general counsel to DANY.

We had tons of work to do just to move forward with the investigation of the financial statements, and pressure to make progress began to mount. Cy Vance had made it clear to me and Carey that he wanted to bring criminal charges against Trump by the end of the year, if warranted. Though Cy had not made a final decision, and a set of charges had not been teed up for his approval, everyone knew that he was leaving office at the end of 2021. His looming departure became the elephant in the room that nobody on the team wanted to discuss. The topic was virtually taboo. Indeed, Carey chastised me after one team Zoom call for alluding to the fact that only a few months remained in Cy's tenure. The team did not want any arbitrary deadlines to be set, and there was a feeling that Cy's planned departure should not dictate the pace of the investigation. His decision not to run for another term was seen as his personal choice, and not something that ought to influence our work.

We had not yet explicitly discussed whether we would or should be seeking to indict Donald Trump. Everyone knew, of course, that we were gathering evidence directly related to that issue, but charging Trump was not a declared intention. Our mission was to gather the evidence so that at some future point, when we were ready, we would take stock of what we had and then the district attorney would make a charging decision. When would we be "ready"? There was no clear-cut or legally defined decision point. Generally, prosecutors make charging decisions when they have a handle on the facts. They

make decisions when they know what the legal and factual issues are likely to be, what the critical witnesses will likely say,
and how the proof will likely stack up at a hypothetical trial.
Perfect knowledge is not possible, and there is always more to
do. In our case, heading into the fall of 2021, the end of the year
seemed like a natural and reasonable decision point. There was
even a waning hope that, if we were going to go ahead with
charges, it might be possible to present evidence to a grand jury
and get an indictment by then.

As the pace of our work quickened, Carey and I discussed
the need for a "drill sergeant" who could keep the team moving
to finish the investigation quickly. I could not fill that role. I
was outside the office's regular chain of command, and I was
completely submerged in the fact investigation, doing witness
outlines and interviews, parsing documents, reading through
testimony transcripts, and doing a million other things. By this
point I was working days, evenings, and weekends. I could determine priorities and come up with lists of "to-dos" and tasks,
but I could not dictate who should do what, set completion
deadlines, and make sure everybody was doing what they were
supposed to be doing. That was the role of a chief of staff; in
a large private law firm working on a big case it would be the
job of the junior partner on the case. Unfortunately, there was
no suitable candidate from within the office. We would just do
the best we could, moving forward in a somewhat shambolic
fashion.

On September 21, the pressure of all that we had to do
reached a boiling point. After a court appearance in the Weis-
selberg/Trump Organization case, where the judge had set a
schedule for defense motions, we had an "all hands" in-person
meeting to go through a witness list for the SOFC investigation. Of course, Michael Cohen's name was on the list, and

the meeting became contentious as soon as his name was mentioned. Julieta Lozano, the head of the Major Economic Crimes Bureau, said she could not see ever calling Cohen to testify about anything, because she did not trust anything he said. I completely disagreed. I thought Cohen was telling the truth, and what he told us had been corroborated. I was not the only person in the room who said as much, and we spent some time belaboring what was obvious: Cohen had liabilities as a witness, but virtually all cooperators have liabilities. Prosecutors have to rely on flawed witnesses. I had used cooperators as a prosecutor or attacked them as a defense lawyer in dozens of cases. I had called witnesses who had been drug addicts, killers, and sociopaths. I had cross-examined a cooperating witness who had assassinated a judge. Other prosecutors had similar experiences. Criminal cases feature a rogues' gallery of witnesses, and Cohen was eligible to testify as a witness in the view of most of us.

There were other disagreements at the meeting involving a different witness and our potential timetable for moving forward. Toward the end of the meeting, I said explicitly what we all knew but had not discussed: Our investigation might well lead to an indictment of the former president. We decided that, in light of the discussion, it would be prudent to reconvene the following week to lay out the potential case against Trump and to get people's reactions to it.

Carey had lunch with the team on the following day and called me to relate that there had been a mini-revolt, focusing on the potential timeline for moving forward. The team thought it would be irresponsible to try to indict the case before the end of the year. I quickly agreed. Too much work remained to be done, and there was no compelling law enforcement reason to act by year's end. Cy's planned departure had nothing to do

with the merits of the case. Perhaps I was naive, but I thought
it was more important to get the investigation done properly
than to get it done quickly. Also, I thought it would be impossible to push people who did not want to be pushed and who
had legitimate concerns about doing the work in a thorough
and deliberate way. Put simply, we did not want to screw up the
case just to get it done before Cy left. In light of what happened
later, that may have been a fateful—and horrible—decision. At
the time, we gave it no further thought or debate.

I was more concerned with the questions that some had expressed to Carey about whether the evidence being developed
would justify bringing a criminal case. As far as I knew, the
prosecutors who raised the questions (primarily Julieta and another person who had been working on tasks unrelated to the
SOFCs) had not studied the witness testimony elicited by the
attorney general, parsed the financial statements, or educated
themselves about how the values reflected in the financial
statements had been developed. They spoke about the need to
follow the evidence, but to my knowledge they had not actually
looked at much of it.

Notwithstanding my pique, we had to pay attention to the
substantive concerns they had expressed. As I heard them from
Carey, they were as follows: First, we didn't have any "flesh and
blood" victims. Deutsche Bank had loaned lots of money to
Trump, but perhaps the bank knew that Trump was a serial liar,
had never trusted his financial statements, and therefore was
not deceived by them. Maybe they loaned him money because
he had good collateral and he was worth a lot of money, even
though they knew he was not worth as much as he claimed. Everyone in the world—so the argument went—knew that Trump
was not worth as much as he claimed. And what of Mazars,
Trump's accounting firm? Perhaps the accounting firm, how-

ever much it might now claim to have been deceived, was like the police captain in the classic film *Casablanca*, shocked that there was gambling going on in this casino! Though Bender was now telling us that he had not known that the financial statements overstated the value of Trump's assets, maybe he and his colleagues at Mazars had intentionally closed their eyes to what was happening and helped prepare statements that they knew were not accurate. And, on top of this, there was the argument that "everybody does it." Real estate moguls commonly overstate their wealth. Perhaps this ought not be the basis for a criminal case without a "flesh and blood" victim.

There were answers to these concerns, and in the coming weeks we would gather more facts and refine our thinking about the potential charges in order to address them. In retrospect, though, we should have spent more time working through the issues with the lawyers who had expressed the doubts. Maybe this would have prevented their doubts from festering in silence. At the time, though, I was tired and frustrated. As I saw it, the doubters had not been immersed in the SOFC fact gathering, and they did not know the case well. Also, they seemed to me to be exactly the kind of traditional, "let's do things the way we have always done them" prosecutors that kept the district attorney's office from being resourceful and successful in white-collar cases. Cy had privately complained many times to me and Carey about the slow-moving and "gun shy" culture in the office, saying that even he, as the district attorney, had not always been able to crack through it.

In any event, the concerns did not stop us from continuing. Carey and I were determined to move ahead with the investigation, and we had Cy's enthusiastic support in doing so, as well as the support of the rest of the team. After several more team Zoom meetings, we thought that the negativity we had heard mainly had to do with the amount of work and the schedule. The solution, in the short term, was to make it clear that there would be no artificial end-of-year deadline. Also, at their request, Julieta and one of her colleagues agreed not to be part of the SOFC investigation moving forward. They would focus on handling the pending executive compensation case against the Trump Organization and Weisselberg.

As we moved into October 2021, people were working productively on the SOFC investigation, and the facts were becoming more and more compelling.

We got some important information from Jonathan Greenberg, a reporter who had worked at *Forbes* magazine. Beginning in 1982, *Forbes* had published a list of the four hundred most wealthy Americans. Greenberg was a young researcher for *Forbes* in the early 1980s, and he had been responsible for gathering facts about the real estate entrepreneurs who were being considered for the Forbes 400 list. Greenberg's work led him to speak directly with Donald Trump. Greenberg told us that Trump had lied to him about his real estate assets in order to get Greenberg to include him on the list. Importantly, Greenberg had taped a conversation in which Trump had falsely passed himself off as "John Baron," a vice president and "finance officer" working for the Trump family. In fact, there was no "John Baron," only Trump posing as "Mr. Baron." Greenberg had kept the original tape, along with his research notes and other materials, and he sent copies to us. When we listened to the tape we heard the distinctive voice of the former president, speaking as "John Baron" and explaining why Donald Trump should be listed in the Forbes 400 in lieu of his father, Fred Trump. According to "Baron," Fred Trump had already transferred ownership of the vast majority of his real estate interests to his son, Donald. Greenberg had researched this claim and discovered that it was false, along with other untrue statements "Baron" made about Donald Trump's real estate assets and their supposed value. Greenberg's information helped to establish that Trump had always been fixated on the public perception of his wealth and was willing to lie about his wealth to enhance his image and reputation.

Greenberg's information dovetailed with other information that *Forbes* had put into the public record about its dealings with Donald Trump over the past thirty-five years. Randall Lane, a senior *Forbes* journalist, had written articles describing what he called Trump's "net worth fixation." He described "wrestling" with Trump annually with regard to his net worth, and Lane concluded that Trump was "worth a lot less than he says." He claimed that Trump "care[d] more about where he ranks on the Forbes 400 list" than any of the wealthy people who had ever appeared on that list. Of particular interest to us were some statements that Lane said Trump had made directly to him, which made Lane a witness to what are legally termed "admissions." Lane recounted conversations he had with Trump in which Trump said, "I look better if I'm worth $10 billion than if I'm worth $4 billion." Trump also admitted having "stretched the facts" regarding his net worth in his dealings with *Forbes*, and he told Lane that a higher net worth was "good for financing." This was good evidence of intent and once again corroborated what Michael Cohen had told us.

Later in October I renewed my conversations with Donald Bender, the Mazars accountant who was the main client contact for the Trump Organization. Bender explained the process by which the SOFCs had been compiled and confirmed that the purported asset values all had come from the Trump Organization. Bender merely received the numbers and, unless there were glaring problems, he incorporated them into the financial statements. He explained that he did not have a professional responsibility to validate the numbers or attest to their accuracy; he relied on his client to give him honest valuations, and he was not a "real estate guy" who could or would second-guess the values he was given. He told us that critical information had been concealed from him with respect to many Trump assets, such as appraisal reports showing much lower valuations for certain assets than the numbers that Bender had been given. However, Bender could not explain to our satisfaction why he had been willing to go along with valuations and valuation methodologies that we thought he should have recognized as illegitimate. Nevertheless, Bender's shortcomings as an accountant did not provide Trump with a defense. On the contrary, we thought jurors who heard from Bender would quickly realize that it suited Trump's purpose to employ an accountant who was not disposed to raise questions about the valuations of Trump's assets. Bender struck me as the accountant's embodiment of the proverbial three monkeys: he made it his business to see no evil, hear no evil, and speak no evil. I did not believe that he was an active participant in a scheme to prepare false financial statements, and Bender was never charged with wrongdoing. However, I thought he displayed a remarkable lack of curiosity about the numbers that he received from Trump, who was his largest client.

We also learned in October, again from the attorney general's office, that a former employee of Trump's golf club in Briarcliff Manor, New York, could provide us with useful information. The former employee had been in charge of recruiting new members and negotiating the initiation fees that they had to pay to join the club. According to the former employee, Donald Trump personally had to approve each membership deal. Trump frequently allowed people to join without paying any initiation fee, but he instructed the former employee to conceal the fact that many new members were paying no initiation fees. At the same time, the financial statement valuation for the golf club was very high, based substantially on the six-figure initiation fees that supposedly were being paid by new members. Further investigation indicated that the same thing had happened at other Trump golf clubs—they were valued based on notional membership fees that had little to do with reality.

In mid-October, my wife and I traveled to Sonoma, California, to spend time with one of my sons, his wife, and their new daughter (our eighth grandchild), who had just been born. While in Sonoma, I took part in the Zoom interview of a former Deutsche Bank senior credit risk officer. The risk officer had approved financing for the Trump Organization, and he could speak with authority about how Trump's financial statements had factored into the bank's lending decisions. He explained that Deutsche Bank's more recent loans to Trump had come through the bank's Private Wealth Management business. This business made loans that involved personal guarantees by wealthy individuals like Trump. The bank had given Trump money to buy the Doral resort in Miami, to refinance the Trump International Hotel & Tower in Chicago, and to renovate the Old Post Office in Washington, D.C. In each case, Trump had given the bank a personal guarantee. The bank accepted the guarantees based on Trump's personal financial statements. For each loan, Trump had certified to the bank that the financial statements were accurate in all material respects, and he had reissued those certifications each year. If he had not provided the financial statements and the certifications, the bank would not have accepted his personal guarantees and would not have made any loans to him. The risk officer told us that he and others at the bank viewed the SOFCs as documents that had been prepared honestly and in good faith. If they had known that the financial statements were intentionally over-stated, they would not have accepted them and would have done no further business with Donald Trump.

Carey and I thought that this information, which had been echoed by other Deutsche Bank personnel, would support a claim that the bank had been defrauded. By this point, we thought we could prove that Donald Trump was involved in a scheme to prepare false financial statements. The bank had loaned money based on the belief that it had gotten honest financial statements, but it had been deceived. Maybe it should have known better than to accept Trump's SOFCs, and maybe some bank personnel thought that some of the valuations were aggressive, but we were told by the bank's employees that they accepted the financial statements as having been prepared in good faith, which is what Trump had represented.

Not everyone on the team agreed with this analysis, and later it became a bone of contention. But we thought we could move forward, and the case seemed to be coming together.

CHAPTER FIFTEEN

MOVING TOWARD A DECISION

November 2, 2021, was Election Day in New York. Alvin Bragg won the election for district attorney of New York County, and on January 1, 2022, he would succeed Cy Vance. In heavily Democratic Manhattan, Bragg's election had been a foregone conclusion for months. The real competition for the job had come in the Democratic primary election in June 2021, when voters had to pick from among a large handful of candidates. I did not know any of the candidates, but I knew that Bragg, like me, had been an assistant United States attorney for the Southern District of New York. He had been endorsed by the *New York Times* and by Preet Bharara, the former United States attorney whose opinion I respected. Bragg had reminded voters during his campaign of his involvement in lawsuits that had been brought against Trump. I did not reside in New York County, but I told relatives who lived in Manhattan that they should vote for Alvin Bragg.

Neither the primary election nor the general election had provoked much discussion in the district attorney's office, at least in my presence. I did not even know who Cy favored as his successor. When Bragg won the general election we had no telephone calls or meetings to discuss what it would mean for the investigation. I just assumed he would pick up where Cy left off.

I cared only that we were moving forward with our investigation. On November 4, the *Washington Post* published a story reporting that the Manhattan district attorney's office had convened a long-term grand jury to probe the accuracy of Trump's financial statements. The story quoted from Michael Cohen's congressional testimony and referenced "incorrect figures" in Trump's SOFCs. For example, it noted that Trump had valued his Seven Springs estate at $261 million, even though local tax assessors had pegged the value at $20 million.

Carey and I had some discussions in early November about having a "summit meeting" or retreat in early December so that Cy could get the team's views and make a decision whether we were going to bring charges arising out of the SOFC investigation. We socialized this with the team during the second week of November and got the sense that it would be better to make this decision sooner rather than later. The lawyers on the team were working hard on the investigation, and they told us, in substance, that we needed to "cut to the chase." After months of effort, they wanted to know whether we were just treading water and accumulating facts and testimony or were we going to be bringing criminal charges.

There was a regular update Zoom call on the SOFC investigation scheduled for November 12, and Carey and I decided to use that call to take stock of where we were. In advance of the Zoom call, I prepared and sent around to the team and to Cy and Carey an "issues outline" that summarized the questions we had to decide and the additional work we had to do. I intended the outline as a discussion piece that would get people talking about how they saw the case.

The outline noted that "[t]he evidence of a pervasive, on-going pattern of substantial overvaluation" in the SOFCs was "compelling." It explicitly raised the question whether "the facts support a charge that Donald Trump was culpably in-volved," and summarized the evidence that would support such a charge.

The document also made reference to potential defenses and litigation risks. There was not an extensive analysis of Trump's potential "witch hunt" defense (referred to in the memo as a "selective prosecution/political prosecution" argu-ment), because everyone in the room knew that this argument had no facts to support it, and it was Trump's standard rhetori-cal claim trotted out whenever he faced any legal jeopardy. But I did want people to focus on the risk that indicting Trump "might trigger civil unrest, or . . . public tumult," and I also asked in the memo whether it would be possible to guarantee a fair trial both for the People and for Trump. I asked whether there were security issues that we needed to consider, and the memo ended with a reference to something I regarded as the central question: "How do we assess the possibility of an ac-quittal? Should we refrain from charging a former President unless we are virtually certain of conviction (i.e., 'if you shoot for the king, you best not miss'), or does the need to hold even the most powerful person accountable for criminal conduct warrant bringing a charge even if conviction is not a foregone conclusion?"

Before writing the outline I had considered these questions for myself. I thought the security risks and the danger of civil unrest could be handled by the New York City Police Depart-ment, maybe with help from federal law enforcement authori-ties. In any event, we could not allow ourselves to be intimidated by a possible repeat of what had happened on January 6, 2021, or anything like it. Prosecutors are supposed to make decisions "without fear or favor." No one could know exactly what the security dangers might be if we indicted Trump. I assumed that the "MAGA" crowd would make its presence felt, but we had to trust that our institutions and personnel could be secured no matter how events might unfold. We simply could not let the danger of violence or unrest deter us from acting.

Nor did I believe that we should require a different and higher standard of proof with respect to Trump than we would apply to anyone else. For decades I had been listening to judges instruct jurors that "all parties stand as equals before the bar of justice." I felt deeply that a former president should be weighed on the same set of scales we would use for any other person. We were no longer dealing with a sitting president; Trump's term had ended, and we were looking at conduct that had predated his presidency. I could not embrace the notion that we needed a superabundance of proof with respect to Trump, or evidence of guilt that went beyond the traditional standard of "proof beyond a reasonable doubt." Indeed, I thought there might be an argument that Trump, having assumed an office that required him to "take care that the laws be faithfully executed," and having urged the country to trust him to uphold the law, should be held to a *higher* standard of personal conduct than the average citizen. Certainly, though, he was not entitled to more favorable treatment.

As the meeting approached, I prepared to make my views explicit. While I thought that everyone on the team knew that I was in favor of bringing the case, this was not a topic that we had squarely addressed. Neither Cy, nor Carey, nor I had ever had a lengthy conversation on the ultimate issue, and we had never had a serious and substantial discussion with the team focusing on whether we should charge Trump with crimes. I prepared talking points for myself to use at the meeting. I felt a bit like I would be summing up a case to a jury, and I wanted to be ready. In my mind's eye, I would close my remarks by saying that this case had to be brought in order to demonstrate that Trump was not "above the law." Prosecutors, I intended to remind the audience, were the palace guard for the rule of law; we had to protect it as our sacred duty and had sworn oaths explicitly to support the Constitution and all applicable laws and rules. I was prepared to quote John Adams, who had observed hundreds of years earlier that we were a "nation of laws and not men."

I never delivered that speech, and the meeting was a bust. No one on the team spoke very much, except for Chris Conroy, the head of the Investigations Bureau, who spoke about his misgivings based on the bad result that the district attorney's office had received in an earlier case involving the collapse of a large Manhattan law firm. That case also had involved false financial statements and accounting fraud. There was some discussion of Michael Cohen, and Cy (who was in attendance) jumped in to say that Cohen could be a persuasive witness if handled properly. I had to remind the group what Cohen had told us about the SOFCs, which I had recently reviewed and which no one else really remembered. We did not go around the table to seek people's views on the merits, and the focus shifted to what work had to be done over the next few weeks to get ready for a more substantive huddle.

I was disappointed that the team did not display a lot of energy or enthusiasm. I wondered if the people in the room were being cautious or reluctant to take a position with Cy in attendance. Perhaps they were even a bit fearful about bringing charges against Trump. This would not have been surprising. Trump's stock in trade when confronted by people scrutinizing his conduct is intimidation. It is a tactic that I found dismaying, and I pondered whether it was working even within the confines of a law enforcement agency. I hoped to myself that I had misread the room, perhaps because I had attended by Zoom, which may have been a mistake. But the meeting left me shaken and wondering whether I should continue working frantically in the effort to bring the investigation to closure. I knew that a new district attorney would be arriving in a few months, which would mean even more work bringing him and his team up to speed. I did not want to "kick the can down the road" indefinitely.

When the meeting ended I did not know what the ultimate charging decision was going to be. Even Carey, a sophisticated, highly intelligent, and savvy lawyer, who had kept the investigation on track, had not stated his views at the meeting. Nor had Cy, who had been listening carefully but had not said much. I wondered whether my views about the case matched up with how others, and particularly Cy, saw the case. If we saw it the same way, that was great, and I would keep on going. If not, I needed to think about my personal plans for the future.

I decided to send this memo to Cy and Carey on November 14:

Dear Cy and Carey,

After the team meeting on Friday, I spent a lot of time thinking about the investigation and my own personal situation. I am hopeful that we can have a discussion after I have shared these thoughts. Here's what I think:

1. We need to make a "go/no go decision" within the next few weeks. We have gathered the essential facts, and the basic landscape of the case is not going to change in the

foreseeable future. That is not to say that we have completed all investigative work or the other steps necessary to indict. If we were to decide to proceed with charges based on the false SOFCs, we would have at least several months of work ahead of us before asking the grand jury to return an indictment. But we are not going to discover a hitherto-unknown financial institution that loaned money based on the SOFCs and lost its shirt, and a new cooperator is not likely to fall out of the trees in the foreseeable future. . . . We have enough information to make a responsible decision in the immediate future.

2. My personal view of the facts and the applicable law lead me to the conclusion that this case should be brought. I will elaborate on these views at the proper time and place. I will just say here that, with all due respect to the rest of the team, no-one has spent as much time as I have in gathering and understanding the facts. I wish it were otherwise. As I see the facts, there is no doubt that the asset values and net worth figures contained in the SOFCs were the product of systematic, intentional, and substantial inflation. . . . I won't restate all the facts here, but there is no doubt that [Deutsche Bank] insisted on receiving DJT's personal guarantees, and that they therefore required the submission of accurate and honestly-prepared financial statements before they would accept DJT's guarantee. That's not what they got. They got false financial statements, and DJT personally certified to their accuracy. I believe, based on the totality of the evidence, that there is no doubt that DJT personally directed that his subordinates prepare financial statements that overstated the value of his assets, knowing and intending that the statements would be submitted to

banks in connection with financings. To me, that is criminal conduct that should be prosecuted. Obviously, this is a discretionary decision, but a multitude of factors—not the least of which are the magnitude of the overstatements in the SOFCs and DJT's history of breaking the law and avoiding accountability—point overwhelmingly toward a decision to prosecute.

3. I completely recognize that, at least on the current factual record, the likelihood of obtaining a conviction is not virtually certain. While the "paper trail" is compelling, the proof has some weaknesses. Our cooperator has his issues. We do not have a classic "victim" who plainly lost money by relying on the defendants' false statements, though I think it clear that we can meet the statutory and legal requirements for establishing a scheme to defraud. To be sure, the possibility of an acquittal, and the consequences of an acquittal, must be part of the calculus on making a decision whether to proceed. I will just say that my personal view, based on some considerable experience, is that a jury would be much more likely to convict than to acquit. But perhaps more importantly, I believe that a prosecutor's overriding obligation is to reinforce the rule of law, and I think that the rule of law would suffer more if we failed to bring this case than if we brought it and lost it.

4. As for my personal situation, by mid-January I will have spent a full year basically working full-time to help pursue our efforts. If we decide to go forward with a prosecution, and if the new administration wants me to continue on, I will do whatever I can do to aid in the effort. I will rearrange my plans for the first half of 2022, and do whatever is necessary; as we've discussed, part of what

is necessary is to add personnel who can strengthen the team's investigative and trial capacity. But, to put it bluntly, the existing team does not require my help in order not to bring a case, or to defer further the making of a prosecutive decision. If that's what the future holds, I will quietly take my leave and resume my retired life of travel, bad golf, and spending time with my wife, children, and grandchildren.

I look forward to discussing this with you in the days ahead.

Best,

Mark

My memo was fairly blunt, which was not unusual. The reference to "rearrang[ing] my plans for the first half of 2022" had to do with a scheduled sojourn in Sonoma, where my wife and I had rented a house in the hope that we would spend a few months of the winter getting to know our new granddaughter. We decided later to abandon that plan so I could stay in New York and keep working on the investigation.

I got a rapid email response from Carey. He wrote that he had been speaking with Cy, and "so can report that we both agree with your analysis." He also agreed that we needed "to come to grips with the important directional decision," and added that he agreed with my "take on the strength of the evidence, as well as the risks, and the likely jury reaction."

Then came the punch line: "Cy and I both believe that, if we had to decide now, it should be a 'go' decision." Carey opined that he didn't "think that view would change, or be overridden," but noted that we had a few weeks to finalize the decision, perhaps with the benefit of "outside advice."

The reference to the decision not being "overridden" was

interesting, at least with the benefit of hindsight. Cy was the district attorney; there was nobody who could "override" his decision. Perhaps this was Carey's shorthand reference to the fact that Cy would be leaving office at the end of the year, and to Carey's confidence that the incoming district attorney would ratify, rather than "override," a decision to charge Trump. The reference to "outside advice" was an allusion to the prospect of reconvening the outside brain trust.

When I got Carey's response, I believed that we had passed a critical threshold. The district attorney agreed that the case against Donald Trump should be prosecuted. This had never been stated explicitly before, so I saw it as a watershed moment. It seemed to me that the hard work and hand-wringing over the last year had been worth the effort. On a professional level, what mattered to me was that Trump committed serious and provable crimes that I firmly believed should be charged. Prosecutors (and defense lawyers as well) have to divorce their decisions from their personal feelings, though of course it is easy to be cynical about any human being's ability to separate personal thoughts from professional decisions.

I think I was able to put aside my personal feelings about Trump as I went about my work. But certainly I had personal views. I had prosecuted and defended a lot of bad people: drug dealers, killers, Mafia chieftains, corrupt cops, disgraced politicians, and con men of all shapes and sizes. Society had the obligation to deal with them, and my role was to make sure that they were dealt with according to the law. Usually, dealing with these people did not generate much emotion. It was my job, and eventually we would all go our separate ways. Trump was different. He had been president, and he would have a continuing presence in the life of the country. I saw him as a malignant narcissist, and perhaps even a megalomaniac who posed a real danger to the country and to the ideals that mattered to me. His behavior made me angry, sad, and even disgusted. But on a professional level, I could not allow my emotional reaction to Trump to affect my activities; it was completely irrelevant. I was happy with Cy's decision, but I knew that I had to keep my emotions out of any actions or decisions I would take as a prosecutor.

Cy, Carey, and I spoke on the following day. Cy was generous, telling me that no one else could have put it all together. We agreed to reconvene our panel of outside legal experts to see if they agreed with how we saw the case. I welcomed this idea. We identified our potential experts and considered whether to incorporate the new district attorney and his team into these discussions. We did not do so, because the decision would be Cy's and the new team was not yet in place. I told Cy that I could make one certain prediction: If we indicted Trump and the case crashed and burned, it will have all been his case and his decision. If the case was a success, it will have been Alvin Bragg's decision and his case. Of course, my prediction was entirely beside the point, as neither of those things happened.

We scheduled the summit meeting with our outside advisors for December 9, 2021, to be followed by an internal meeting the next day. We prepared materials for these meetings, with the goal of giving everyone a fair summary of what a case against Trump would look like. We also wanted to summarize the arguments that we could anticipate from the defense. I prepared draft charging language that described a scheme to create and use false financial statements to obtain bank financing and other business advantages. It detailed the many respects in which the SOFCs overstated Trump's asset values and made the point that Trump's whole business model had been permeated by deception. Trump's modus operandi was to overstate his wealth and success and conceal any failures. The SOFCs had been compiled accordingly.

Carey drafted a lengthy outline of defense arguments. The defense outline claimed that a prosecution would be politically motivated and would violate Trump's constitutional rights. It noted that the district attorney and the attorney general were Democratic politicians who supposedly were trying to prevent Trump from becoming president again. It detailed some of New York State attorney general Letitia James's public statements about Trump and referenced Alvin Bragg's campaign statements about having repeatedly sued the Trump administration. It suggested that Trump would move to disqualify the prosecution and seek a transfer of venue out of New York City. It characterized the case as a political vendetta that had wasted vast resources in the hunt for a viable theory of criminal liability as to Trump, all at a time when murders and violent crime were increasing. It argued that subjective opinions about the value of real estate cannot support a fraud charge and claimed that anyone who received Trump's SOFCs had been on notice that it contained the company's opinion; sophisticated bankers and others could come up with their own valuations if they doubted Trump's. The outline argued that there had been no intent to deceive anyone, that the financial institutions had not relied on the SOFCs, and there were no victims and therefore no fraud. It also faulted the prosecution for a lack of direct evidence, and lambasted Michael Cohen as a convicted perjurer making an avowed effort to "bring down" Donald Trump. Finally, it argued that Trump had been surrounded by financial experts within his own company, outside lawyers, and outside accountants, none of whom had suggested to him that anything illegal was going on.

As we got ready for our summit meeting, the press drumbeat about our investigation was getting louder. A *New York Times* article appeared on November 24, 2021, titled, "Trump Investigation Enters Crucial Phase as Prosecutor's Term Nears End." The article referenced new grand jury subpoenas for records, disputes over document production and sealed litigation on that topic, and a recent Deutsche Bank interview. It reported that the prosecutors were "zeroing in on whether Mr. Trump or his company inflated the value of some of his properties while trying to secure financing from potential lenders." Once again, we wondered whether there was a leak. I read through the many comments to the article, which illustrated the huge differences of opinion among the readers about a potential charge, and also provided a good cross section of reactions ranging from "what's taking you idiots so long" to "no harm no foul" to "valuation is not a basis for a case." I resolved to make sure we would consider the views of the skeptics at our upcoming meetings.

In the same article, there was a reference to a comment from a spokesperson for Alvin Bragg saying that Carey and I would be "retained" when Alvin took over as district attorney. This struck me as odd. Neither Alvin nor anybody from the incoming transition team had asked me to stay on, but I gave it no further thought.

On November 29, we had a call with the team to discuss what additional materials we needed for the upcoming meetings. The team said virtually nothing on the call, and I mentioned to Carey that this group of lawyers was unusually reserved. I was perplexed about the reasons for the team's reserve. They seemed on edge to me, and reluctant to engage in a free-for-all about the case. It may have been the enormity of the decision we were getting ready to make, or it may have been lurking discomfort with the merits of the case and a concern about making a mistake.

Whatever the reasons, the team's lack of excitement led me and Carey to speak again about the need to energize the team with additional resources. This was a topic we had discussed with each other, and with Cy, for months. We had lost one prosecutor because she left the district attorney's office for a job in the private sector. We had lost another when he decided in September to work solely on the executive compensation case against the Trump Organization and Weisselberg. We were not sure how much longer the associates we had "borrowed" from Davis Polk and Paul Weiss would be able to stay with us. We knew that if we went forward with an indictment of the former president, we would need some legal superstars to join the prosecution team. The resulting case would be a blockbuster and would surely be met with a scorched-earth response from Trump, who undoubtedly would be hiring new lawyers, or at least more lawyers.

The prosecution of *People vs. Donald Trump* would be one of the most consequential and sensational criminal cases ever brought, and it might take some years to litigate. I was already over seventy years old, with some health issues. Carey was in his sixties. Neither of us wanted or planned to walk away from the case if it was charged, but we also could not commit to staying with it no matter how many years it might take to wind its way through pretrial proceedings, a long trial, and possible appeals in state and federal courts. Cy, Carey, and I had therefore decided that we needed to hire some lawyers to join the prosecution team. We needed experienced trial lawyers and veteran prosecutors who would take leadership roles on the case. Obviously, though, we could not hire the kind of people we wanted to recruit before we made the decision to go forward with the prosecution for which they would be hired. Also, Cy's term was coming to an end in a matter of weeks. We did not think it was fair to the incoming district attorney to start hiring new senior prosecutors to handle DANY's most significant case before the new boss had even set foot in the office.

As we approached the upcoming summit meeting with Cy and the outside advisors, as well as the internal meeting scheduled for the following day, my agenda was clear. I wanted a direction to go forward with a prosecution of Trump and a commitment to reenergize the team with additional resources, subject to the approval of the incoming district attorney.

CHAPTER SIXTEEN

THE "SUMMIT MEETING" AND CY'S DECISION

Finally, we arrived at December 9, 2021, the day for our summit meeting with the outside advisors. All the lawyers on the team, including me, Carey, and Cy, came to the meeting, along with the five outside advisors, our reconstituted "brain trust." All the outside advisors were former prosecutors whose views we respected.

Michael Dreeben had been deputy solicitor general of the United States for more than thirty years and had argued over one hundred cases before the Supreme Court of the United States. He had been in charge of the Justice Department's criminal docket in the Supreme Court. He had taught law at Georgetown and Harvard and had worked with Robert Mueller in the special counsel's investigation of Russian interference in the 2016 election. We regarded Michael as the ultimate "wise man" on issues of criminal law. He left government in 2020 to become a partner at O'Melveny & Myers, a prominent law firm.

Greg Andres had been a federal prosecutor in the Eastern District of New York, where he had prosecuted members of the Bonanno crime family. Greg had gone on to be Criminal

Division chief in the Eastern District and later a deputy assistant attorney general for the Justice Department. He, too, had worked on the Mueller investigation, and had led the successful prosecution of Paul Manafort, Donald Trump's former campaign chairman. In December 2021 he was in private practice at Davis Polk.

Harris Fischman was a partner at my old law firm, Paul Weiss. He had served as an assistant United States attorney in the Southern District of New York, where he had been the chief of the Violent and Organized Crime Unit. Harris also had been a prosecutor at the Office of the Prosecutor of the International Criminal Tribunal for the former Yugoslavia, where he had worked on the prosecution of Slobodan Milosevic, the former president of Yugoslavia, for attempted genocide and other war crimes.

Scott Muller also had been an assistant United States attorney in the Southern District of New York, where he and I had been contemporaries. Scott had served as general counsel of the Central Intelligence Agency and had taught an advanced course in federal law enforcement at Georgetown Law School. He and Carey had practiced law together for many years at Davis Polk.

Rich Girgenti had been a longtime prosecutor in the Manhattan district attorney's office under Bob Morgenthau, where he had been a contemporary of both Cy Vance and Carey Dunne. Rich had been on the board of KPMG, written several books on managing the risks of fraud and misconduct, and was himself a Certified Fraud Examiner. He also had been New York State's director of criminal justice.

The meeting took place in a large conference room near the suite of offices occupied by the district attorney's executive staff. Unlike most of the office's moth-eaten physical plant, the executive conference room was large and well equipped. Even the furniture matched. Remarkably, there were some refreshments in the morning, and a platter of sandwiches arrived in time for lunch. This was the height of luxury. Conference room snacks and meals are a staple in the private sector; there is an informal competition among the big law firms to see who serves the best food. At Paul Weiss, a giant bowl of popcorn and a platter of freshly baked cookies were required at every afternoon meeting. Morning meetings usually featured pastries, coffee, fresh fruit, and orange juice (freshly squeezed, of course). At the district attorney's office it was a triumph to find drinking water.

I started with a presentation about the nuts and bolts of the SOFCs, giving examples of falsified asset values and some of the evidence proving that the falsification had been by design. The first example I discussed was Trump's Mar-a-Lago estate, which Trump bought in 1985 for a reported price of $7 million. After buying the property, Trump sought permission from the town of Palm Beach, Florida, to turn the property into a private club. His engineers, architects, and lawyers filed a plan with the town saying that, as a private residence, Mar-a-Lago was a "white elephant" that no one wanted to buy. They told the town that it was "[i]mpractical for a[n] . . . individual to continuously own MAL as a private estate." Later, in order to get a tax deduction, Trump donated a preservation easement that prevented changes to important features of the property, including things like the light fixtures and the windows, so that the physical appearance of the estate would remain unchanged. Some years later, after a dispute with the Internal Revenue Service, Trump signed a deed acknowledging that he had no right to use Mar-a-Lago for anything other than a private club. These limitations on the use and development of Mar-a-Lago substantially diminished its value. Nevertheless, Trump claimed in his financial statements that Mar-a-Lago had a value as a private residence exceeding $400 million. This purported value was vastly larger than the values stated in appraisal reports that the Trump Organization had itself commissioned, and it was based on valuation techniques that our experts told us were inappropriate and misleading. Trump's valuations for Mar-a-Lago, in the seven years reviewed in detail by our experts, had exceeded the actual reasonable value of the property by an average of more than 1,000 percent per year.

I went through some other examples of how the financial statements had inflated the value of Trump's assets, but this was not a sticking point at the meeting. Everyone accepted that the SOFCs were false, and that they had been intentionally falsified. Although Trump had delegated the valuation process to others, the group acknowledged that he had created the process and "owned" it; he could not credibly claim that he did not know how the SOFCs were created. However, there was a long discussion probing whether we could prove that Trump subjectively knew that the stated asset values were false. Some questioned whether Trump had "smoked his own dope" and actually believed that his properties had the outlandish values ascribed to them. The concern that Trump might not be able to distinguish between actual truth and "alternative facts" had apparently vexed the Mueller team as well. In a similar vein, we discussed whether Trump's claims that he actually had won the 2020 presidential election were just lies, or whether he truly believed what he was saying about the election notwithstanding the lack of any credible basis to believe he won. Was Donald Trump suffering from some sort of mental condition that made it impossible for him to distinguish between fact and fiction? Put otherwise, the group discussed whether Trump had been spewing bullshit for so many years about so many things that he could no longer process the difference between bullshit and reality.

The discussion at the "summit meeting" also explored other issues in the case. Everyone understood that Trump had not defaulted on his recent Deutsche Bank loans. (He had defaulted on an earlier financing that had taken place in 2008, but that transaction took place years before loans we had investigated, and there had been a settlement of the disputes arising from the earlier default.) The fact that we did not have a "victim" that had lost money because of the false financial statements was not a fatal legal flaw, but it weakened the case's appeal to a potential jury.

We also spent time discussing the issues of "causation" and "reliance," focusing again on Deutsche Bank. It was easy to prove that the bank had made loans to Trump, and that a condition of the loans was the receipt of accurate financial statements. Trump had repeatedly certified, in signed writings, that his financial statements were accurate, and we were prepared to prove that they were anything but accurate. Was this enough to establish fraud, or did we also have to prove that the bank would not have extended credit if it had understood Trump's true finances? Put otherwise, did we have to show that the bank had relied on Trump's phony numbers in making loans, or was it enough that the statements had been intentionally falsified, even if the actual values of Trump's assets would have led the bank to approve the loans no matter what? This divided the group, in terms of both fact and law. Factually, some witnesses had supported the idea that, while Trump was clearly very wealthy, he was not so wealthy that the bank would have made the same loans on the same terms if it had been given accurate financial statements. Maybe we would be able to prove that, but maybe not. Legally, the question was whether we even had to prove it. Was it sufficient to show that the bank had bargained for accurate financial statements, and that was not what it received? This was a construct that a number of team members seemed not to accept. The issue troubled some of the outside advisors as well, but eventually they seemed to agree that Trump's representations about the accuracy of his financial statements, and the bank's decision to lend money based on those false representations, were enough to establish fraud if we could prove that the SOFCs were false in meaningful ways. Carey and I strongly believed that it did not matter whether the bank would have made the same loans if Trump had provided accurate financial statements. That was not what he had done, and prisons are full of people who commit "stupid" crimes—crimes that they did not have to commit to get what they wanted.

As the meeting ended, the sense of the group seemed clear: we had a case, but it was not without issues, and certainly could not be described as a slam dunk. We needed to be strategic about how we would present it:

First, we would have to simplify the proof that the SOFCs were false. We did not want protracted battles between expert witnesses over arcane metrics like capitalization rates; it would be better to rely on clear instances of deceptive conduct. We concluded that it might be hard to demonstrate the breadth and depth of the overstatements without showing some of the more subtle and "deep in the weeds" techniques that were used. Ultimately, though, it would be a matter of trial tactics to decide how to present the case if we went forward.

Second, to rebut the claim that Trump believed his own "hype," and really thought that his assets had the ridiculous values reflected in the financial statements, we would have to show, and stress, that Donald Trump was not legally insane. He had just recently completed a term as president of the United States; he had not lost the ability to separate truth from fiction. He could not possibly have believed that "only he" could value real estate. All the wild valuations were off in only one direction—higher than warranted. This reflected intentional deception, not random detachment from reality. Ultimately, we agreed that Trump did not have the right to make up "alternative facts" in a courtroom.

Nor did Trump have the right to bury his head in the sand and deliberately avoid learning the truth about his net worth and the value of his assets. In that regard, judges usually give jurors a "willful blindness" instruction, sometimes referred to as an "ostrich" instruction. This instruction tells jurors that a defendant cannot avoid guilty knowledge by taking intentional steps to avoid learning facts that the defendant does not want to know. The precise formulation of the instruction varies slightly from jurisdiction to jurisdiction, but almost all of the states and all of the federal courts have adopted some version of this principle. When this came up at the outside advisors meeting, I was told bluntly by one DANY lawyer that New York does not follow this doctrine. Some quick legal research, later bolstered by a more in-depth research memo from Paul Weiss, indicated to the contrary. New York law supported the "ostrich" instruction, but Manhattan prosecutors had not been asking for it on a regular basis. I thought it would be helpful if the Trump case ever went to trial, but even asking for the instruction ran into the objection that "this is not what we usually do."

Finally, the extensive debate at the meeting about causation meant we would need to be careful about how we defined the charges. If we went forward, we would need to stress that Trump had repeatedly certified to the banks that he was supplying them with honest financial statements. The banks unquestionably relied on the certifications and would not have made loans without them. We would later refine the charges to eliminate any need to show that the banks had relied on Trump's inflated wealth in deciding to extend credit, but we were convinced in any case that our legal theory was sound, and the outside experts seemed to agree with us.

After the meeting with the outside advisors, Carey and I huddled briefly with Cy. Cy told us that the meeting had reinforced his inclination to bring the case; it certainly had not convinced him to "pull the plug" on a prosecution. Carey and I then went to Forlini's to have a drink, and Cy joined us there as well. Forlini's was a legendary downtown watering hole for lawyers and judges, located a few blocks away from the courthouse. More than thirty-five years earlier, Ron Fischetti (Trump's lawyer) and I had met at Forlini's and had decided there to become law partners.

Cy, Carey, and I sat at Forlini's to reflect on the meeting and to tell some war stories, a favorite pastime of virtually all lawyers. During the conversation, Cy expressed some regret that he would not be around for what seemed likely to be the next act in the long investigation—Trump's indictment. He never expressed regret about deciding not to run for another term. I asked him what he would do after leaving office. He said that he would be practicing law in some capacity. I was surprised. If he was going to keep practicing law, why not do it as the district attorney? I did not ask that question, understanding that it had been a personal decision.

For his part, Carey reported that the conversation with the "brain trust" had left him "on the fence" about charging Trump. I was not certain whether the discussion had left him with questions or whether Carey wanted to preserve his options until we made a final decision. His body language and dialogue had convinced me that he had decided long ago that the case should be brought, but Carey is a very deliberate and cerebral lawyer. He kept his opinions to himself, not wanting firmly to "declare" himself until necessary. By contrast, I wore my opinions like a sandwich board; no one had to guess what I was thinking.

I met with Carey again the next morning, before the internal meeting with the lawyers on the investigative team. Again, Carey said he was "on the fence." I said, with obvious irony, that I was not.

After speaking briefly with Carey, we started to head into the meeting with the team. Cy had decided not to attend the meeting, because he did not want the conversation to be "chilled" by his presence. He stopped me on the way into the meeting. He said he wanted me to promise him something. I asked, "What?" He said he wanted me to promise I would not leave the meeting and immediately quit without speaking with him. After the first hour, I knew why he wanted that promise. Many of the lawyers were relentlessly negative, dwelling on all the difficulties and issues with the case, and seemingly refusing to acknowledge the positives. Everyone thought the case would be stronger if it was brought in federal court, and there was some discussion whether the case could be passed off to federal prosecutors at the Department of Justice.

Whether the Department of Justice would have taken the case, whether it belonged with the feds, and why the Justice Department sat quietly by during the district attorney's criminal investigation of Trump's finances are all interesting questions, which came up at the very end of my tenure.

Returning to the meeting with the internal lawyers, there were references to our case as "weak," and one lawyer opined that it had "many fatal flaws." Another disagreed about whether there were fatal flaws and referred instead to "many small imperfections" and a "lack of clarity" on the causation issue. Causation took up a lot of time, and there was a long debate whether we had to prove that Deutsche Bank would not have loaned money to Trump if it had known his true net worth and had received accurate asset values. One person asked the question whether the banks really had been fooled, because perhaps "everyone" knew that Trump was a "fraudster." Some on the staff pointed to the civil case that the attorney general was getting ready to bring and observed that that case would provide some accountability. Another person asked, "What are we getting ourselves into?" and expressed a view that the case might be "way out there." Another voice opined that, while the legal theory was legitimate, "it's not the strongest case in the world." The discussion was not all negative. One prosecutor was worried about making a status-based distinction and questioned whether declining prosecution of a wealthy and powerful defendant would be applying a double standard. Several people asked the question whether this was a good case to "test the limits" of our prosecutorial power, and thought we were outside the "heartland" of the statutory definition of "scheme to defraud" under New York law because we had no victim who had lost money.

I made a fairly impassioned speech saying that I would be in favor of prosecution even if the defendant was not Donald Trump, or a politician, but just "Joe Blow from Kokomo." I explained that I had made a deliberate effort not to think about the damage Trump had done to politics, the rule of law, respect for the truth, or the fabric of our democracy. I said that it was strictly Trump's conduct as a businessman that required prosecution, and I would feel the same way about any businessman who had engaged in this conduct. Carey made reference to a comment that one of our outside advisors had made the day before about the need to bring the case against Trump, even if there was a substantial risk of loss, to stand up for the rule of law.

A telling exchange took place toward the end of the meeting. I commented that the one thing that no one in the room had said was that Donald Trump was innocent. Everyone then affirmed that they thought he had committed serious criminal conduct, but they were concerned whether it fit within the strictures of New York's Penal Law. Everyone agreed that the financial statements were false, and there was general agreement that Trump was responsible. But if charging a "scheme to defraud" under New York law meant that we had to prove that Deutsche Bank had lost money because it relied on the false asset values in Trump's SOFCs, there were strong views that the case was too weak to proceed.

The meeting broke after three hours, and Carey and I retreated to his office. Cy and Marlene Turner joined us. Marlene was Cy's special assistant and a lawyer; she had been on most of our calls and meetings during the past year. Marlene is a warm and friendly person, and I had enjoyed getting to know her. We had chatted a bit every time I had come up to the executive suite. Marlene had attended the internal staff meeting and had grown frustrated with the discussion. She said it was a good thing she was masked (as we all were), because otherwise she was sure that her face would have betrayed her disgust. When Cy asked me how the meeting went, I told him that after the first hour, I just wanted to "open my veins." Notwithstanding the pessimism about our case, I told Cy that no one thought Trump was factually innocent.

It quickly became apparent that Cy had made up his mind, and Carey too was no longer "on the fence." The three of us all had the same view—the case should go forward. Of course, we knew that the new administration arriving in three weeks would have to ratify the decision. But none of us thought that would be a problem, and Cy opined that there was really no question but that the incoming folks would agree with us.

The conversation then turned to the team, and Cy expressed his frustration with their negativism. He said that there had been many other occasions that he had run into the same problem, including the internal discussions that had attended a number of other high-profile cases. We talked about the need to find new blood, either within or outside the office, with the latter being more likely than the former. I also said that it was frustrating to feel like we were about to march into battle, and were strapping on our guns and equipment, but when we looked around at the rest of the platoon we saw a lot of conscientious objectors. This turn of phrase seemed to capture Cy's fancy, and for the next half hour he made repeated reference to the "conscientious objectors."

I left the DA's office that Friday afternoon to go back to my suburban home and enjoy the weekend. I knew that the work would begin anew on Monday. We had to beef up the team, brief the incoming administration, plan for a grand jury presentation, and prepare for the indictment of the former president. On Sunday evening, December 13, Carey sent an email to the team announcing that the decision had been made to go forward.

It was gratifying to know that, after a lengthy investigation and a somewhat ponderous decision-making process, the prosecution of Donald Trump had gotten the green light. I marveled at the thought that I might soon be at the center of what might become one of the most consequential criminal cases ever brought. My only similar experience, which was not really comparable, had come in November 1998, when I was chief of the Criminal Division at the United States Attorney's Office in Manhattan and we announced the indictment of Osama bin Laden and other members of al Qaeda for the bombing of the United States embassies in Kenya and Tanzania. But I had been a tiny, bit player in that investigation and had played a vastly more important role in the Trump investigation.

There were now just three weeks left in Cy Vance's tenure as DA. The week after the summit meeting saw the end of a long fight with *Forbes* regarding our efforts to secure testimony from *Forbes* reporters about their dealings with Donald Trump. I cannot disclose details about grand jury proceedings, but grand jury witnesses can freely describe events in the grand jury. Randall Lane, *Forbes*'s chief content officer, wrote a piece for the magazine, published on December 17, 2021, titled, "Forbes Testified Before the Trump Grand Jury Yesterday— Here's Why We Fought Their Subpoena." The article described "months of objections" that *Forbes* had made about subpoenas for testimony, and Lane described all the questions I had put to him in the grand jury about the magazine's dealings with Trump, including questions relating to Trump's net worth fixation and his description of his triplex as containing 33,000 square feet. Lane complained in his article about the "creeping use of subpoenas to undermine a free press." But he also made clear that his testimony had been limited to matters he had already disclosed to the public in the pages of the magazine. Reporters and media outlets have no statutory or constitutional privileges to resist giving testimony about matters they already have disclosed. I can understand why a media outlet would categorically refuse to cooperate with prosecutors. However, *Forbes* and Lane had climbed up on their First Amendment high horse about giving testimony that the First Amendment did not protect.

On the morning of December 18, I had my first contact with Alvin Bragg, in the form of a very nice email. I assumed we would be talking in the near future, and I looked forward to getting to know him. Our paths had not crossed before, perhaps because I had spent the last ten years in semi- and then complete retirement. Everyone told me that Alvin was a "good guy," which I think is how people generally described me as well. I figured we would see eye to eye on most things and anticipated no friction or difficulty.

CHAPTER SEVENTEEN

FRICTION AND DIFFICULTY

As we raced toward the end of Cy's tenure as district attorney, we had not had any discussions with the incoming DA about the investigation. There had been no outreach from Alvin Bragg or his transition team, and no request for a briefing. Carey and I had scratched our heads about this but assumed that the transition team was busy. Regime change is not a routine event at the Manhattan district attorney's office. Alvin Bragg would be only the fourth newly elected DA to run the office since 1942. Cy Vance had been district attorney for twelve years, and before him Bob Morgenthau had run the office for thirty-four years and Frank Hogan had been district attorney for more than thirty years.

Carey and I were anticipating an indictment of Donald Trump in the first quarter of 2022, so we decided to press the incoming team to become familiar with our investigation. We sent them the materials that we had prepared for the summit meeting earlier that month. On December 20, Carey sent an email to Alvin and to Peter Pope, who would be one of Alvin's close advisors in the new administration. I did not know Peter, but I had had lunch with him and a mutual friend in early November. (We had not spoken about the substance of the Trump investigation, but even at that time I had begun to talk about the need to add new staff to the team.) Carey's email suggested that we get together to discuss the case before the new year, and he urged the new team to speak with us as quickly as possible.

Peter responded very promptly. He called Carey to say that Alvin was "completely underwater" getting ready for his new job. With respect to staffing, Peter said that he and Alvin were hoping to recruit some senior trial lawyer from within the office. As Carey and I later discussed, this was not likely to be a solution. We had spoken many times with Cy about the need to beef up the team, and we had canvassed the office roster many times to identify someone from within DANY who could join the team. But we were looking for a potential first chair and team leader—someone who could take over the case down the road if Carey and I could not finish the job. I did not know the DANY roster myself, but Carey and Cy, who both knew the office's personnel inside and out, had already determined that there was no DANY superstar who was a candidate for the job.

Substantively, Peter expressed concern about the pitfalls of a case in which there was no classic victim who had been fleeced as a consequence of relying on Trump's financial statements. While it could be argued that the American people generally had been hurt by Trump's deceptions, we were speaking about a victim in the legal sense—a person or entity that had received the SOFCs, relied on them to give money to Trump, and then suffered a financial loss. The absence of such a victim had been a major focus of the "conscientious objectors."

Peter thought that we might refocus the charges to feature allegations that the SOFCs were false business records, rather than building the charges around one central scheme to defraud. Under the New York Penal Law, the baseline charge of falsifying a business record is a misdemeanor and not a felony. Peter's view, as related to me by Carey, was that strong misdemeanor charges might be preferable to felony fraud charges because it would be hard to prove that anyone had lost money by relying on Trump's false financial statements.

It is conventional wisdom among lawyers that white-collar criminal cases are all about "lying," "cheating," or "stealing." We had been looking at Trump's conduct as a species of "cheating," but Peter Pope's essential notion was that we could recast the case as being more about lying. This seemed a very good idea to me, but I was not in love with bringing a criminal case against the former president that contained only misdemeanors. I thought a misdemeanor case would be a "chickenshit" maneuver, because misdemeanor charges would undervalue the seriousness of the misconduct we had been investigating. Trump had been using inflated financials for many years and had employed the financial statements to obtain hundreds of millions of dollars in financing. This conduct required felony treatment.

After spending some additional hours parsing the New York Penal Law and the cases interpreting it, I thought there was a better way forward—a way in which we could focus on the "lying" and the false financial statements but bring felony charges either in addition to or in lieu of charging Trump with participating in a scheme to defraud. Under the Penal Law, falsifying a business record becomes a felony if the actor intends both to defraud and to commit another crime. "Intent to defraud" is broadly defined under this statute, and generally includes any intent to deceive, with no requirement that a victim lose money or even that the defendant intends a victim to lose money. Under the cases, any intent to deceive the recipient of the false business record is good enough. We would not have to prove that the recipient actually had been deceived. This was critical for us. It would moot the whole debate about what Deutsche Bank had known about Trump's real net worth and the value of his assets, and we would not have to prove that the bank would have refused to extend credit if it had been presented with accurate financial statements.

But had the SOFCs also been used to commit other crimes, which would allow us to bring felony charges relating to the falsification of business records? We had faced this issue months earlier when we were considering the "zombie" case involving the coverup of the hush money payment to Stephanie Clifford, but with respect to the SOFCs the answer was clearly "yes." There were other eligible crimes, but the one that fit best was the crime of "uttering" a false financial statement. To "utter" simply means to issue, distribute, or put into use. This crime is also a misdemeanor. But if a person falsifies a business record with the intent to utter a false financial statement, that's a felony. This crime was exactly what I thought Trump had done. He had repeatedly signed certifications claiming that his attached financial statements were accurate. The certifications were false business records, and Trump's intent in providing them to Deutsche Bank had included the intent to utter false financial statements. The crime would be a completed felony even if Deutsche Bank had taken the financial statements and locked them in a cabinet without looking at them. Of course, that's not what happened, but charging the case in this fashion would eliminate a potential defense and moot the objections of the "conscientious objectors" on our team. At least, so I thought.

We featured the new legal approach when we finally had a Zoom conversation with the new leadership on December 27, 2021. Alvin, Peter, and other incoming members of the new administration were on the phone. This was the first time I had ever met or spoken with Alvin Bragg. We talked through some of the merits of the case, along with our desire to move quickly. We also addressed our staffing needs, which were pressing. I was encouraged by the conversation, although Alvin did not take charge of the discussion and he dropped off after an hour or so. Carey also thought it was a good conversation. After the call he emailed me to say, "That seemed to go well." I responded by saying, "I think so. It's hard to know—early days."

After the conversation, I wrote a memo sketching out the evidence and the witnesses that we would need to present to the grand jury, and I sent the memo to the team and to Alvin and his advisors. I also agreed with my spouse that we would have to cancel our stay in Sonoma for most of the winter, even if it meant forfeiting the large deposit we had paid to rent a house there. There was just too much to do to finalize the charges and get ready for the return of the Trump indictment.

January 1, 2022, marked the arrival of the new year and the installation of the new district attorney. Unfortunately, things started to go south almost immediately.

Carey, who had been a "power behind the throne" during Cy's tenure, and who was one of the most respected lawyers in New York City, was told he had to vacate his office immediately. He managed to relocate to vacant space many floors away, but in the meantime he was given a small cubicle as the new place for him to hang his hat. Also, we now understood that the process of educating the new team would be far slower and more painful than we had anticipated. The new regime had not jumped in to embrace the investigation or to learn the facts. Our telephone conversation on December 27 had been the only substantive conversation we had had with Alvin since he was elected.

In the meantime, our staffing needs had grown critical. Another lawyer on the investigative team had decided to leave the case for personal reasons and would soon leave the district attorney's office. The associate who had been "seconded" to us from Davis Polk had to return to the law firm at the end of January. Defense motions were due to be filed in the indicted case at the end of the month, and that would involve responding to hundreds of pages of legal and factual arguments. There was no doubt about what the lawyers for the Trump Organization and Weisselberg would do. Their approach would surely be to throw crap against the wall to see what, if anything, might stick. We knew we would be reading about a "witch hunt" and the supposed political nature of the prosecution. Sorting out the arguments and responding to them would involve months of work. And we needed to present evidence to the grand jury. We were going to require the full attention of the new regime if we were to fill out the team and do everything that had to be done.

In early January, having heard nothing after the December 27 telephone call, Carey and I noted our mutual and growing unease. Carey told me that he was losing patience for a "lon[g] deliberative effort," and was concerned that we needed to add "a good number" of new prosecutors who could be on the case for the long haul. I responded by noting that "I keep reading that Alvin has asked me to stay on. He must have done that in a very quiet voice," since we had spoken only during the group call on December 27. I also suggested that we send an email "shot over the bow" to the new team, because "the next two weeks are critical to our ability to move forward with the investigation."

We decided that we needed to prod the new team to focus on our investigation. Carey sent an email asking to meet and received word that maybe something could be arranged for later in January. The lack of interest prior to and during the holidays, and the lack of any apparent sense of urgency, left me and Carey feeling that the whole investigation, and us along with it, had been pushed off to the side of Alvin's agenda. I wrote to Carey that "[i]t feels a bit like we are some aging food leftovers that are still lurking in the refrigerator—we were once sought after, but we're not yet fully rotten, so we can be kept around for another short while to see if there is a use for us." Carey's one-word reply: "Compost."

More email exchanges persuaded Alvin and company that it was urgent to speak soon, and we arranged to have a Zoom call during the first week of January. The dialogue we had on that call struck me as superficial and negative in tone. The new team spoke about the difficulties in the case—Michael Cohen's credibility, the lack of a "victim," the absence of Trump's "fingerprints" on the valuation spreadsheets—without appreciating its strengths. The heart of the case was the many and varied ways in which the SOFCs were false, which had taken months to understand. I knew that the new group could not possibly have delved into these complicated facts, let alone mastered them, when we spoke in early January.

The discussion left me despondent, and I wondered what to do if we could not get a commitment to move forward. Then Carey told me that one or more of the "conscientious objectors" were talking to the new team behind the scenes to disparage the case. Of course, everyone had the right to communicate his or her opinion, but the notion that the charging decision might turn on private conversations taking place behind closed doors, rather than an open dialogue in everyone's presence, left me cold. This was not the protocol that I had seen in my earlier stints as a prosecutor. I had worked under three United States attorneys, all of whom had encouraged an open dialogue when making decisions on cases.

I had been working night and day for months, and I was

anxious to add some new talent to the team very quickly. As we had discussed with the new management, we had a pressing need to find a true superstar, someone who could lead the team and also do the "nuts and bolts" work of completing the investigation. Carey was a sober, intelligent, and mature lawyer, with excellent judgment. During Cy's tenure, he had functioned as both chief of staff and secretary of state, dealing with all of the people involved in the case and moderating the discussion. However, he had not spent time combing through documents looking for financial irregularities, and he had not been outlining the facts that we needed to elicit from critical witnesses. This work, the basic "blocking and tackling" that takes place in every criminal investigation, had been left to the team, and I had done a lot of it. I told Carey that we urgently needed to find someone who could share this work at the highest level, because I could not do it all myself and would have to quit if we could not get more help soon.

Carey replied that if I quit, the investigation would be over, and we would have to fold our tent and "call it a day." I said that it was unfair for him to put that responsibility on me, and he responded that it might be unfair, but that's the way it was. It left me unsettled and thinking that I had to soldier on or else accept responsibility for a failure to hold Donald Trump accountable for his financial crimes. It was not a cheery thought.

There was some hope on the immediate horizon. I had started a conversation with a recent alum from the Southern District of New York. By all accounts, the potential recruit was a true superstar, who had enjoyed a long stint as a federal prosecutor, had been an office leader, and had extensive trial experience. He was also a congenial fellow who got along well with people. He was interested in joining the team, and Carey and I thought he would be just who we needed. Carey also had been exploring the addition of a lawyer from Davis Polk with whom he had worked. The lawyer was a gifted writer and an experienced legal eagle who would give us some much-needed capacity for turning out legal briefs quickly and competently.

Carey sent a message saying that we wanted to move forward with these new hires, and heard only "crickets" in response, until finally we got two emails from Alvin that left us pulling our hair out. In the first one, Alvin said to hold off on hiring our hot superstar prospect while the new administration finished "poking around a bit" to identify current assistant district attorneys (ADAs) who could join the Trump team. In the second email, Alvin said he also wanted to "put into the mix" two former assistant United States attorneys who had expressed a general interest in joining DANY. The emails struck both of us as missing the urgency of the situation and underestimating the special needs of the Trump investigation and potential prosecution. In our minds, we needed to find some unquestioned all-stars, lawyers who are hard to find and hard to recruit. We were not seeking out itinerant lawyers looking for a new home. Carey was particularly aggravated because we had been trying for months to identify ADAs from within the office who could help us. Carey knew the office and its people intimately, having worked there for years, but Alvin was telling us that he and his team, who had been in the office for all of a week, would "poke around" to see who was available. This did not give us confidence.

I wanted to have a one-on-one conversation with Alvin, with whom I had never spoken other than as a participant in two Zoom calls with a lot of others involved. We arranged to speak on Saturday, January 8. As luck would have it, I could not have picked a worse day to have my first private conversation with the new district attorney. A media furor had broken out that day over Alvin's "first-day memo." The memo, which Alvin had issued on January 3, had laid out a progressive agenda for the office, including directives to ADAs not to charge certain relatively minor crimes (including, under some circumstances, resisting arrest). Prosecutors also were told not to seek prison time for some robberies, assaults, thefts, and gun possession cases, and not to argue to have defendants kept in jail prior to trial except in certain serious cases. The city's new police commissioner, Keechant Sewell, had sent an email letter to NYPD officers on January 7, telling police officers that she had studied Alvin's memo and was "very concerned about the implications to your safety as police officers, the safety of the public and justice for the victims." I had heard about Sewell's memo from my son, a lieutenant with the NYPD, who told me that cops were exchanging message after message about difficult new arrests and the sentiment that Alvin's new policies had left police officers feeling unsupported. My son also wondered, as did I, about Alvin's apparent decision to issue the first-day memo without first resolving any disputes it might create with the Police Department. In any case, the police commissioner's response to the first-day memo had resulted in a firestorm of criticism directed at the district attorney. All of this took place just before my first one-on-one conversation with Alvin Bragg.

I started the conversation by saying that I had been reading in the newspapers that Alvin wanted me to stay on. Alvin interrupted to apologize for not having spoken to me directly. I then described the work I had been doing and made a pitch for immediate new hires, saying that I could not continue doing what I was doing without more help. I also made sure that Alvin knew that the case was ready to be charged. I described it as a "rocket" that we were ready to "launch," assuming that he could be comfortable that it was a case that should be brought.

We talked about that at some length. I told him that the case was a good and solid case, but not a "slam dunk." I mentioned that we were retooling the charging theories to moot the objections about the lack of financial injury to Deutsche Bank or other victims. He asked, appropriately, whether it was the kind of case we would bring against somebody other than Donald Trump. I said that I had asked myself, and the team, whether we would pursue the case if the defendant was "Joe Blow" and we had the same conduct, just with smaller dollar amounts. For me, the answer was unquestionably "yes" because of the brazenness and blatant illegality of the conduct. I told Alvin that rich guys who inflated their financial statements to get bank financing were prosecuted every day of every week across the United States. Alvin was responsive, and in general I thought he was professional and pragmatic. Nothing was said about the first-day memo and the criticism from the police commissioner, other than my pregnant comment that I knew Alvin had "a lot going on."

I thought it was a good conversation. Toward the end, Alvin said he better understood the staffing needs, and he commented several times that I had given up a year of my life to the investigation, which had been a "noble" thing to do. He also said that he wanted to get a briefing on the key parts of the case in the very near future.

I took some heart later in the day when Alvin sent an email authorizing us to make an offer to the former federal prosecutor who was our potential superstar recruit. Unfortunately, Alvin never reached out personally to the potential recruit, and after much consideration, the person decided not to join us.

Our next meeting with Alvin and the new team took place on January 11, 2022.

Early that morning I visited with Carey in his new office on the fifteenth floor of 100 Centre Street, the Manhattan Criminal Court. Carey had left his tiny cubicle and somehow had found a large area in the courthouse (connected to the district attorney's office) that would be suitable for the whole prosecution team in the Trump case. The space would have been perfect for us if we had gone forward, with a large conference room and enough offices not only for the existing team but also for a new infusion of lawyers we hoped would soon be joining us. Having everyone in the same space, we thought, would be good for morale and might increase team cohesiveness.

Later that day, we convened for our in-person meeting. Alvin was there, along with his new management team, including Susan Hoffinger, the incoming chief of the Investigation Division. Susan attended the meeting even though she had not yet assumed her new job. She is an assertive, confident person, and she had a lot to say. In this respect she took after her father, Jack Hoffinger, who was an accomplished criminal defense lawyer in his day. I had been in several cases with Jack, and meeting his daughter made me remember that I was old enough to be the father of everyone in the room (other than Carey), if not the grandfather. I was finishing law school when Alvin was a toddler.

At the meeting I made a presentation on the essentials of the overvaluation of the SOFCs, focusing on Mar-a-Lago, Seven Springs, 40 Wall Street, Trump's Briarcliff golf course, and his triplex apartment. I then gave a quick overview of the evidence establishing Trump's personal culpability. Everyone seemed convinced that the SOFCs had been falsified, but the part of the presentation about Trump's involvement came at the end, when people had lost some focus, so Alvin said he wanted another presentation on this topic. There was considerable "angst" about using Michael Cohen as a witness. In part, the reluctance was because the new team had not heard him in person, and they did not appreciate his ability to provide first-hand testimony about Trump's role in the fabrication of asset values. It seemed that we were starting from the very beginning to educate people about the case. I was frustrated that we had lost valuable time and lamented that Alvin had made no effort to get briefed about the Trump investigation during the weeks that had gone by since he had been elected.

Our efforts to recruit lawyers from within DANY was not producing a throng of applicants. Alvin had assigned the recruitment task to Chris Conroy. Since Chris seemed to be exuding negative vibes about the case, it was no wonder that he was having little success in speaking to well-regarded ADAs about joining the team. It was common knowledge in the office that there had been "defectors" from the Trump investigation, and ADAs realized—quite accurately—that they would not have a lot of autonomy working on the case. But I was still hopeful that, when and if we got Alvin's green light to go forward with a prosecution, the sensational nature and obvious importance of the case would make it easy to build out a bigger team. In my own mind, I figured that any younger lawyer interested in public service would jump at the chance to be part of the Trump prosecution team.

Substantively, we were continuing to pivot away from scheme to defraud as the central charge in the case and moving toward charges focused on falsifying business records with the intent to commit other crimes. Because we were now contemplating an indictment that featured false business records, Carey and I spoke about reviving the hush money allegations, which would bring the "zombie" theory back from the dead once again. The thought was to charge as false business records not only the documents relating to the SOFCs but also the phony invoices for "legal services" that had been used to reimburse Michael Cohen for the money he had paid to Stephanie Clifford.

When we had considered these facts in early 2021, we did not want to bring the falsification of the hush money records as a stand-alone case against Donald Trump. As I've explained, there was a legal problem that could result in felony charges being reduced to misdemeanors: Claiming that the false records were created in order to commit or conceal a *federal* election violation might not hold water as a felony charge under a literal reading of the New York Penal Law. But, even if the false business records relating to the hush money were reduced to misdemeanors, they would not be standing alone in the larger case we wanted to bring. Even as misdemeanors, those charges would buttress the other false-business-record allegations that would be at the center of the prosecution. Those other charges, based on the false SOFCs and related documents, could unquestionably be brought as felonies. The right way to proceed, we thought, was to bring felony charges based on the full panoply of false business records that Trump had helped to generate: the phony documents relating to the hush money payment and Michael Cohen's reimbursement, the false financial statements, the false certifications attesting to the accuracy of the financial statements, the false accounting spreadsheets that were created to support the financial statements, and so forth. We could allege that the records had been created with the intent to commit or conceal a variety of state and federal offenses. Even if the federal offenses were ruled out of bounds as a legal matter, we would be left with felony charges as to the financial statement records and misdemeanor charges as to the hush money records. Those charges would be immune from legal attack, and we were confident that we would reach a jury with them.

As we worked to formulate a precise set of charges, New

York State attorney general Letitia James filed a detailed petition on January 20, 2022, in support of an application to compel Trump and members of his family to give depositions in her
civil investigation. The petition was thorough and well done,
and reflected the work the attorney general's office had done to
establish that the asset values in the SOFCs had been inflated
and fabricated. Carey's reaction was that the filing of the petition would be helpful to us—it contained allegations similar
to those we hoped to bring, and it would allow us to gauge
the reaction of the pundits, analysts, and others who would see
the petition. The petition also suggested that the attorney general was getting closer to bringing a civil fraud lawsuit against
Trump and his business. If we got the green light to bring a
criminal case against Trump, we had hopes that DANY and the
attorney general's office could coordinate the filing of the criminal case and the civil case and bring them at the same time.

As it turned out, the attorney general's filing of the petition
had a boomerang effect that none of us could have foreseen. Michael Cohen could not restrain his enthusiasm for the attorney
general's lengthy public disclosures about the falsification of the
SOFCs. He made several public appearances saying that Letitia
James "had the goods" on Trump, and he took credit for her
work, telling everyone that he had brought all the bad conduct
to light and was the key witness in the case. Cohen's congressional testimony had identified Trump's financial statements as
false; in that sense he had started the investigative ball rolling.
However, his relentless focus on his own importance had not
been helpful to his credibility. Unfortunately, he had studied the
art of self-aggrandizement at the feet of the master. Cohen's pen-
chant for publicity, exaggeration, and grandiose statements had
played into the hands of people who distrusted him, just as the
same qualities had turned some people off to his former boss.

Cohen could not have picked a worse time to blow his own horn. Although Alvin had told us on January 11 that he wanted to have another meeting to discuss the evidence about Trump's personal involvement in the SOFC falsification, his schedule had been too full (in part because of the chaos caused by the controversial "first-day memo") for him to give us any time until Monday, January 24, 2021. When we convened on January 24, the meeting quickly degenerated into a whirlwind of negativity. As I started to detail Cohen's potential testimony against Trump, Susan Hoffinger brought out her phone to play a recording of one of Cohen's recent media appearances, in which he had taken credit as the person who had first spoken about the false financial statements and had crowed about his importance as a witness in the case. This was exactly opposite to the point I was making at the meeting, which was that Cohen could provide the jury with the basic story of why the financial statements had been fabricated, but the strength of the case would be the corroboration—all the documents, expert testimony, appraisals, and other evidence showing that Trump had caused the value of his assets to be massively and systematically inflated.

To make matters worse, the defendants in the indicted case, Weisselberg and the Trump Organization, had just filed motions to dismiss that case. Weisselberg's motion papers, which had been circulated to the new team on the night before our meeting, made a convoluted and meritless argument that the case against him was the product of his own compelled testimony, which supposedly was being used against him in violation of the Fifth Amendment. Weisselberg had testified before a grand jury in the federal hush money investigation. DANY had never seen or made use of that testimony, but Weisselberg claimed that his federal testimony had convinced Cohen to cooperate with our investigation. Cohen, according to Weisselberg's argument, decided to cooperate and give evidence that led to the charges against Weisselberg because he wanted to get back at Weisselberg for having testified under immunity for the feds. Cohen's cooperation, according to Weisselberg, ultimately had led to our charges against him and amounted to the use of Weisselberg's compelled testimony to incriminate him. This argument, apart from being illogical and hard to follow, was completely fallacious. Cohen had had nothing to do with the tax charges against Weisselberg. Cohen had not even known about the executive compensation scheme and was not a witness in that case. The tax charges against Weisselberg had not derived from Cohen's cooperation, and Cohen had not been induced to cooperate by Weisselberg's immunized testimony.

Although the new team knew nothing about the underlying facts, and nothing about how the Weisselberg case had been put together, they had read the defense motion papers attributing critical importance to Cohen, dumping all over him, and claiming that he had tainted the prosecution. Cohen, having made appearances referring to himself as the key witness in the whole investigation, had unwittingly reinforced the defense arguments. And then I came into our meeting to do a presentation on Trump's involvement with the false financial statements, and I referred to Cohen's testimony as part of our proof. The discussion degenerated into chaos and confusion. On top of it, Alvin came into the meeting late, spent much of the time looking at his phone, and then left early, saying he just wanted to see the important documents, as though the whole sprawling case could be reduced to a collection of a few crucial documents, which made no sense. This was the key meeting for the new district attorney to "vet" our incipient case against the former president!

Later that day, perhaps realizing that the train had gone off the rails, Susan Hoffinger called me at home. She told me that the new team was trying to sort through everything quickly, but then started asking how we could "shore up" the case. I had mentioned at the meeting that we had evidence that Trump had exerted iron-fisted control over the Trump Organization's finances. Trump had insisted, for instance, that he had to sign all but the most routine checks and personally initial invoices to approve payment. Susan wanted to know whether we had witnesses other than Cohen who could testify to these facts, reflecting her aversion to using Cohen as a witness. The conversation, and the meeting that had preceded it, left me convinced that the new team was not prepared to give us a green light to charge Trump, notwithstanding Cy's earlier decision and our strong recommendation. As I wrote to Carey later that day, "it seems increasingly likely to me that we will lurch along at an uncertain pace toward an uncertain result, with the demands of the indicted case siphoning off more and more of the team's attention. . . . I am not prepared to bet that we will ever cross the finish line. I hope you can give me some reason to be more optimistic."

Carey responded that "I can't give you a reason to be more optimistic," adding facetiously that "it's nice they have all kinds of suggestions for improvement to the evidence that we doubtless never considered." He then told me that he was mulling over a decision to leave DANY, perhaps as early as March 1, "unless a decision to proceed with a further indictment is made prior to that date."

I responded that there would be no prompt decision to proceed with a further indictment. I told Carey that "[t]hey perceive it to be a difficult decision, so they will do what usually happens in such situations: pressure us to keep digging and defer making a final decision in the hope that the equation will change." I also raised with Carey the question whether it made sense to press forward with presenting our grand jury case. I had spoken with another lawyer on the team earlier in the day, telling him that we were getting extremely "bad vibes" from the new regime about whether a prosecution of Donald Trump was going to be authorized. The lawyer, quite sensibly, had pointed out generally that there are legal risks involved with presenting evidence to a grand jury before deciding to ask the grand jury to return charges. If that grand jury was not asked to return an indictment, a defendant who was charged later by a different grand jury could claim that the prosecution had pulled the case from the first grand jury in order to present it to a different, more receptive grand jury. New York law does not look kindly at such tactics. In general, if charges are contemplated, it makes sense to present the evidence to the grand jury that will be asked to approve those charges, and it is unwise to present a case to a grand jury unless the prosecution is planning to ask for an indictment.

I suggested to Carey that perhaps we should tell the new team that it made no sense to put additional evidence before a grand jury until Alvin reached a decision to authorize charges. As I put it to Carey, if the new team wanted us to hold off on a grand jury presentation, "that is tantamount to a vote of 'no confidence' in our efforts, which—however disappointing and wrong it would be—I would rather get sooner than later." Carey agreed and added that we also needed to tell the new team that it was impossible to recruit superstar lawyers from outside DANY to join the investigation without being able to tell them that the prosecution of Donald Trump would go forward.

The die was now cast: we would tell the new team that, unless we got a prompt decision to allow us to prosecute Trump, we should not be calling grand jury witnesses and we would need to hold off recruiting outside lawyers to work with us. This would effectively sound the death knell on the case. I hoped that sending this dire message might provoke another discussion, but I knew at least it would force the issue. If Alvin agreed that there should be no grand jury presentation, and agreed that we needed to stop recruiting people to work on the case, we would know that the investigation would be going nowhere.

Carey sent his email and got a prompt response from Susan Hoffinger: "Thanks and agree with your assessment." This meant that there would be no witnesses heading to the grand jury, and no "superstars," or even lesser "stars," hired to continue putting together a case against Trump. The prosecution of Donald Trump was now on life support. I sent an email to Carey telling him how I felt: "[E]ither they haven't seen the ball since the kickoff or they truly don't think there is any case against [Trump], a determination they have made without making a serious and intensive effort to understand that case. Either way, they clearly have no confidence in the judgments we have made, and I have no confidence in their judgment. That is not a recipe for success, and I will be advising the DA shortly that my active participation in the Trump investigation will be coming to an end. . . ."

Carey did not lobby me to stay on. On the contrary, he saw no path forward, and was heading toward his own decision to leave DANY.

CHAPTER EIGHTEEN

THE LOOMING END OF THE INVESTIGATION

O ur disastrous meeting with the new team took place on January 24. I had been scheduled for surgery on January 27. The surgery was relatively minor; I needed to have a hernia repaired. I had delayed the procedure because work had become so frenzied over the last six months. But now I had a date for the operation, and I would be out of commission on the day of the surgery and for a short time afterward.

In advance of the surgery, I prepared a resignation letter. The letter informed Alvin that I did not want to continue "in the absence of clarity about a decision to prosecute and without the ability to secure the resources that I believe the case requires." I finished the letter on the evening of January 26 and sent it to Carey in draft to get his reaction. I told him that I was going to "sleep on it," but I planned to press SEND in the morning before leaving for the hospital. Carey then sent me a draft of his own resignation letter, saying that he too would be heading out the door. He, like me, decided to "sleep on it."

I could not sleep at all that night. I tossed and turned thinking not about the surgery, but about all of the work that I and others had done in the past year. While I was sad for having invested a lot of personal time and effort, I was haunted by the thought that there were many people everywhere who had been counting on us to hold Trump accountable for crimes that we would never get a chance to prove in court. Those people out there were the "People" we represent in the courtroom, and on whose behalf we act when we bring criminal cases in their name. They might not have known or cared about Trump's financial crimes as a businessman, but they were looking for some reassurance that he was not wholly immune to the rule of law.

As I tossed and turned, I asked myself whether we had done everything we could to convince Alvin to let us bring our case against Trump. I kept thinking that maybe we were being rash. I also thought about Alvin's relative youth and wondered if he was in over his head. From what I knew, he had never run an organization anywhere close to the size of the district attorney's office, and he had scant experience in leading or defending high-profile prosecutions. I was disheartened about where we were and a little angry. I felt that we had been given short shrift, and that Alvin had not really understood the work that had gone into the case or the evidence that we had put together. I began to wonder if there might be a chance to turn the situation around if I told Alvin exactly how I felt and gave him a chance to reconsider and perhaps reverse course.

I got up in the wee hours of the morning and composed a new letter, to take the place of the resignation email I had planned to send before leaving for the hospital. The new message was blunt, perhaps too blunt:

> Alvin,
>   I am out today because I am having some surgery, but we need to speak urgently. I am not happy, and I know that

Carey is not happy, with the status of the Trump investigation and with how you are handling it—or not handling it. We are both ready to quit. If that is what you want, or if you have reached a considered opinion that a case against Donald Trump should not be brought, then so be it. We will leave, and you can deal with the resulting consequences. But both of us are telling you that there is a case that should be brought, which is a conclusion we reached after months of effort and after the extensive personal participation of your predecessor, who agreed with our judgment. Neither Carey nor I are rash, immature, starry-eyed young lawyers. You need to respect our judgment, our decades of experience as prosecutors and defense lawyers, and the work that we have put into the case, more than you have to this point. Of course, you are the elected DA, and you must make your own judgment. And we know that you have been distracted. But, with all due respect, it is not appropriate for us to be told that it is virtually impossible to get a meeting with you to review Donald Trump's culpability, and for you to come to that meeting late, spend most of the meeting looking at your phone, and then leave before we are finished. You need to take the time to review this case in detail, and that does not mean just looking at a bunch of testimony or documents without understanding the full context and texture of an extremely involved fact pattern. And you also need to spend some time with the investigative team. Now that we have stopped the grand jury presentation pending the need for more clarity from you on whether a case will be brought, every one involved in the case is wondering what is going on. I hope and believe that the situation can be turned around. But that is not going to happen without your direct involvement.

Please excuse the bluntness of this memo, but it is not a time to mince words.

Mark

I felt badly for switching up on Carey, but I was much more comfortable with the new message than the letter quitting the case that I written the night before. I thought about it some more, talked with my wife, and then sent the email. We left immediately for the hospital. I was happy that I had not yet quit, and that maybe we could mount a last-ditch effort to change Alvin's mind. It was probably the anesthesia I got for the surgery, or maybe the lack of sleep the night before, but that night I slept like a baby after returning home from the hospital.

Alvin's response to my blunt email was somewhat encouraging. He wrote that he "definitely" did not want me to quit and said that he had not "reached a determination" but had "significant questions." He also was willing to meet whenever and as often as necessary to review the case. We agreed to have a telephone conversation on Sunday, January 30.

Our telephone conversation that Sunday was somewhat awkward. Alvin said he would give us as much time as we wanted to discuss the case, and said he knew that the decision was important, perhaps even "the most important legal decision" he would ever make. He also said that he had not made any "considered decision," with emphasis on the word *considered*. When I thought about this after we hung up, it seemed to me that his emphasis on *considered* spoke volumes. I took it to mean that he was leaning against bringing the case but had not yet thought that decision completely through. We left it that I would speak to Carey and then send Alvin an email suggesting a process for moving forward that would give him whatever data he needed to make a final decision. He seemed to welcome that. It was a business-like conversation, but not warm or friendly, which was hardly a surprise in light of the strongly worded email that preceded it.

After Carey and I huddled about the logistics, I suggested to Alvin that we should schedule a number of extended Zoom meetings, each lasting a few hours. (In-person meetings would have been better, but I was recouping slowly from the surgery.) I told Alvin that our goal was to lay out the case, answer his questions, and enable him to make an "up or down" decision before the end of February 2022. I told Alvin in an email that there was "nothing magical about [the] date, but with the grand jury presentation on hold, Carey and I are anxious to get clarity about our future course as quickly as reasonably possible." By this point, it was public knowledge that the new grand jury we had convened in early November 2021 would be finishing its six-month term in the spring of 2022. We scheduled the first extended Zoom meeting for Friday, February 4.

I prepared for the February 4 meeting for many hours, putting together a written outline. The goal was to summarize the case against Donald Trump, not including testimony from Michael Cohen because we wanted to cover what he had to say, and his liabilities as a witness, in a separate meeting. I began by pointing out that the fabrication of values in the SOFCs had been pervasive, substantial, and continuous over many years. As an example, I talked about the values that had been assigned to Trump's golf courses. Our experts had put together some charts with yearly statistics on the purchase and sale of golf properties. Trump's valuations of his golf courses were literally "off the chart." I argued that he had to have known this, because he was a real estate entrepreneur in the business of building, owning, and running golf courses, just as he surely knew that the apartment he built and in which he lived had not contained 33,000 square feet. The brazen, pervasive, and outlandish nature of the overvaluations, I argued, was important proof of Trump's intent.

I then spoke about the evidence tying Trump to the preparation of the financial statements. I noted that the SOFCs on their face were directed to Trump, contained language saying that he was responsible for their preparation and presentation, and repeated over and over that the valuations had been "prepared by Mr. Trump," working in conjunction with others. The assets described in the SOFCs were the assets that Trump had spent his business life to build and acquire. Trump, as a person obsessed with his wealth and net worth, surely had familiarized himself with the SOFCs and how they had been prepared. And he had certified, time and again, that the SOFCs had accurately presented his financial condition.

I next displayed some documents reflecting Trump's review of the financial statements and addressed some witness testimony that we had gathered from the attorney general or civil case files. The testimony established that Weisselberg and Trump had reviewed the SOFCs before they were finalized, and at least some of the valuations had come directly from Trump, though Weisselberg and Jeff McConney, the Trump Organization comptroller, had been key players.

I reviewed Trump's admissions from the defamation case he had brought against Tim O'Brien, in which Trump had acknowledged keeping his financial statements on his desk, going over the asset values with Weisselberg, and giving his opinions on the value of certain properties. Trump did not distance himself from the asset values in the financial statements; on the contrary, he complained that they were too low. I emphasized Trump's extraordinary control over the Trump Organization's financial workings, including his personal signing of checks, close review of expenses, and approval of the financial terms on which every new member joined one of his golf clubs.

I next turned to Trump's history of making up facts regarding his wealth. I spoke about the evidence we had received from Jonathan Greenberg, including the "John Baron" tapes and Trump's correspondence with the *Forbes* staff regarding his wealth. I also alluded to the information that *Forbes* had made public regarding Trump's net worth obsession, his admission that he had tried to mislead *Forbes* about his wealth, and his statement that a high net worth was "good for financing." I argued that the back-and-forth that Trump had with *Forbes* over the years, on which the magazine had reported, had put Trump "on notice" that his asset values were unreasonable. Yet the pattern continued, and Trump had not taken any of the steps he could have taken if he wanted to ensure their accuracy. I then turned to Trump's many public statements and tweets about his wealth, noting that those statements helped prove that the size of his net worth was of central importance to Trump's public persona.

I said that if we were presenting our case to a jury, I would ask the jury to consider some simple questions as they decided whether Trump bore responsibility for the false valuations: Whose assets were these? Who benefited from the overvaluations? Who was out there trumpeting his net worth and his wealth? Who was the boss, who ran the company with an iron fist? And who had a documented history of exaggeration and outright lies about his wealth?

Finally, I said that the case should be brought even if conviction was not certain because we had to vindicate the rule of law. I argued that the facts warranted prosecution of anyone who had done what Trump had done, and his prior service as president was not something that should make us reluctant to prosecute. I closed by stressing the need for a prompt decision on whether we would proceed. I told the group that there was "complete unanimity" from everyone on the investigative team that the time had come for a decision because the nature of the case and the nature of the evidence were clear.

My remarks took a long time. I spoke, with hardly any interruption, for about ninety minutes. Incredibly, there were virtually no questions. It was exactly like summing up to a jury, except I was speaking to about twenty people on a Zoom call, and not twelve jurors in a jury box. I was flabbergasted that there was no real discussion. I felt as though I was speaking to people who were listening politely but not engaging. At the end of the meeting, Alvin and his team thanked me for the presentation and left the room to have a meeting among themselves behind closed doors.

In the course of my career, I had made hundreds of oral presentations. Over the years, I had made presentations to prosecutors, defense lawyers, judges, jurors, appellate courts, clients, prospective clients, partners, witnesses, young lawyers, bar groups, and others. After making so many presentations, I had a pretty good idea when I was "talking to the wall," and I was certain when I finished speaking on February 4 that I had been doing just that. The feeling in the room was as though I was speaking to adversaries. Neither the district attorney nor the people on his team did anything to make me, Carey, or the other team members who attended feel like we were connecting with them or that we had been taken into their confidence. They projected the feeling that they had little confidence in us, and little respect for our work or our judgment. As I wrote to Carey in an email I sent to him about scheduling our remaining meetings with the new team, "we seem to be as welcome as skunks at a garden party."

At least the meeting moved us closer to a decision. Alvin promised that he would make up his mind within the next two weeks or so. I was left drained. I was glad that at least I had been able to deliver what amounted to a summation in the case of *People vs. Donald Trump*, but I was fairly certain by this point that my remarks were the only summation that anyone would ever give in that case.

After the meeting broke, I got some very nice emails from the team, including an email from Marlene Turner, who had listened to the presentation. She wrote: "Today was a master class in compelling and persuasive presentation. I find it almost impossible to see a side that would lead to not going forward. . . ." I responded by saying that "I fear that my comments amounted to the only summation that will ever be given in this jurisdiction with respect to the crimes of Donald Trump. . . . It's like speaking to the Politburo."

Our next Zoom meeting took place on February 9, 2022, and the agenda was to discuss the "pros" and "cons" of using Michael Cohen as a witness. A number of us spoke again with Cohen a few days beforehand, making sure that we knew the details of the testimony he could provide. He told us, as he had in the past, that he had had conversations directly with Trump and Weisselberg about jacking up the asset values in the financial statements so that the bottom-line net worth figure would meet Trump's expectations and requirements. When we had our Zoom meeting, Carey spoke about what Cohen could add to the case (the "pros") while I spoke in detail about Cohen's liabilities as a witness (the "cons"). I wanted to speak to Cohen's liabilities so I would not always be the primary spokesperson for bringing the case against Trump. I was worried that I had become a "Johnny-one-note," always arguing the reasons for prosecuting Trump until I was blue in the face and nobody wanted to hear me anymore.

I made sure not to understate the risks of using Cohen as a witness. I talked about his hatred for Trump, his perjury conviction, his inflated views of his own importance as a witness, his many press appearances, and his other liabilities. I said that the defense would portray him as an inveterate liar, though in truth I did not see him in that light. I had gotten to know Michael, and he was a complicated person. He would be the first to admit that he can be a complete pain in the ass. I had been dealing with his tortured psyche for months; there were times he was demanding and defensive and other times when he was down in the dumps. He spoke to me once about his daughter, who had blamed him for his involvement with Trump and the pain that this had caused for the family. His daughter had needed surgery, and Michael had not been able to be with her because of his legal situation. Whatever his sins, Michael dearly loved his family. I listened to him and told him that I felt very badly for the impact that his legal problems had had on his family. And I did feel badly. I had learned over the years that it is often the people in a defendant's family who suffer the most from a criminal prosecution. I had also learned that being professional does not mean you have to check your humanity at the door to your office.

The February 9 meeting was more interactive than the last one had been, but some of the questions that arose were uninformed or confused. Here is an example: Under New York law, no person can be convicted of a crime based on the uncorroborated testimony of an accomplice (that is, someone who testifies that he or she committed a crime along with the defendant on trial). The point of requiring "corroboration," or supporting testimony, is to make sure that no one goes to jail just because a "squealer" tries to shift blame away from himself or herself by pointing a finger at the defendant. There needs to be some independent supporting proof, in addition to the accomplice's testimony, for a jury to return a guilty verdict. (Federal crim-

inal law is different; in federal court, the unsupported word
of an accomplice is enough to support a guilty verdict if the
jury believes the accomplice beyond a reasonable doubt). I was
well familiar with this peculiarity of New York law. Many years
earlier, I had argued an appeal in New York's highest court, the
New York Court of Appeals, claiming that my client should not
have been convicted of murder based solely on the testimony
of a witness who testified that he had helped my client dispose
of the victim's body and destroy the physical evidence of the
crime. I won the case, which became one of the leading prec-
edents on New York's accomplice corroboration requirement.
(Fortunately for society, my client—who had killed not only
the victim, but also the victim's pet Chihuahua—was convicted
on a retrial.) At our February 9 meeting, I was asked whether
the "accomplice corroboration" requirement might prevent a
conviction if we called Michael Cohen as a witness. The question reflected a complete lack of understanding about the case.
We had boatloads of testimony to corroborate Cohen's testimony that the financial statements had been fabricated, and
that Trump had been involved in the fabrication. I had summarized some of that testimony just a few days earlier. Whatever
the legal issues were in the case, accomplice corroboration was
not one of them.

At one point during the meeting, Alvin commented that he
"could not see a world" in which we would indict Trump and
call Michael Cohen as a prosecution witness. This was a telling comment. Whether or not we could bring the case without calling Cohen as a witness, Alvin had never met Cohen or
listened in when Cohen was interviewed. We had never taken
Cohen through a "dry run" of his testimony, or even prepared
him to give testimony. Witness preparation cannot turn a sin-
ner into a saint, but prosecutors can and do work with wit-

nesses to smooth out the rough edges of their testimony and help them answer questions more directly and honestly. I had one trial as a federal prosecutor in which we had met with the main witness more than eighty times before he took the witness stand. (He was still a terrible witness at the end of that process, but better than he might have been otherwise.) Alvin's dismissal of Cohen as a witness seemed to presage his decision to drop the idea of charging Trump on the evidence we had accumulated so painstakingly over the last year.

We had the last in our series of preplanned meetings on February 14. The topic for this meeting was the charges we were proposing to bring against Trump and the legal issues that might come up in connection with those charges. I spent some long days and nights before the meeting preparing an elaborate and lengthy memorandum discussing the proposed charges in detail. During this time, there was radio silence from the front office, and I had the premonition that my lengthy legal analysis, and the elegant plan that Carey and I had developed for structuring an indictment, would not be appreciated by our audience. I remarked to Carey that we might be about to disregard the biblical advice not to waste effort by "casting pearls before swine."

When the meeting took place, our audience did not act like swine; they were perfectly polite and attentive, but also restrained and unresponsive. Once again the room had an "us vs. them" flavor that was alien to me; we were all on the same side, wearing the "white hats," and trying to decide collectively on the right course of action. But the mood in the room resembled the many frustrating meetings I had during my years as a defense lawyer trying to dissuade prosecutors from coming after my client. I would be allowed to speak my piece, but nobody's mind was likely to change.

Carey and I exchanged emails after the meeting. He was

disheartened, as was I. He talked about setting Friday, February 18, as his personal mental deadline. If we did not get a green light by that date to go forward with our charges against Trump, he would resign. I was disgusted and knew that I certainly would not stay on if Carey decided to leave. I started to think about how it would feel to abandon the effort; I took some comfort in telling myself that I had done everything I could to bring about a different result.

Oddly, just as these events were playing out, the press reported on a pleading that the state attorney general had filed in her civil investigation. The pleading disclosed that Trump's accounting firm, Mazars, had sent a letter to the Trump Organization advising that it was no longer standing behind Trump's financial statements. It is very unusual for an accounting firm to take this kind of action, akin to telling anyone who had received Trump's financial statements that they would be well advised not to believe them. The Mazars letter caused a mini-furor. The Trump Organization, in keeping with its customary practice of spinning the facts in a distorted reality field, put out a statement saying that Mazars's repudiation of Trump's financial statements was some sort of positive attestation that rendered the investigations of him "moot." Only in Trump-world could a letter like this, stating that the SOFCs should not be relied upon, be characterized as a good thing. The judge presiding over the attorney general's investigation of Trump, Arthur Engoron, issued an opinion saying that claim of "mootness" was "as audacious as it is preposterous." The pundits opined that the letter was a very bad thing for Trump and had provided the district attorney's office with more ammunition for its forthcoming charges. The pundits did not realize that the ammunition had arrived just as the general was deciding to leave the battlefield.

On February 16, we got some confirmation that our fears were well founded, and that Alvin would not permit the prosecution to go forward. I came home from walking the dog in the early afternoon and saw an email from the lead ADA on the investigative team referencing a conversation with Alvin Bragg earlier that day. Alvin had mused for a bit about charging Weisselberg but not Trump in connection with the financial statements—a notion that we had never discussed, and that made little sense to me. Alvin also had said that it was tempting to take time and not make a final decision, but he understood that the team did not want to leave the case in limbo. Alvin added that the consensus among the group of prosecutors with whom he had been speaking was not to go forward.

My first reaction was dismay. Whatever "group of prosecutors" was speaking to Alvin apparently did not include anyone who had spoken with the witnesses or who had a detailed understanding of the facts. I shook my head over the decision-making process that had evolved, in which we made formal "presentations" to members of the new regime, who then went off to deliberate among themselves. Not once had Alvin suggested that we meet one-on-one so that he could explain his reservations or discuss at length his view of the case. Of course, he had no obligation to do that. He was the district attorney, and he could make his decisions as he pleased. However, I believed that Alvin was on the verge of making a historically bad decision, which would be hugely destructive to public confidence in the rule of law. Having spent forty-five years in service to the rule of law, I could not passively accept this decision. I wondered if there was a way to ask Alvin to reconsider that might resonate with him.

CHAPTER NINETEEN

A "LITTLE PIECE OF JUSTICE"

When I researched Alvin Bragg's career, I learned that he had counseled the family of Eric Garner, a Staten Island man who had died in July 2014 after being placed in a chokehold by NYPD officers who were trying to arrest him for selling untaxed cigarettes. Police officers in New York had been trained for years not to use chokeholds to restrain people because chokeholds can be dangerous and even fatal.

Eric Garner's death had led to state and federal criminal investigations, but no criminal charges had been brought, notwithstanding community protests and the efforts of Garner's family, represented by Alvin. I had followed the Garner case, both because my son was a New York City police officer and because I had led the prosecution many years earlier of Frank Livoti, another NYPD officer who had applied a chokehold that led to the death of a person he was trying to arrest.

The Livoti prosecution took place in 1998, when I was chief of the Criminal Division in the United States Attorney's Office in Manhattan. Livoti, a Bronx police officer, had been sitting in a squad car with other cops one night just before

Christmas 1994. Anthony Baez and his brothers were playing football in the street in front of their home, and the football bounced off the police car. Words were exchanged, and then the football bounced off the police car again. The cops told the Baez brothers that the football game was over, and the situation escalated. Eventually Officer Livoti decided to arrest Baez, who was twenty-nine years old, overweight, and suffering from asthma. Livoti put Baez in a chokehold, and Baez lost consciousness and died. Local prosecutors tried Livoti in state court for criminally negligent homicide and he was found not guilty. The United States Attorney's Office conducted an investigation to determine whether Livoti had violated Baez's civil rights by using excessive force in connection with his arrest.

At the end of the investigation, the United States attorney, Mary Jo White, had to decide whether to charge Livoti. The decision was difficult. Livoti already had been tried and acquitted in state court, and the Civil Rights Division of the U.S. Department of Justice, with whom we were discussing the case, advised us not to bring charges. They had reviewed the evidence and had concluded that the case was "unwinnable" because Livoti's fellow police officers had testified on his behalf, and the medical evidence about whether a chokehold had caused Baez's death was subject to dispute. From my own review of the evidence, I thought Livoti was guilty, and that his acquittal in state court had been a miscarriage of justice. Mary Jo White agreed; she too believed that there had been a miscarriage of justice and that we had to bring the prosecution to reinforce the rule of law, in part because Livoti had a long history of using excessive force as a police officer. So, notwithstanding the probability that we would lose the case, we decided to charge Livoti with violating Baez's civil rights.

We thought it would be a better result to bring the case, even if we lost it, than not to bring it at all.

I volunteered to try the case, along with Andy Dember and Serene Nakano, two fine lawyers who had handled the investigation. We brought the indictment and then went to trial. Livoti was found guilty, notwithstanding the dire predictions of the Civil Rights Division, and he was sentenced to a long prison term.

The scene in the courtroom after the jury returned the guilty verdict has stayed with me for more than twenty years. The courtroom was packed, as it had been throughout the trial. The jury verdict was announced, and the defendant and his family were somber as they dealt with the shock of the result. I made my way through the crowd to speak for a moment with Anthony Baez's parents. His mother, Iris Baez, had been a vocal and visible activist leading demonstrations calling for her son's killer to be charged. When I came up to her, she thanked me and said that, at long last, she had gotten a "little piece of justice." Her words—a "little piece of justice"—were what stayed with me. I took from those words that she never expected a full measure of justice. She believed that to be impossible, because poor people of color had learned not to expect much when they asked the criminal justice system to hold police officers to account. A full measure of justice was not possible. Livoti's conviction would not give her son back to her, and she already had been through years of public strife, including Livoti's acquittal in state court, seeking whatever quantity of justice might be available to her. In that moment, though, she was grateful for the "little piece of justice" that the guilty verdict represented. I made my way back to the office. We had won our case, but I was not elated as I walked back. It had been a sad scene. Livoti's life had been ruined, even though he was guilty and deserved punishment. The Baez family had suffered unspeakable grief and sorrow that a guilty verdict could not erase. The criminal justice system had given them a "little piece of justice," but could not undo the damage that had been done. Nevertheless, Mary Jo White later described the Livoti prosecution as the case that had made her most proud during her long tenure as United States attorney.

I thought about the Livoti case as we came down to the wire in deciding what to do about Donald Trump. That experience had convinced me that even hard cases could be won, because jurors usually cut through the legal process and reach the right result. More importantly, bringing the Livoti case had been the right thing to do notwithstanding its difficulty and the high risk that we would lose it. Justice sometimes requires prosecution, even if conviction is far from certain.

I believed that indicting Trump was the right thing to do even in the face of the risk we would lose the case. In my view, the Trump case was not "unwinnable." Just the opposite—I thought we could bring it and win it. But even if the risk of losing the case was substantial, that had to be weighed against the damage to the public's trust in the rule of law that would occur if we walked away from the case.

Thinking that perhaps my experience with the Livoti case would resonate with Alvin, I sent him a long email talking about the Livoti case and urging him to let us proceed against Trump even if the odds of conviction were not as high as he would like:

Dear Alvin,
    Unfortunately, we have not developed the kind of personal relationship that would make it easy to have a "heart to heart" conversation. I hope, therefore, that you

will simply read this letter as you ponder the decision about whether to go forward with the Trump prosecution.

I know that the case against Donald Trump is not an easy one, and there is a big risk that it will not end in a conviction. It is impossible to quantify that risk. I believe that the prosecution would prevail, but a lot of uncertainty is baked into the situation. I am certain, however, that Donald Trump committed the crimes for which a prosecution would attempt to hold him to account. As far as I know, everyone who understands the facts, and the full story of Trump's history of lies about his finances and his assets, believes that he is guilty. The question is not whether he committed crimes; it's whether we could convince a jury of his guilt.

I would like to share with you a personal experience that informs my belief that in these circumstances the "right thing to do" is to bring the case. More than twenty years ago, when I was the Chief of the Criminal Division at SDNY, we were investigating a New York City police officer, Frank Livoti, in connection with the death of Anthony Baez, a young man who died after a street encounter with Livoti and other officers from the 46th precinct. Baez and his brothers had been playing football in the street in front of their Bronx home, and had kept on playing football even after the cops told them to stop. Words were exchanged, and the situation escalated. Finally, Livoti decided to arrest Baez and placed him in a "chokehold." Baez died. Livoti was charged with homicide by the Bronx DA's office, and he was acquitted. . . . SDNY opened a civil rights investigation, and the time came to make a charging decision. . . .

I tell you this story because I firmly believe that Donald Trump is a criminal, with a history of lying about his finances. I believe he should be prosecuted for his crimes, just as I believed that Frank Livoti had to be prosecuted for what he had done, in part because he had a history of using excessive force as a cop. We undertook the Livoti prosecution, notwithstanding the high risk of loss, because we ultimately thought that justice would be better served by bringing the case—even if we lost it—than by allowing an injustice to stand without challenge. As it happened, we won the case, but I believe that we were on the "right side of history" even had there been an acquittal.

Please do not misunderstand. I am not suggesting for a moment that we should bring a case that is unsupported by proof sufficient to establish guilt beyond a reasonable doubt, or that we should bring a case that poses no real prospect of conviction. But I am suggesting that there are circumstances where a high risk of loss is outweighed by the need to confront a possible miscarriage of justice, and a lack of accountability for criminal conduct. I would therefore bring this case even if the defendant was not Donald Trump. The fact that he is who he is certainly raises the stakes, but it does not change the calculus. If anything, respect for the rule of law and the need to reinforce the bedrock proposition that no man is "above the law" reinforce the need to bring this prosecution.

Thank you for indulging me by reading this letter.
Sincerely,
Mark Pomerantz

Alvin did not respond right away, but eventually I got an email saying that he had appreciated my note and had been thinking about it. He proposed that we speak on the telephone on Sunday afternoon, February 20. I offered to come see him in person at his home, but it was left that we would have a telephone call.

In my responding email, I also added a bit more about the Livoti case, sharing with Alvin that the case had meant a great deal to me. I told him about the conversation I had had with Iris Baez, hoping that he might appreciate that when it came to Donald Trump, many people felt like Mrs. Baez. They believed that it was impossible to hold a man like Trump accountable for anything, and they doubted that the criminal justice system would provide even a "little piece of justice." They were cynical that there would be a good-faith effort to prosecute Donald Trump. In my mind, it was critical that we at least try, even if ultimately we might not succeed.

CHAPTER TWENTY

"HAIL MARY" PASS

On Friday and Saturday, before my scheduled Sunday telephone call with Alvin, Carey and I predicted to each other that Alvin would not tell us or anyone that he was ending the Trump investigation. Rather, we thought Alvin would tell people he was not going to indict right now but would see how the investigation developed. If Letitia James could compel Trump to testify about his financial statements, or if Allen Weisselberg decided to cooperate after being convicted on the pending tax charges, Alvin would revisit the matter. This would make it sound like the investigation was continuing. But, as Carey and I discussed, there was little chance that a "continuing investigation" would change the result, or that the office would pursue an aggressive further inquiry after Carey and I left. Prosecutors who are concerned about a negative reaction to closing down a case often claim that their investigations are "continuing"; the reference to a "continuing" investigation is a fig leaf to avoid confronting or admitting the fact that an investigation is not going to ripen into an indictment.

I decided to try one last "Hail Mary" play. I spoke with an intermediary I knew and trusted. The intermediary was well acquainted with our investigation and could speak to Alvin. I told the intermediary about the difficult conversations we had

had with Alvin and his team and the likelihood that Alvin would not approve an indictment. We also spoke about the many law enforcement reasons that the Trump investigation should have been handled by the U.S. Department of Justice, rather than by the Manhattan district attorney's office. The intermediary agreed to contact Alvin directly to try to persuade him to consider referring the investigation to the federal authorities. By this point we knew that the *New York Times* was getting ready to print a story saying that our grand jury investigation had hit a "pause." The intermediary would counsel Alvin that referring the Trump case to federal prosecutors would be better for the case—and for him—than simply declining to bring it.

Referring the investigation to the feds, and specifically to the United States Attorney's Office for the Southern District of New York, was not a sudden brainstorm. Carey and I had discussed the idea months earlier, and the investigative team had proposed a federal referral in our December 10 meeting.

There were many sound reasons that the financial statement investigation might better have been handled by federal authorities. For one, a federal criminal statute applies directly to Trump's conduct. It is a federal crime to make a false statement, or to overvalue any property, "for the purpose of influencing in any way" the action that a bank will take on a loan application. In a nutshell, federal law prohibits giving false financial statements to a bank, whether or not the bank relies on those statements or loses money. The crime is punishable by up to thirty years of imprisonment. This statute was right on point; federal prosecutors would not have to torture or massage its language to charge Trump with a violation. The potential penalty was more serious than for any state crime we could charge, and there was a much longer statute of limitations as well—ten years as opposed to the five-year limitations period that generally applies to felonies committed in violation of New York State law. Federal prosecutors also would have the FBI, with all of its resources, available to investigate the case, and they enjoyed nationwide service of process, meaning they could serve subpoenas throughout the United States. In the district attorney's office we could not compel an out-of-state witness to testify before a New York grand jury without going through an elaborate legal process involving authorities in the state where the witness was located. Also, witnesses who testify before a federal grand jury do not automatically receive immunity. As a consequence, witnesses are much more likely to speak voluntarily with federal prosecutors in informal interviews than they are with local prosecutors. Federal grand jury practice is also vastly less complicated. The federal authorities simply have stronger and better legal tools at their disposal than we had in a local prosecutor's office. And those tools were better suited to the Trump investigation than the ones we were using.

Of course, there was no guarantee that the Department of Justice would pick up the investigation if Alvin referred it to them. We knew that federal prosecutors had not been investigating Trump's financial statements. If they had been, we would have heard about that from the witnesses and likely would have been urged by federal authorities to keep away. We did not know why the feds had not gotten involved. Until Trump lost the 2020 election, perhaps they stayed away because they could not indict a sitting president under any circumstances, and if Trump had won the election he would have had another four years of constitutional immunity. But once Trump lost the election, the United States Attorney's Office could have mounted an aggressive investigation of Trump's tax filings and his finances generally. Michael Cohen had testified publicly about Trump's financial shenanigans, and the *New York Times* had run a series of long articles in the fall of 2020 raising questions about Trump's nonpayment of taxes. Either of those events, and certainly that combination of events, along with other available information, would have been sufficient to warrant a federal investigation. Nevertheless, the feds had not gone near Trump's financial statements or his tax returns. Maybe they had stayed their hand because they knew the district attorney's office was doing a criminal investigation and the attorney general was working toward bringing a civil fraud action. Typically, however, the feds do not defer to state authorities in such matters. In fact, they are usually quick to tell state investigators to "get lost" if they want to do their own investigation, as they had done with respect to DANY's early efforts to look into the Stephanie Clifford hush money payment.

Within DANY we surmised that the federal authorities had not dug into Trump's finances because the Department of Justice regarded an investigation of Donald Trump as more than just a "hot potato." It was a blistering, giant, radioactive man-eating potato, with the potential to burn anyone holding it. The new United States attorney for the Southern District, Damian Williams, had a good reputation, but any decision to investigate the former president would likely be made not by Williams, but by Attorney General Merrick Garland. Williams had been a law clerk for Garland during the latter's tenure as a federal appellate judge. It was inconceivable that Williams would decide to investigate the former president if Garland wished him not to do so.

Even though the Department of Justice had not begun an independent investigation of Trump's financial statements, that did not mean they would refuse to pick up the case if Alvin decided to ask them to do it. Obviously, if Alvin asked them to investigate, the feds could not claim to be deferring to him.

In my mind, it was vastly better for Alvin to try to "lateral" our investigation to the United States attorney than simply "take a knee" by keeping the case in the district attorney's office to die a lingering death.

I knew that the odds of the Department of Justice taking the case and deciding to bring charges against Donald Trump were long, even though that would be a great result. Given where our own investigation was heading, it would be the equivalent of a legal Houdini act. Still, I allowed myself to wonder what Michael Cohen's reaction would be if the investigation magically transferred over to the Southern District of New York. Cohen hated the Southern District prosecutors with a passion—they had prosecuted him and had sent him to prison. Cohen also hated Trump with a passion. I wondered whom he hated the most—would he cooperate with the feds in an effort to convict Trump? I also wondered whether federal prosecutors would accept Cohen's cooperation. Maybe they didn't "hate" Michael Cohen, but they had already rejected him as a cooperator. Could there be some kind of rapprochement? My head hurt from thinking about these complexities.

Finally, on Sunday evening, February 20, 2022, I had my telephone call with Alvin. It was the last time I spoke with him. Alvin started by saying that he was in "purgatory" about the Trump case, which I took to mean that he didn't want to drop the investigation but also didn't want to bring the case. He then asked for my thoughts about the impact of the applicable statutes of limitations, a sure signal that he was thinking about letting more time go by before making a final decision. Then Alvin brought up, very softly, the notion of referring the case to the feds. He asked whether we had considered this. I took from his question that the intermediary had successfully planted the idea of a federal referral, and I jumped on it. I went into a long riff that I had outlined in writing before our call. I said that I knew Alvin was not comfortable with authorizing the immediate prosecution of Trump (a gross understatement), so referring the investigation to the Justice Department would be the wisest course—a "win" for justice, for the case, for the district attorney's office, and for Alvin personally.

I elaborated on each of these ideas. For justice, it was much better for the feds to take on the investigation than for the case to die a slow death within our office. I think I mentioned an editorial that had appeared in that day's *Washington Post*, titled "Prosecuting Trump Would Set a Risky Precedent. Not Prosecuting Would Be Worse," a title I thought applied perfectly to our case.

For the case, federal prosecution would be a godsend. There was a better statute, a longer limitations period, the certainty of getting a "willful blindness" charge, the investigative ability of the FBI, and nationwide service of process. (Something that I did not mention to Alvin was that the federal prosecutors who would handle the matter surely would be "all-stars," with years of experience in handling complicated financial prosecutions.)

For the district attorney's office, shifting the investigation to the United States attorney would free up resources and allow the team to focus on prosecuting the case we already had brought against Weisselberg and the Trump Organization. There would be no more debates about whether to prosecute Trump.

For Alvin personally, I said that a decision not to bring charges would provoke my departure, which he surely knew already. Although I did not speak for Carey Dunne, I predicted that he also would resign. I said that the press would learn of these resignations very quickly, and the *New York Times* already was working on a story about the pause in grand jury proceedings. If the press also learned that Cy Vance had reached a different judgment and had directed the team to press charges against Trump, the result would be a public "hue and cry" that would not be good for the office or for Alvin. Alvin said that he had not put that chronology together.

I went on to say that, by referring the case to the Justice Department, the whole narrative would change. Alvin would be perceived as taking the unusual step of "giving up" the case because the federal authorities had better legal tools to deal with it. It would be a statesmanlike decision made in the public interest. It also would be a decision that the whole team would welcome.

After I made this pitch, we spoke briefly about the possible reaction of Damian Williams, the United States attorney. Alvin said he knew Damian and had attended his swearing-in. Alvin commented that Merrick Garland also had attended, and Garland had spoken very warmly about Damian at that event, making it clear that they had a close relationship. I urged Alvin to call Damian as soon as possible. He responded that he was not schooled in the protocol for such matters, but it sounded to me like he would reach out to Damian soon. He also said he would be calling Cy Vance to get his views. I was stunned by that remark, amazed that he had not yet spoken to Cy about the charging decision. When I later mentioned this part of the conversation to my wife, she erupted, asking me, "Are you kidding? What the hell has he been waiting for?"

Although this was the last time I spoke with Alvin, and we had completely different opinions about whether to bring charges against Trump, it was not an angry conversation. There was never any yelling or screaming; in fact, it was a cordial discussion. I had learned over a long career that angry conversation rarely persuades anyone. After practicing law for forty-five years, I could recall only one incident when I had screamed at another lawyer. (That had occurred during a deposition when opposing counsel insulted my younger colleague by addressing her as "little lady." I am not proud of my reaction, which was to ask him why he had to be such an "asshole." The conversation degenerated from there.)

After my call with Alvin, I spoke with Carey to bring him up to date and to suggest that he give Cy a call to tell him that Alvin would be calling him.

I had now thrown my last Hail Mary pass, and there was nothing left to do. The next day was Presidents' Day. Americans are supposed to honor and celebrate the men (all men, regrettably) who have served as the country's leader, and reflect on their patriotism and accomplishments. There was no celebration in my house. I commiserated with my wife, who had lived through the last year with me, with all its ups and downs. She knew, and I knew, that my tenure as a prosecutor was likely coming to an end in a day or two.

CHAPTER TWENTY-ONE

LEAVING DANY

After the Presidents' Day holiday, I spoke to Carey about his most recent conversation with Alvin. It had been teed up as the call in which Alvin would disclose what he had decided, after sleeping on the decision one more time. Carey told me that there had been no discussion of a possible referral to the feds. It seemed that Alvin did not want to give up the case because he wanted to preserve a possible future prosecution. So my Hail Mary pass, and the effort to persuade Alvin to throw a lateral to the feds, had fallen incomplete. Carey also told me that Alvin had spoken with Cy, but the conversation had been pointless; Alvin apparently told Cy he was not even sure why he had called.

Carey then relayed the news that I knew was coming but that nevertheless felt like a punch in the stomach. Alvin had told Carey that he still had not reached a *final* final decision. But he had decided that he would not authorize a prosecution on the facts we had developed. He wanted to "wait and see" how future events unfolded.

For me, this was the end of the line. I already had told Alvin that I was not going to stay on just to "kick the can down the road." We had made it crystal clear that the case was ready for an up-or-down decision. The entire team had agreed on this point. Everyone wanted a decision, and everyone thought that we had developed the facts to the point that a decision could and should be made. No one had pushed back on the timing for a decision or suggested that it was premature to decide whether to ask a grand jury to indict. A decision to "wait and see" was simply a decision not to bring charges, with no expectation that there would be a different decision in a month, or in six months, or in a year, or ever. I could continue to work on the case, hoping that one day we might catch some unanticipated "break," or that one day Alvin and his team of advisors might reach a different decision. But I was not even a member of that team. Ironically, Carey and I were now the "former guys," whose judgment had been rejected. I had promised myself and my wife that I would not just hang around hoping for a change of heart. As I had told Alvin in our first conversation, the team did not need my help in order *not* to make a case. The new team could manage that task all on its own.

That night I drafted a resignation letter. I did not draft it for publication, but I wanted it to be accurate, direct, and thoughtful. I laid out my reasons for leaving the case without either overstating my differences or pulling my punches about why I disagreed with Alvin's decision:

Dear Alvin,

    I write to tender my resignation as a special assistant district attorney and to explain my reasons for resigning.

    As you know from our recent conversations and presentations, I believe that Donald Trump is guilty of numerous felony violations of the Penal Law in connection with the preparation and use of his annual Statements of Financial Condition. His financial statements were false, and he has a long history of fabricating information relating to his

personal finances and lying about his assets to banks, the
national media, counterparties, and many others, including
the American people. The team that has been investigating
Mr. Trump harbors no doubt about whether he committed
crimes—he did.

In late 2021, then–district attorney Cyrus Vance
directed a thorough review of the facts and law relating
to Mr. Trump's financial statements. Mr. Vance had been
intimately involved in our investigation, attending grand
jury presentations, sitting in on certain witness interviews, and receiving regular reports about the progress of
the investigation. He concluded that the facts warranted
prosecution, and he directed the team to present evidence
to a grand jury and to seek an indictment of Mr. Trump and
other defendants as soon as reasonably possible.

This work was underway when you took office as district
attorney. You have devoted significant time and energy
to understanding the evidence we have accumulated with
respect to the Trump financial statements, as well as the
applicable law. You have reached the decision not to go
forward with the grand jury presentation and not to seek
criminal charges at the present time. The investigation has
been suspended indefinitely. Of course, that is your decision
to make. I do not question your authority to make it, and I
accept that you have made it sincerely. However, a decision
made in good faith may nevertheless be wrong. I believe
that your decision not to prosecute Donald Trump now,
and on the existing record, is misguided and completely
contrary to the public interest. I therefore cannot continue
in my current position.

In my view, the public interest warrants the criminal
prosecution of Mr. Trump, and such a prosecution should

be brought without any further delay. Because of the complexity of the facts, the refusal of Mr. Trump and the Trump Organization to cooperate with our investigation, and their affirmative steps to frustrate our ability to follow the facts, this investigation has already consumed a great deal of time. As to Mr. Trump, the great bulk of the evidence relates to his management of the Trump Organization before he became President of the United States. These facts are already dated, and our ability to establish what happened may erode with the further passage of time. Many of the salient facts have been made public in proceedings brought by the Office of the Attorney General, and the public has rightly inquired about the pace of our investigation. Most importantly, the further passage of time will raise additional questions about the failure to hold Mr. Trump accountable for his criminal conduct.

To the extent you have raised issues as to the legal and factual sufficiency of our case and the likelihood that a prosecution would succeed, I and others have advised you that we have evidence sufficient to establish Mr. Trump's guilt beyond a reasonable doubt, and we believe that the prosecution would prevail if charges were brought and the matter were tried to an impartial jury. No case is perfect. Whatever the risks of bringing the case may be, I am convinced that a failure to prosecute will pose much greater risks in terms of public confidence in the fair administration of justice. As I have suggested to you, respect for the rule of law, and the need to reinforce the bedrock proposition that "no man is above the law," require that this prosecution be brought even if a conviction is not certain.

I also do not believe that suspending the investigation pending future developments will lead to a stronger case or dispel your reluctance to bring charges. No events are likely to occur that will alter the nature of the case or dramatically change the quality or quantity of the evidence available to the prosecution. There are always additional facts to be pursued. But the investigative team that has been working on this matter for many months does not believe that it makes law enforcement sense to postpone a prosecution in the hope that additional evidence will somehow emerge. On the contrary, I and others believe that your decision not to authorize prosecution now will doom any future prospects that Mr. Trump will be prosecuted for the criminal conduct we have been investigating.

I fear that your decision means that Mr. Trump will not be held fully accountable for his crimes. I have worked too hard as a lawyer, and for too long, now to become a passive participant in what I believe to be a grave failure of justice. I therefore resign from my position as a special assistant district attorney, effective immediately.

Sincerely,

Mark F. Pomerantz

The following morning, before transmitting my resignation letter, I had a long Zoom call with the lawyers on the team. I thanked them for their hard work and effort and assured them that it had not been in vain. I read them my resignation letter and asked the team members to tell me if anyone disagreed with the two points in the letter that referenced the agreement of the entire team: (1) Trump was guilty of crimes, and (2) there was no good law enforcement reason to postpone a decision whether to prosecute. There was no disagreement. I later spoke with most of the team members individually to wish them well and to say good-bye.

When the team Zoom call was done, I pressed SEND on the letter to Alvin. Later that day, I was walking the dog, having promised her that I would now be taking her on longer and more frequent excursions. I got a call from Carey, who had decided to send his own resignation letter.

Later, Carey told me that when he arrived at his office earlier in the day, Alvin had been waiting outside. He was somber. He asked Carey not to resign, but Carey already had done so. Carey asked Alvin if he had spoken to me about my resignation and suggested that it would be a good thing if he called. Alvin did not call, that day or ever.

That afternoon I spoke with Cy Vance, to let him know that I had resigned and also to thank him for having given me the opportunity to work on such an incredibly important matter. Cy was gracious as always, reminding me that we had accomplished a great deal, especially for a local prosecutor's office. I agreed that we had done important work, but we both knew that much more important work could have been done. Once again, Donald Trump had managed to dance between the raindrops of accountability.

CHAPTER TWENTY-TWO

WHAT HAPPENED?

After Carey and I resigned, the media covered our departure extensively. The *New York Times* did a long piece on the events that led to our departure, and eventually published my resignation letter. I got phone calls, emails, and a stream of requests to do live appearances on radio and television, all of which I declined. Most of the feedback was positive; some was not. One email read simply, "Sayonara, you piece of shit."

Hundreds of people made comments in the newspaper and tweeted about Alvin's decision and our resignations. Many of the comments and tweets suggested that Alvin's decision had been corrupt and urged that he be investigated for refusing to prosecute Donald Trump. The suggestions that Alvin had acted in bad faith were ridiculous, and I am sure there will never be a shred of fact to support them. The people who accused Alvin of corruption or bribery had no clue about how these prosecutorial decisions are made or were bloodthirsty for some action against Trump. If they could not get that, they wanted the scalp of the guy who let him off. But, baseless though these suggestions were, they reflected a deep cynicism about how the criminal justice system works, especially when it confronts political actors. The comments represented to me a growing lack of public confidence in the rule of law. The people who insinuated that Alvin was corrupt viewed his decision as proof that prosecutors could be "bought," and that it was foolish to expect rich and powerful people to be treated the same as everyone else. The cynicism was disturbing, because we had missed an opportunity to push back against it by showing that well-founded charges could be brought even against a former president. The missed opportunity seemed cruelly ironic to me, because much of the cynicism has been fueled by Donald Trump himself. By politicizing the Department of Justice, pardoning political cronies for their crimes, and in countless other large and small ways, Trump has weakened public confidence in the rule of law, and fueled doubt about the integrity of the legal system.

Of course, after leaving the investigation, I spent many hours wondering to myself why things had gone the way they had. What happened? Why had I and other serious and experienced lawyers, including Cy Vance and Carey Dunne, been convinced that we should bring a criminal case against Donald Trump, while other serious and experienced lawyers had reached the opposite conclusion? Did some of us see the case as strong while others thought it too weak? Was it as simple as some people seeing a glass of water as half full, while others see the same glass as half empty?

Here are my thoughts about it, with the caveat that I don't really know why Alvin reached the decision that he did. He never shared his thinking with me or spoke to me about why he decided not to prosecute on the record we had built. He did not have to do that, but it would have been the right thing to do in light of the effort I and others had put into the investigation. I wish he had.

In any case, I am not sure that we had vastly different views about the strength of the case against Donald Trump.

The odds of winning or losing a case cannot be quantified with certainty. There are no formulas or algorithms that tell lawyers that they have a 47 percent or an 84 percent chance of winning a case that they will try years down the road before a jury of unknown people. At the margins, lawyers can agree whether a case is a "slam dunk" or, conversely, a "dead bang loser" for one side or the other. Even at the margins, mistakes are made. Most lawyers who have tried a lot of cases can point to "unwinnable" cases that they won, or "slam dunk" winners that they lost.

I suspect that Alvin and his advisors saw the case against Trump in much the same terms that Carey, Cy, and I saw it: it was by no means a certain winner, but it was far from hopeless. It was somewhere in between, in that large gray area in which one finds most of the cases that get tried to verdict. I personally thought that the odds of obtaining a conviction were significantly better than 50/50, perhaps in the neighborhood of 70/30 or so. But this is a meaningless number, because nobody can "handicap" a case with precision. Experienced lawyers speak not in terms of numbers, but with adjectives—a case is "weak" or "strong," or "triable" for both sides if either side might prevail assuming that the evidence comes in as expected. I thought the case against Trump was "triable" for the prosecution and the defense. In my mind, the trove of evidence showing that Trump's financial statements had overvalued his assets, year after year and in large amounts, would eventually overwhelm the defense. Interestingly, neither Alvin nor his advisors ever took issue with the strength of the evidence showing that Trump's assets had been valued falsely, and that was the heart of our case.

To the extent that we did evaluate the case differently, what then accounts for the differing views? It is an impossible question to answer with certainty, but here are some educated guesses:

First, we had different levels of familiarity with the evidence. Those of us who wanted to proceed knew the case inside and out. We had met the witnesses and lived with the documents. The financial statements, and the backup to the SOFCs, were like old friends to me; I had reviewed different pieces of them hundreds of times and could recall many of the numbers by heart. I had spent many hours speaking with Michael Cohen and Donald Bender, who both would have been important trial witnesses in the case I wanted to bring. I felt I knew their strengths and weaknesses and understood what made them tick. It was impossible to download this familiarity in a series of Zoom meetings.

Second, we all fall prey to confirmation bias. We interpret information in a way that supports our different interests, hopes, and fears. Alvin was at the beginning of his first term as district attorney. Though the stakes were high for all of us, they were perhaps higher for him than for anyone else. If we brought the case and lost it, the loss might have defined and ruined his tenure as district attorney. Such uniquely high stakes can lead people to see issues and problems around every corner. He may have put the case under a powerful microscope that he would not otherwise have used, and under that microscope every flaw or imperfection may have become magnified. Every case is imperfect, and the imperfections may have loomed particularly large to Alvin because he may have thought he could not afford to make a mistake.

One could also turn this argument around the other way. The district attorney, and only the district attorney, bears the burden of being the ultimate decision maker, and his job is to apply exacting scrutiny to the cases he brings. The rest of us, me included, were sitting in the "cheap seats," where the view of everything is not quite as good. Indeed, Alvin may have thought that some of us, and perhaps me most of all, had become Captain Ahabs in search of Donald Trump as the "great white whale" of criminal defendants, and that we had lost our perspective and our ability to read the facts accurately because we so wanted to bag this target of a lifetime. Maybe Alvin believed that, after investing so much time and effort, we had lost the ability to weigh the facts dispassionately, particularly as to a person whose politics we reviled. I don't think that this is what happened. I would like to believe that I had the professional experience, training, judgment, and familiarity with high-profile cases to evaluate the facts correctly, but none of us is a perfect judge of our own critical thinking.

However we all viewed the facts, and whatever biases and different viewpoints we all brought to the table in gauging the strength or weakness of the case against Donald Trump, I think Alvin made the wrong decision for a different reason. He erred not because he misperceived the strength of the case, but because he failed to recognize that the case had to be brought to vindicate the rule of law, and to demonstrate to the public that no one can hold himself above the law.

Prosecutors have discretion about which cases they bring. They do not have to bring every case in which they have evidence that a person is guilty of a crime. Indeed, even if the evidence against a particular person is overwhelming, there is no obligation to prosecute. If the interests of justice would not be served by a prosecution, prosecutors are free not to prosecute even the most guilty of defendants. A defendant may be unusually sympathetic or suffer from a terminal illness and pose no threat to society, or a prosecution might jeopardize national security, or frustrate a larger investigation, or conflict with other priorities and interests. There are many compelling reasons not to bring particular cases.

By the same token, prosecutors are free to bring a case that is in the interests of justice even if a conviction is highly uncertain. Of course, this does not mean that prosecutors can go after people they know to be innocent, or as to whom there is little or no evidence. Under standards put forward by the American Bar Association, a prosecutor's office should not file charges against a person it believes to be innocent, no matter how much evidence it may have. But if it believes a person to be guilty, it can charge that person with a crime if the charges are supported by "probable cause" and the evidence is legally "sufficient" to support conviction beyond a reasonable doubt.

In discussing the case against Donald Trump, none of the prosecutors who heard the evidence claimed to believe that he was innocent. On the contrary, when I resigned from the district attorney's office I asked the investigative team whether I could say in my resignation letter that the entire team believed him to be guilty, and there was no dissent. Nor did Alvin or anyone advising him ever voice the belief that Trump was innocent. I also believe that the proof we gathered provided ample "probable cause" to believe that Trump had committed crimes in connection with the false financial statements, and that our evidence would have been legally sufficient to support a guilty verdict.

Importantly, evidence can be "legally sufficient" to support a guilty verdict even if a prosecutor thinks that a jury will vote to acquit the defendant. "Legally sufficient" evidence is proof on which a reasonable jury *may* base a guilty verdict, not so much evidence that a jury *must* convict the defendant if it is doing its job. The sufficiency of evidence is a question of law, not a measure of the likelihood of conviction.

In plain English, what all of this means is that Alvin Bragg could have decided to authorize the case against Donald Trump even if he thought we might lose it. The federal guidelines about the exercise of prosecutorial discretion, contained in a document called "Principles of Federal Prosecution," make this crystal clear. They say that "the likelihood of an acquittal due to the unpopularity of some aspect of the prosecution or because of the overwhelming popularity of the defendant or his/her cause is not a factor prohibiting prosecution. For example, in . . . a case involving an extremely popular political figure, it may be clear that the evidence of guilt—viewed objectively by an unbiased factfinder—would be sufficient to obtain and sustain a conviction, yet the prosecutor might reasonably doubt, based on the circumstances, that the jury would convict. In such a case, despite his/her negative assessment of the likelihood of a guilty verdict . . . the prosecutor may properly conclude that it is necessary . . . to commence or recommend prosecution. . . ." These are federal guidelines, but state prosecutors typically follow the same principles.

To be clear, I thought we would win the case against Trump, but Alvin was free to bring the case even if he disagreed with that judgment and thought it was likely that we would lose the case. Should he have done so? Asking the question differently, should a prosecutor bring cases where an acquittal is not only possible, but likely? Are there circumstances in which a prosecutor should charge someone with a crime even if the case may be "unwinnable"? Conversely, are there circumstances in which a prosecutor should refrain from charging a defendant even if there is a legitimate case to be brought?

There are no hard-and-fast rules for deciding these issues, and there are several competing considerations. Again, I don't know what actually went into Alvin's calculus, since he did not tell me. But he may have believed that it would have been imprudent to go forward if there was a big risk of losing the case. He could have thought that an acquittal in a case against a former president would be catastrophic for the district attorney's office and for public respect for the rule of law. He may have feared that it would be irresponsible to risk an acquittal in such a high-profile and consequential matter, and that a loss would reinforce Trump's claims that the prosecution had been a "witch hunt" and a political vendetta, perhaps even adding to Trump's quest for political power. He may have agreed with the view that to prosecute a former president you should have proof of guilt that is not only "beyond a reasonable doubt," but *way beyond* a reasonable doubt. The *Wall Street Journal* recently put it this way: "The evidence should be so compelling that it persuades fair-minded Republicans, not merely MSNBC or CNN anchors."

I do not share this view. In my mind, the same evidentiary standard should apply to presidents and paupers alike. Requiring prosecutors to produce an extra helping of evidence because of Trump's political popularity and support would create a double standard, and inject politics into the charging decision, not remove it. And what of the politically powerless person, perhaps someone loathed by the entire community? Should we require a lesser quantum of evidence to charge that person, because everyone—including all of the television anchors at all of the networks—would applaud the bringing of charges?

When I left DANY, we believed that Trump committed serious crimes over many years, and we had evidence on which a jury could have found him guilty. The failure to bring charges in these circumstances reinforced public skepticism about our ability to apply the rule of law to rich and powerful people. It suggested to the public that Trump was correct when he boasted that he could shoot somebody on Fifth Avenue in Manhattan and not lose voters—that he had virtual impunity and would never be found guilty of anything.

If anything, the fact that Trump had been president of the United States might have been a reason to be more aggressive about prosecuting him, not less. People who seek high public office, and who are successful in representing the public, have to be held to a higher standard in their private business dealings, not a lower one. Their crimes tear at public confidence in our government; they rip the social fabric more deeply than the anonymous wrongdoer.

Of course, no lawyer likes to contemplate losing any case, let alone a "once in a lifetime" criminal case. Losing the Trump case would be a ghastly outcome. But I thought, and still think, that not bringing the case was an even more ghastly outcome in terms of our obligation to enforce the law. I thought we owed it to the public to bring the case to trial. While I thought we would win it, I also thought that losing it would be better than not even trying.

The argument to the contrary is not foolish or irresponsible. Pundits have observed that half the country believes in Trump, and that charging him would fuel their resentment, convince them that he is being persecuted, and risk political violence and perhaps even the breakdown of the democratic system. Trump's supporters would believe that charging him was a perversion of the rule of law, and a failed prosecution would fuel the perception that the prosecution was an unjustified act of partisan warfare. On this view, bringing a prosecution that "misses" would create an intolerable political risk.

Arguments like this put me at a loss. I am a lawyer, not a politician, historian, philosopher, or social engineer. As a law-yer, I think in terms of doing justice and following the legal and ethical rules that are supposed to guide our decisions. I have no special expertise in weighing the political impact of a prosecu-tion. Considering the political impact of bringing a case, or of not bringing a case, puts me in unfamiliar territory. If we are to consider the destructive impact of a failed prosecution, are we also free to consider the impact of a successful prosecution on Trump's political future? Such thinking is dangerous for a prosecutor. Prosecutors have no special competence to weigh conflicting political belief systems, and they have the duty to enforce the law without regard to competing political crosscur-rents. Once prosecutors start handicapping the historical and political impact of their decisions, they start forfeiting their own legitimacy, and eroding confidence in the rule of law that is supposed to be their touchstone.

I understand that trying to do justice is not the only thing that matters in our deeply divided country, and justice is an elusive concept. The decision whether to prosecute anyone, including a former president, of course involves weighing the risk of losing the case. But the decision ultimately should rest on right and wrong, the law, and the need for evenhanded law enforcement. We do our work in courts of law, not the courts of public opinion. Under our system, other actors make po-litical judgments, like whether to grant pardons or to render judgments of impeachment. Prosecutors do not make such judgments; they enforce the law and make legal judgments ac-cording to established principles that should apply equally to princes and paupers alike.

I concede that a failed prosecution of Donald Trump could foster the belief that the prosecution was motivated by politics, and result in an erosion of public confidence in the rule of law.

But even a successful prosecution would be viewed by many as an act of political warfare rather than a legitimate law enforcement action. I do not think we can allow unfounded cynicism about charging decisions to deter us from making proper decisions in the first place. Half the population might come to the belief that the earth is flat; that ought not lead to a change in our mapmaking practices.

The best remedy for cynicism about political charging decisions is to make charging decisions that are not motivated by politics, and to explain those decisions publicly, not to avoid making them entirely. In the Trump case, the risk of eroding public confidence by bringing and losing the case had to be weighed against the erosion of public confidence by failing to bring charges that were justified by the law and the facts. People can assign different weights to these conflicting risks, but for me the right answer was to apply the time-honored standards that should shape a prosecutor's decision: Did the defendant commit serious crimes? Is the evidence sufficient to establish guilt beyond a reasonable doubt? Is it likely (even if not certain) that a jury would convict? If the answer to these questions is "yes," the case should be brought absent a compelling reason to decline prosecution. The job is to enforce the law when criminal charges are appropriate, not to speculate whether the world will be a better or safer place if no prosecution is brought.

I am not sure what thinking Alvin did about these issues, if any. He may have just disagreed about the merits of the case or have been fearful about losing it. But I am prepared to give him the benefit of the doubt in at least one respect. I did not get the sense that he based his decision on political expedience, which of course would have been wrong. The politically expedient thing to have done might have been to charge Donald Trump in early 2022 and worry later—perhaps years later—about a possible verdict, claiming victory if there was a conviction and perhaps even blaming a loss on a decision made by Cy Vance on his way out the door.

Maybe, though, "politics" was a factor in a different sense. Like all elected prosecutors, Alvin Bragg is a political actor. He cared deeply about his progressive agenda. Perhaps he did not want his entire tenure, legacy, and political future defined by this single prosecution. I would like to think that this was not on his mind, but people are people. Arguments like this can easily be turned around on the person making them. Some might believe I was a lawyer at the end of my career, and I wanted one more turn under the bright lights, a final "coda" as a prosecutor. Was I willing to bring a case I would have steered away from earlier in my life? I don't think so—I never was a lawyer who sought out the bright lights in my high-profile cases. I wanted the Trump case brought because I thought a prosecution was necessary to serve the public interest. I was proud of my role in the investigation, but I never felt that it was about me.

All I know for sure is that the investigation turned into the legal equivalent of a plane crash. Trump was not charged, and naturally he claimed vindication when news broke about Alvin's decision. Carey and I left the district attorney's office, Alvin was heavily criticized, and many members of the public were disappointed, angry, and suspicious about what had happened. Most plane crashes have more than a single cause, and this one also may have had multiple causes. The biggest one, in my opinion, was "pilot error." Alvin made the wrong decision about whether to charge the case, but I won't belabor that further. If you think he made the right decision, I salute your willingness to keep reading this book.

"Pilot error" aside, there were other causes that contributed to the crash of the investigation. Fundamentally, the case always should have been investigated by the Department of Justice, not the Manhattan district attorney's office. The legal advantages of federal prosecution that I spoke about in my final conversation with Alvin were all real and important. I am convinced that a federal investigation into Trump's financial statements would have turned out differently. Why the feds never took on the investigation, either at the beginning or later, is a question I cannot answer.

Another cause of the "plane crash" was the process by which the new management team became involved in the investigation. In my view, it was both rushed and bungled. The factual complexity of the SOFC investigation was mind-boggling, and the new team—especially the incoming district attorney— could and should have started learning the case months earlier. Before he took office we had gotten a court order allowing us to share information, including grand jury information, with Alvin Bragg and several members of his transition team. Alvin knew since he won the Democratic primary election in June 2021 that he would be the new district attorney on January 1, 2022. He surely knew, or easily could have found out, that the Trump case would be sitting on the launching pad when he arrived. I believe he waited too long to get his arms around the case, and there was too much to absorb in a very compressed time period. He jumped into very deep water, and immediately was in over his head.

Timing aside, Alvin never tried to forge any kind of personal relationship with me or Carey, notwithstanding our experience and our long work on the investigation. I never had a one-on-one meeting with Alvin, and I never set foot into his office. We had two telephone conversations; the rest of our dealings were by email or via Zoom meetings. Reading in the newspaper that

I would be "retained" when Alvin became district attorney was not a very good way for us to get to know each other.

It is also unfortunate that the new administration immediately became involved in controversy over the "first-day memo" laying out the district attorney's progressive law enforcement agenda. It's not my purpose to criticize that agenda, but as Alvin later conceded, its public rollout was mishandled; the resulting criticism and repair effort became a distraction. In order to make a sound and prompt decision on the Trump investigation, Alvin needed to "hit the ground running" when he became district attorney. Instead, he landed with a thud.

I have also thought about my role in the "plane crash." Carey and I put a lot of pressure on the new administration by pushing for a speedy resolution. Did we make a mistake thinking that Alvin would plainly see the merits of the case, particularly since we knew the case had attracted "conscientious objectors" even among some colleagues in the district attorney's office? In retrospect, we were too blithe in our assumption that Alvin and the new team would see the case the same way we did.

Still, there were legitimate reasons we wanted a prompt decision. As had been publicly reported, a grand jury with a limited term had begun to hear evidence. If we were going forward with a prosecution, it was important for legal reasons to finish presenting the facts to the same grand jury that had started to hear them. Also, the entire team wanted to know whether we were going to be seeking an indictment. We were leaning hard on the throttle because time was of the essence.

I also have asked myself whether we quit rashly or prematurely. Given the stakes, should we have opted in favor of "the long game"? Should we have tried to cultivate more of a relationship with Alvin and the new regime? Maybe, with the advantage of hindsight, we did too much Zooming and not enough schmoozing. In my own defense, I thought it was important and in the public interest to go forward as quickly as possible. It was not a friendly environment. Alvin and the new team were not looking for camaraderie. They made no effort to build any sort of professional relationship, which might have promoted some trust and confidence. They wanted the facts and the law, so that's what we gave them. When they rejected our conclusions, it was time to leave.

Many people criticized Cy Vance for not having indicted Donald Trump before he left office at the end of December 2021. If we had had a better crystal ball, of course we would have charted a different course. But Cy had been pushing us to finish the investigation for months. The whole investigation had been delayed by Trump's stalling tactics, including two trips to the Supreme Court. Cy wanted no foot-dragging, and we were working as quickly as we could, even to the point of incipient mutiny from the team over the pace of the investigation. I do not think we could have worked much faster with the resources we had. In any case, our crystal ball malfunctioned. We all believed that the new regime would agree with our conclusions and would promptly authorize us to proceed with the charges. It did not work out that way.

CHAPTER TWENTY-THREE

NOW WHAT?

What happens now?

In September 2022, New York State attorney general Letitia James brought her civil fraud case against Donald Trump and the Trump Organization. That case brings out into the open many of the facts and events we were investigating in the district attorney's office. The attorney general's lengthy complaint lays bare the details of the fraud; it recites how Trump's financial statements were massively and routinely falsified. It also explains their use to deceive banks, insurers, and others over many years.

For me, reading the attorney general's complaint was gratifying but frustrating. It was gratifying because the complaint is chock-full of facts that, if proved, establish that Trump and his confederates intentionally and repeatedly broke the law. Some of the details involved facts that I helped to develop; other details were new to me. But, with all the details pulled together and made public in the complaint, the strength of the evidence is undeniable. If the facts alleged in the complaint are accurate (and there is no reason to doubt their accuracy), then Trump surely committed the crimes I believe DANY should have charged, including the falsification of business records and the issuance of false financial statements. Put simply, Cy Vance, Carey Dunne, and I were correct in believing that there was a strong case to be made against Donald Trump. If Alvin Bragg thought that the evidence of Trump's culpability was too weak to warrant prosecution, the facts laid out in the attorney general's complaint show that he was wrong.

The judge presiding over the attorney general's case, after reviewing just some of the evidence described in the complaint, issued an opinion in early November 2022. The opinion referenced the complaint's "comprehensive demonstration of persistent fraud," and noted that the defendants had "failed to submit an iota" of contrary evidence. Given what he termed "the persistent misrepresentations throughout every one of" Trump's SOFCs, the judge restrained the transfer of Trump's assets and ordered that a monitor be appointed "to ensure there is no further fraud or illegality" attending Trump's financial disclosures.

While it was gratifying to read the complaint (and the judge's opinion), it was frustrating that the fraud was charged only as a civil case. The civil case will take a long time to litigate and will likely end in some negotiated settlement. In any case, a civil judgment is a pale substitute for a criminal conviction. A conviction represents society's pronouncement that a defendant engaged in criminal conduct. It amounts to a public declaration and finding of guilt, and cannot easily be dismissed as a compromise or a business decision. A conviction can lead to imprisonment, and has a gravitas, and a significance, that a civil resolution lacks.

When she announced her civil case, Letitia James also announced that the facts "plausibly" violated federal law, and she therefore referred her factual findings to the United States attorney for the Southern District of New York. This, of course, was what I had urged Alvin Bragg to do shortly before I resigned from DANY. Will James's criminal referral prompt a federal investigation or prosecution based on Trump's fraudulent financial statements? I doubt it. The United States attorney has long been aware of many of the underlying facts. Indeed, the feds considered whether to investigate Trump's financial statements right after Carey Dunne and I resigned from DANY. I don't know for certain whether the United States attorney took any steps at that time, but nothing happened publicly to suggest that the feds began an active investigation. The attorney general's public "referral" of her findings to the United States attorney is a new development, and some of the complaint's factual allegations may be new, but I would be surprised if the United States attorney now decides to take action given his previous inaction. I hope I am wrong about this, but time will tell.

Interestingly, the attorney general referred the "plausibl[e]" violations of federal criminal law to the United States attorney but made no criminal referral of the state law violations that she alleged in her complaint. Presumably, James made no "referral" of state crimes because Alvin Bragg and DANY are already conducting a "continuing" and "active" criminal investigation.

This, at least, is what Alvin is telling the public. Alvin has made several public statements referencing a "continuing" investigation of Donald Trump, including a statement made right after the attorney general filed her complaint. As of this writing, I don't know in what respect DANY's investigation of Donald Trump may be "continuing." The investigation of Trump's financial statements seems to have died. Nothing has happened to move the case forward that has been reported publicly. New discussions with Trump's accountants, bankers, or other witnesses likely would have become known to the press, but few such discussions appear to have taken place. No one has reached out to me with any questions about all the work that was done previously; I am persona non grata in the district attorney's office. Michael Cohen has said he will no longer cooperate with that office.

Most recently, DANY has suggested that it may move forward with the "zombie" case. Alvin Bragg may pursue charges that Trump falsified business records to conceal the hush money payment to Stephanie Clifford. As of this writing, I do not know if DANY actually intends to bring this case. If so, the prosecutors will have to mend fences with Michael Cohen, as I believe he would be an indispensable witness in such a case. He could be compelled to testify, but trying to convict Donald Trump by using Michael Cohen as a reluctant or hostile witness is a recipe for disaster. DANY also would have to overcome the legal problem I described back in chapter three: Falsifying business records is only a misdemeanor unless the defendant intended to use the false records to commit or conceal "another crime." The statutory language—"another crime"—may or may not include a *federal* crime. So far as I know, there is no eligible state crime that Trump or Cohen intended to conceal by falsifying the hush money payment or reimbursement records. So, if DANY does resurrect and bring the "zombie" case, it will run the risk that the charge will be reduced to a misdemeanor before a jury even hears it.

If the "zombie" case is the only case that DANY brings against Trump, notwithstanding the trove of evidence that has now been made public about Trump's fraudulent financial statements, that would be a very peculiar and unsatisfying end to this whole saga. The more important prosecution, by far, was the criminal case that should have been brought to hold Trump accountable for the "persistent fraud" that permeated his financial statements. Nevertheless, I hope that DANY does pursue the "zombie" case. That case also involves serious criminal conduct, even though it pales in comparison to the financial statement fraud.

One way or the other, Alvin Bragg has pledged to tell the public when the Trump investigation is complete. Presumably this will happen at some point before Alvin completes his four-year term as Manhattan district attorney. He is eligible to stand for reelection in November 2025.

If DANY does not move forward with a prosecution, and if the United States attorney likewise takes no action, then almost certainly there will be no prosecution of Donald Trump for the crimes committed in connection with his financial statements. The only path forward would lie with the governor of New York. The governor has the legal authority to appoint a special prosecutor to bring the case against Trump. The governor also could give Attorney General Letitia James the ability to charge Trump with crimes. James already has investigated the facts and has alleged in her civil case that Trump committed criminal violations of New York State law; she has the resources to move forward quickly with a criminal case. But, notwithstanding her public pronouncements about Trump's crimes, James has made no request for the authority to prosecute him, and the governor has taken no action.

Unfortunately, financial statement fraud is neither the beginning nor the end of the criminal conduct that prosecutors have had to consider with respect to Donald Trump. On November 18, 2022, attorney general Merrick Garland decided to appoint a special counsel to investigate other potential criminal conduct by the former president, having to do with obstructing the lawful transfer of presidential power to Joe Biden and the presence of sensitive documents at Trump's Mar-a-Lago estate. Those matters are being handled by experienced federal prosecutors with resources and legal tools that should enable them to get to the bottom of the facts and make sound charging decisions. Of course, Trump has already labeled their efforts as "political" and a "witch hunt."

As for me, I was disappointed and sad when Alvin made the decision not to bring the SOFC fraud case against Donald Trump. But lawyers who have spent years doing criminal defense work learn not to let the rejection of one's legal position crush the spirit. I felt sad mainly for the people that Trump's misbehavior hurt along the way. Back in the spring of 2021 I had come across an article in the *Washington Post* about a small business owner who had sold Trump pianos for Trump's Taj Mahal casino in Atlantic City, New Jersey. The piano dealer had delivered the pianos, tuned and ready to go, without demanding payment in advance because he was dealing with Donald Trump, who had "lots of money." Trump stiffed him, and the piano dealer took a $30,000 hit that had hurt his family business very badly. There were many others with similar stories. They had not studied Trump's financial statements, so they were not "victims" of his fraud in the legal sense, but I viewed them as people who had been hurt nevertheless by Trump's decades-long deception about his great wealth and success in business. I was disappointed that those people would not see Trump held accountable for his financial lies.

Life goes on. I was not working for public praise or for the thrill of victory. I was working for the personal satisfaction of doing something worth doing. As I worked on the Trump investigation, usually sitting alone in my home office, I often thought back to my first job after law school. I was a law clerk in 1975–76 for Judge Edward Weinfeld. Judge Weinfeld was a wizened old man, who was written up as "the ideal judge"; many called him the best federal judge in the country. He had the appearance and demeanor of an Old Testament prophet. He arrived in chambers regularly at 4:30 a.m., usually working seven days a week, and when he was not on the bench he worked in quiet solitude at his little desk, looking out over the Brooklyn Bridge. He never thanked jurors (or, for that matter, his law clerks), and he never sought thanks for himself. He just did his job. His law clerks revered him, and he taught us that public service is not done for "thanks" or adulation or personal aggrandizement. It is done for the satisfaction that comes from doing what is right and making whatever contribution one can to the public good.

I believe very much in that philosophy, and like most of Judge Weinfeld's law clerks I have never forgotten the example he set for us. He kept working his entire life. I don't think I can emulate that, but working on the Trump investigation strengthened my resolve to keep working, and to keep trying to serve the public interest. Carey Dunne and I have started a new law firm, a not-for-profit venture that will litigate cases that protect the public and seek to stem the rising tide of authoritarianism in the United States. It looks like we will not have a problem keeping busy.

As for Donald Trump, he will go on screaming about "witch hunts," and branding anyone who criticizes him as "scum." He put out a statement calling me a "low-life lawyer," and he would surely describe me as a "loser." But no one gets everything he wants, and nobody wins every fight. That does not make somebody a "loser." A loser is someone who does not appreciate what he or she has, whether that is love, power, fame, or money. A loser keeps digging a bottomless pit, never satisfied, just looking for more and more.

As I finish writing this book, Donald Trump has announced that he will once again seek to become president of the United States. For him, as his niece has written, "too much" is still "never enough." At some point, prosecutors will sit in a room at the Department of Justice to decide whether to charge Trump for crimes—perhaps including his role in stirring up the January 6 insurrection, conspiring to obstruct the lawful transfer of presidential power, or mishandling government information. Will those prosecutors give the proper weight to the need to maintain confidence in the rule of law? Will the risk of failure or the fear of political damage cloud their judgment? I don't know, but I hope they will reflect on some of the things I have written about in this book. When it comes to Donald Trump, there are millions and millions of Americans who are still waiting for just a "little piece of justice."

AUTHOR'S NOTE

Under New York law, prosecutors cannot legally disclose grand jury material. I kept this prohibition in mind as I wrote this book and got some legal advice in order to make sure that my account of the investigation did not violate the grand jury secrecy requirement. That is why the book does not describe what happened when witnesses came before the grand jury. Also, some things happened in the investigation that were sealed by court order and therefore could not be made public.

The vast majority of the facts relating to our investigation did not involve grand jury material, and many of the facts I discuss in the book have now become public in the attorney general's lawsuit relating to Donald Trump's financial statements or in connection with the criminal case brought against Allen Weisselberg and the Trump Organization.

While the book does not disclose grand jury material, it does reveal what happened when we spoke to witnesses outside the grand jury room and when those of us working on the Trump investigation spoke to each other. Usually, material like this does not become public, except perhaps in stray bits or pieces as the result of media reporting or litigation. Prosecutors typically do not describe their work in detail. This is because public disclosure of what goes on in law enforcement investigations can compromise those investigations or the cases that result from them. Also, prosecutors usually do not talk about their investigations because they need to respect the interests of persons who are not ultimately charged with crimes.

I thought a lot about these issues before deciding to go forward with the book. I took comfort, first, from the knowledge that nothing I wrote in these pages would prejudice the case that was brought against Weisselberg and the Trump Organization. As of this writing, Allen Weisselberg has pleaded guilty to the crimes charged against him, which included scheme to defraud, conspiracy, grand larceny, criminal tax fraud, filing false instruments, and falsifying business records. The trial of the Trump Organization began on October 24, 2022, and was underway when this book went to press. At the trial, Weisselberg admitted that he received untaxed compensation from the Trump Organization, which saved money for the company as well. A verdict in the case will have been reached by the time this book is published. In any case, all of the facts underlying the case against the Trump Organization were produced to it in connection with the trial; nothing said in this book impacts that prosecution. The Trump Organization pleaded not guilty. Unless it was proven guilty at trial, it is presumed innocent; the charges against it are merely accusations.

As the year 2022 draws to a close, there has been no New York State criminal prosecution of Donald Trump. The "continuing investigation" that Alvin Bragg has referenced in his public statements may or may not end with a prosecution. In the event that any New York State criminal prosecution is brought against Trump, all the relevant documents and all the witness statements and expert materials will be produced to the defense long before trial, and this book will have no bearing on the litigation of that case. The same is true for any federal prosecution based on Trump's financial statements. In short, I am comfortable that this book will not prejudice any investigation or prosecution of Donald Trump.

Nor am I concerned that writing this book was somehow unfair to Donald Trump because the investigation did not result in his indictment. From the beginning, Trump lambasted DANY's investigation as political, claiming that we were conducting a "witch hunt" aimed at an innocent man, and that the prosecutors involved (me included) were "lowlifes," "racists," and political hacks. Given the statements that Trump made about this investigation and those investigating him— statements made by a former president who has access to a huge media platform and a very loud megaphone—it is in the public interest to tell the real story of the investigation, and to disclose what we were investigating and why no criminal case has yet been brought against Trump. The notion that it is somehow "unfair" to Trump to set the record straight is ridiculous. Simply put, the public has an abiding interest in knowing what actually happened.

I do have some angst about having described the inner dialogue of the investigation. Prosecutors do not usually "kiss and tell" about the work that they do, let alone share the details of internal conversations and emails. If asked, some "talking feds" will engage in pearl-clutching and opine that this kind of disclosure "just isn't done." This criticism is legitimate. Generally speaking, prosecutors should be able to share their thoughts with each other without fear of public scrutiny. I overcame my angst because the Trump investigation was in a class of its own. It attracted a huge amount of public attention; many people speculated publicly, and often incorrectly, about what we were doing and why we were doing it. The public debate about

Trump's conduct, his unique public status, the circumstances under which my work ended, and the extensive news coverage about the progress of the investigation convinced me that writing this book was appropriate and in the public interest. I hope that those who read it will have the same opinion.

NOTES AND REFERENCES

This book is based primarily on personal experience, as well as notes and emails from my work on the Trump investigation. Where excerpts from emails appear, I have quoted the language verbatim, but I have not cited the emails individually. Included below are references to some of the external sources mentioned in the text.

CHAPTER 1: OUTSIDE COUNSEL

9 *yearly rental income*: Russ Buettner, Susanne Craig, and Mike McIntire, "Long-Concealed Records Show Trump's Chronic Losses and Years of Tax Avoidance," *New York Times*, September 27, 2020.

14 *a series of articles*: Ibid. The *New York Times* published a series of articles, collectively titled "The President's Taxes," beginning with the cited article.

16 *Bloomberg had published a story*: Caleb Melby, "Trump's Perks for Weisselbergs Included Free Rent," *Bloomberg*, November 2, 2020.

CHAPTER 2: SWORN IN

22 *later called me a "never Trumper"*: Statement by Donald J. Trump, 45th President of the United States of America, *https://www.donaldtrump.com/news/news-4rvxhjeaba721*.

29 *reduced to twenty years*: See *United States v. Salerno*, 868 F.2d 524 (2d Cir. 1989).

31 *dispute boiled over onto the front page*: Benjamin Weiser, "2 Prosecutors, State and U.S., Fight Over Plea," *New York Times*, December 4, 1997.

CHAPTER 3: THE "ZOMBIE" CASE

36 *a 1973 memo*: Memorandum from Robert G. Dixon, Jr., Assistant Attorney General, Office of Legal Counsel, *Re: Amenability of the President, Vice President and other Civil Officers to Federal Criminal Prosecution while in Office* (Sept. 24, 1973).

36 *reaffirmed in 2000*: U.S. Department of Justice, Office of Legal Counsel, *A Sitting President's Amenability to Indictment and Criminal Prosecution* (2000), 24 Op. O.L.C. 222.

40 *processed each invoice for payment*: Though the checks to Cohen were booked as "legal expenses," there was no evidence that Trump or the Trump Organization treated them as items that would support a tax deduction.

46 *stop her "extortionist accusations"*: John Wagner, "Trump Acknowledges His Lawyer Was Reimbursed After Payment to Stormy Daniels," *Washington Post*, May 3, 2018.

CHAPTER 4: MEETING MICHAEL COHEN

47 *he would "take a bullet"*: Maggie Haberman, Sharon LaFraniere, and Danny Hakim, "Michael Cohen Has Said He Would Take a Bullet for Trump, Maybe Not Anymore," *New York Times*, April 20, 2018.

52 *the* Wall Street Journal *had broken*: Michael Rothfeld and Joe Palazzolo, "Trump Lawyer Arranged $130,000 Payment for Adult-Film Star's Silence," *Wall Street Journal*, January 12, 2018.

52 *she dutifully reported*: Maggie Haberman, "Michael D. Cohen, Trump's Longtime Lawyer, Says He Paid Stormy Daniels Out of His Own Pocket," *New York Times*, February 13, 2018.

54 *statement was videotaped*: Trump's statement was widely reported. See, e.g., Rebecca Ballhaus, and Joe Palazzolo, "Trump Denies Knowledge of $130,000 Payment to Stormy Daniels," *Wall Street Journal*, April 5, 2018.

54 *Rudy Giuliani admitted*: Rebecca Ballhaus, Michael Rothfeld, and Joe Palazzolo, "Giuliani Says Trump Repaid Cohen for Stormy Daniels Payment," *Wall Street Journal*, May 3, 2018.

CHAPTER 6: SCOTUS SPEAKS AT LAST

66 *which the* New York Times *described*: Adam Liptak, "Supreme Court Rules Trump Cannot Block Release of Financial Records," *New York Times*, July 9, 2020.

CHAPTER 8: ALLEN WEISSELBERG'S FREE APARTMENT

79 *called Michael Cohen a "rat"*: Trump's comment was widely reported. See, e.g., Isaac Stanley-Becker, "Calling Michael Cohen a 'Rat,' Trump Brings 'American Underworld' Lingo to the White House," *Washington Post*, December 17, 2018.

CHAPTER 9: DIVING INTO THE FINANCIAL STATEMENTS

91 *Cohen's book*: Michael A. Cohen, *Disloyal* (New York: Skyhorse Publishing, 2020).

CHAPTER 11: ENTERPRISE CORRUPTION

102 *who wrote a book*: Timothy L. O'Brien, *TrumpNation: The Art of Being the Donald* (New York: Warner Books, 2005).

109 *the* New York Times *ran an opinion piece*: Ralph Blumenthal, "Who Said It: Trump or Gotti?," *New York Times,* August 24, 2018.

111 *book of the same name*: Jesse Eisinger, *The Chickenshit Club* (New York: Simon & Schuster, 2017).

113 *He tweeted that he had paid*: Donald J. Trump (@realDonaldTrump), November 19, 2016.

113 *led to a tweet complaining*: D'Angelo Gore, "Trump Spins Court Ruling on Trump Foundation," *FactCheck.org,* November 8, 2019.

113 *tweeted that the hush money payment*: Reuters Staff, "Trump Calls Hush Money Payments 'a Simple Private Transaction,' " *Reuters,* December 10, 2018.

115 *ran a long article*: Ben Protess, William K. Rashbaum, Jonah E. Bromwich, and Maggie Haberman, "N.Y. Seeks Insider's Records, in Apparent Bid to Gain Cooperation," *New York Times,* March 31, 2021.

CHAPTER 13: INDICTMENT

138 *clients like . . . Deutsche Bank*: My prior representations involving Deutsche Bank had nothing to do with the Trump investigation, were disclosed to the district attorney, and posed no conflict of interest.

138 *a policy memorandum*: Daniel R. Alonso, "Considerations in Charging Corporations," Memorandum to All Assistant District Attorneys, May 27, 2010.

142 *calling our investigation a "witch hunt"*: Brett Samuels, "Trump Says NY 'Taking Over' the Witch Hunt Against Him with New Charges," *The Hill,* July 1, 2001.

142 *calling the prosecutors "rude"*: Cammy Pedroja, "Trump Lashes Out at 'Rude, Nasty, and Totally Biased' NY Prosecutors as Criminal Charges Loom," *Newsweek,* June 28, 2021.

142 *"standard practice"*: Corinne Ramey and Rebecca Ballhaus, "Trump Organization Lawyers Make Last-Ditch Effort to Avoid New York Charges," *Wall Street Journal,* June 28, 2021.

CHAPTER 14: BOILING THE OCEAN

152 *an article appeared in* Forbes: Chase Peterson-Withorn, "Donald Trump Has Been Lying About the Size of His Apartment, *Forbes,* May 3, 2017.

163 *had written articles describing*: Randall Lane has written extensively about Donald Trump's net worth. The article of greatest relevance to the investigation was "Inside the Epic Fantasy That's Driven Donald Trump for 33 Years," *Forbes,* September 29, 2015.

CHAPTER 15: MOVING TOWARD A DECISION

168 *the* Washington Post *published a story*: Shayna Jacobs, David A. Fahrenthold, and Jonathan O'Connell, "Manhattan DA Convenes New Grand Jury in Trump Org. Case to Weigh Potential Charges," *Washington Post,* November 4, 2021.

179 *A New York Times* *article appeared*: Ben Protess, William K. Rashbaum, Jonah E. Bromwich, and David Enrich, "Trump Investigation Enters Crucial Phase as Prosecutor's Term Nears End, *New York Times,* November 24, 2021.

CHAPTER 18: THE LOOMING END OF THE INVESTIGATION

229 *put out a statement*: Ben Protess and William K. Rashbaum, "Accounting Firm Cuts Ties With Trump and Retracts Financial Statements," *New York Times,* February 14, 2022.

229 *issued an opinion*: Jonah E. Bromwich, Ben Protess, and William K. Rashbaum, "N.Y. Attorney General Can Question Trump and 2 Children, Judge Rules," *New York Times,* February 17, 2022.

CHAPTER 19: A "LITTLE PIECE OF JUSTICE"

234 *the case that had made her most proud*: Transcript of Interview with Mary Jo White (Feb. 8, 2013; Mar. 1, 2013; July 7, 2015), https://abawtp.law.stanford .edu/exhibits/show/mary-jo-white.

CHAPTER 22: WHAT HAPPENED?

253 *a long piece on the events*: "How the Manhattan D.A.'s Investigation into Donald Trump Unraveled," Ben Protess, William K. Rashbaum, and Jonah E. Bromwich, *New York Times,* March 5, 2022.

259 *"Principles of Federal Prosecution"*: United States Department of Justice, Justice Manual, Title 9: Criminal, Section 9-27.000.

260 *The* Wall Street Journal *recently put it*: "Garland's Special Counsel Mistake," *Wall Street Journal,* November 19–20, 2022.

CHAPTER 23: NOW WHAT?

272 *DANY has suggested*: Jonah E. Bromwich, Ben Protess, and William K. Rashbaum, "Manhattan Prosecutors Move to Jump-Start Criminal Inquiry Into Trump," *New York Times,* November 21, 2022.

274 *an article in the* Washington Post: J. Michael Diehl, "I Sold Trump $100,000 Worth of Pianos. Then He Stiffed Me," *Washington Post,* September 28, 2016.

274 *written up as "the ideal judge"*: The *NYU Law Review* featured a colloquium in 1975 referring to Edward Weinfeld as "the ideal judge." Much has been written about him. See, e.g., David Margolick, "A Lifetime of Law and Quiet Diligence for Judge Weinfeld," *New York Times,* August 18, 1985; William E. Nelson, *In Pursuit of Right and Justice: Edward Weinfeld as Lawyer and Judge* (New York: NYU Press, 2004).

275 *calling me a "low-life lawyer"*: Patricia McKnight, "Trump Slams 'Low-Life,' 'Never Trumper' Attorney for Unjust Prosecution," *Newsweek,* April 8, 2022.

275 *as his niece has written*: Mary L. Trump, *Too Much and Never Enough: How My Family Created the World's Most Dangerous Man* (New York: Simon & Schuster, 2020).

ACKNOWLEDGMENTS

As a reader, I have never cared for long acknowledgments at the end of books. But I must thank Cyrus Vance Jr. and Carey Dunne for asking me to work on the Trump investigation. I must also thank Jonathan Karp, the CEO of Simon & Schuster, and Mel Berger, my literary agent at WME, for believing that this was a book worth writing and helping to bring the concept into reality. Many friends, relatives, and colleagues spoke with me about writing a book or looked at various versions of the manuscript and gave me their advice. I am grateful to all of them, but it is better—and perhaps better for them—if I do not name them.

Finally, there is my wonderful family: My wife shared it all with me and tried to keep the book from making me sound arrogant or stupid. I fear she did not entirely succeed. My children and their spouses listened to me talk about my work and this book for endless hours, and provided edits, comments, and insights that made this a better book and me a better person. My eight grandchildren are not yet old enough to read this book; one day they will be. They helped me nevertheless. As someone who has spent a lifetime dealing with criminals and criminal cases, and thousands of hours thinking about Donald Trump's conduct, who he is, and what he represents, I could have become a pessimist, or even a misanthrope. Instead, my children and grandchildren remind me every day that people can be caring, kind, honest, and moral. They can laugh together and enjoy each other's company, living in freedom and respecting each other, as they embark on the "pursuit of happiness" that is their birthright as Americans. That is their blessing, and mine as well.

INDEX

ABOUT THE AUTHOR

Mark Pomerantz was born in Brooklyn and received a B.A. from Harvard College in 1972 and a J.D. from the University of Michigan Law School in 1975, where he was editor in chief of the *Michigan Law Review*. He served as a law clerk to Justice Potter Stewart of the U.S. Supreme Court and Judge Edward Weinfeld of the U.S. District Court for the Southern District of New York.

He worked as a federal prosecutor in the U.S. Attorney's Office for the Southern District of New York, eventually leading the appellate unit. In private practice, he defended numerous cases involving organized crime and white-collar crime before returning to the U.S. Attorney's Office to head its criminal division, where he supervised all criminal prosecutions, including cases involving financial fraud, corruption, narcotics dealing, police misconduct, and organized crime, including the case against John A. Gotti Jr.

Pomerantz has also been on the faculty of Columbia Law School and has lectured on criminal procedure and white-collar law at Harvard and Stanford law schools. He is a member of the advisory board of the Quattrone Center for the Fair Administration of Justice at the University of Pennsylvania Law School. From February 2021 to February 2022, he worked pro bono as special assistant district attorney in the office of the New York District Attorney Cyrus Vance Jr. to assist with that office's criminal investigation into the personal and business finances of former president Donald Trump.